The
BOWLER's
Holding,
the
BATSMAN's
Willey

The
BOWLER's
Holding,
the
BATSMAN's
Willey

Geoff Tibballs

EBURY
PRESS

9 10

Published in 2007 by Ebury Press, an imprint of Ebury Publishing

Ebury Publishing is a division of the Random House Group

The Random House Group Limited Reg. No. 954009

Addresses for companies within the Random House Group
can be found at www.randomhouse.co.uk

A CIP catalogue record for this book is available from the British Library

The Random House Group Limited makes every effort to ensure that the
papers used in our books are made from trees that have been legally sourced
from well-managed and credibly certified forests. Our paper procurement
policy can be found on www.randomhouse.co.uk

Printed and bound in the UK by CPI Mackays, Chatham, ME5 8TD

ISBN 9780091918415

CONTENTS

INTRODUCTION

In sickness and in health, for better or for worse, for richer or for poorer, whether they are over the moon or sick as a parrot, we hang on the every word of our sportsmen and women. And it's hardly surprising, because frequently neither we – nor indeed they – have any idea what is going to come out of their mouths next. It could be a witty comment, destined to feature in books of quotations for years to come, or some garbled nonsense that is almost as baffling as a Garth Crooks question. In a true labour of love, I have collected over 4,000 of these sporting gems – sharp one-liners and unintentional howlers, not only from participants and coaches but also those whose solemn duty it is to cover the action for the media. Spanning more than 50 different sports, the quotes range from the incisive wit of Brian Clough, Lee Trevino and Muhammad Ali to the studied observations of John Arlott, the colourful phrases of Sid Waddell and the gaffes of Murray Walker, Dan Maskell and their fellow commentators. It was Clive James who once said of the doyen of the gaffe, David Coleman: 'Just by being so madly keen, he helps you get things in proportion. Anything that matters so much to David Coleman, you realise doesn't matter so much at all!' In truth, the same can be said for virtually every sporting utterance, but, as I hope this book shows, sometimes it can be fun to revel in the trivial.

Geoff Tibballs, 2007

GENERAL

Have you noticed that whatever sport you're trying to learn, some earnest person is always telling you to keep your knees bent?
~ DAVE BARRY

I'm glad to say that this is the first Saturday in four weeks that sport will be weather-free.
~ DAVID COLEMAN

The more violent the body contact of the sports you watch, the lower your class.
~ PAUL FUSSELL

Performance-enhancing drugs are banned in the Olympics. OK, we can swing with that. But performance-debilitating drugs should not be banned. Smoke a joint and win the 100 metres, fair play to you. That's pretty damn good. Unless someone's dangling a Mars Bar off in the distance.
~ EDDIE IZZARD

The Olympics. Not a sport but several peculiar sports, each of which only commands your attention every four years, like a dental appointment.
~ DAN JENKINS

When it comes to sports I am not particularly interested. Generally speaking, I look upon them as dangerous and tiring activities performed by people with whom I share nothing except the right to trial by jury.
~ FRAN LEBOWITZ

There's a simple recipe about this sports business. If you're a sporting star, you're a sporting star. If you don't quite make it, you become a coach. If you can't coach, you become a journalist. If you can't spell, you introduce *Grandstand* on a Saturday afternoon.
~ DES LYNAM

I hate all sports as rabidly as a person who likes sports hates common sense.
~ H.L. MENCKEN

The ball is man's most disastrous invention, not excluding the wheel.
~ ROBERT MORLEY

The ribbon-waving rhythmic gymnasts are in. The shuttlecock-chasing badminton players are in. Even the ice-sweeping curlers are in. And poker's out? That's like throwing a party for mankind's greatest inventions and forgetting to invite indoor plumbing.
~ POKER WEBSITE, WWW.POKER.NET, BIDDING TO MAKE THE CARD GAME AN OLYMPIC SPORT

The only thing on the level is mountain climbing. ~ EDDIE QUINN

Men forget everything. That's why they need instant replays in sports. They've already forgotten what happened. ~ RITA RUDNER

Son, when you participate in sporting events, it's not whether you win or lose. It's how drunk you get. ~ HOMER SIMPSON

If the Bible has taught us nothing, and it hasn't, it's that girls should stick to girls' sports, such as hot-oil wrestling, foxy boxing, and such and such.
~ HOMER SIMPSON

Sports are the reason I am out of shape. I watch them all on TV. ~ THOMAS SOWELL

A sports journalist is someone who would if he could but he can't, so he tells those who already know how they should. ~ CLIFF TEMPLE

An astonishing number of international games were invented by the British, who, whenever they are surpassed by other nations, coolly invent another one.
~ PETER USTINOV

Binge-drinking and teenage pregnancies are the only games the English invented where they are still ranked number one in the world. ~ MIKE WALTERS

I always turn to the sports section first. The sports page records people's accomplishments. The front page has nothing but man's failures.
~ JUSTICE EARL WARREN

Of course I have played outdoor games. I once played dominoes in an open-air café in Paris. ~ OSCAR WILDE

ANGLING

Fishing is the sport of drowning worms.

~ ANON

Even a fish wouldn't get into trouble if he kept his mouth shut.

~ ANON

Nothing makes a fish bigger than almost being caught.

~ ANON

A fisherman is a sportsman who catches fish sometimes by patience, sometimes by luck, but most often by the tale.

~ LEO BAKER

The formal term for a collection of fishermen is an exaggeration of anglers.

~ HENRY BEARD

Don't take advice from people with missing fingers.

~ HENRY BEARD

The fishing was good, it was the catching that was bad.

~ A.K. BEST

My biggest worry is that my wife [when I'm dead] will sell my fishing gear for what I said I paid for it.

~ KOOS BRANDT

If fishing is like religion, then fly-fishing is high church.

~ TOM BROKAW

Fishing, with me, has always been an excuse to drink in the daytime.

~ JIMMY CANNON

Three-fourths of the earth's surface is water, and one-fourth is land. It is quite clear that the good Lord intended us to spend triple the amount of time fishing as taking care of the lawn.

~ CHUCK CLARK

I love fishing. It's like transcendental meditation with a punchline.

~ BILLY CONNOLLY

All fishermen are liars; it's an occupational disease with them like housemaid's knee or editor's ulcers.

~ BEATRICE COOK

Even eminent chartered accountants are known, in their capacity as fishermen, blissfully to ignore differences between seven and ten inches, half a pound and two pounds, three fish and a dozen fish.   ~ WILLIAM SHERWOOD FOX

Fishing seems to be divided, like sex, into three unequal parts: anticipation, recollection, and between them, actual performance.   ~ ARNOLD GINGRICH

Fly-fishing is the most fun you can have standing up.   ~ ARNOLD GINGRICH

Give a man a fish, and he can eat for a day. But teach a man how to fish and he'll be dead of mercury poisoning inside of three years.   ~ CHARLES HAAS

Anglers exaggerate grossly and make gentle and inoffensive creatures sound like wounded buffalo and man-eating tigers.   ~ RODERICK HAIG-BROWN

Anglers think they are divining some primeval natural force by outwitting a fish, a creature that never even got out of the evolutionary starting gate.   ~ RICH HALL

Fly-fishing is a very pleasant amusement; but angling or float-fishing I can only compare to a stick and a string, with a worm at one end and a fool at the other.   ~ GEORGE W. HARVEY

On fishing shows they always throw the fish back. They don't want to eat them. They just want to make them late for something.   ~ MITCH HEDBERG

Somebody just back of you while you are fishing is as bad as someone looking over your shoulder while you write a letter to your girl.   ~ ERNEST HEMINGWAY

He's just perfect for mounting.   ~ FISHERMAN MIKE HULBERT ON HIS 8LB 3OZ SON

An angler is a man who spends his rainy days sitting around on the muddy banks of rivers doing nothing because his wife won't let him do it at home.   ~ *IRISH NEWS*

Fly-fishing is like sex: everyone thinks there is more than there is, and that everyone is getting more than their share.
~ HENRY KANEMOTO

If people concentrated on the really important things in life, there'd be a shortage of fishing poles.
~ DOUG LARSON

It is to be observed that angling is the name given to fishing by people who can't fish.
~ STEPHEN LEACOCK

Fishing is the only sport where sitting on your butt under a tree looks like a concentrated activity.
~ JEFF MACNELLY

The two best times to fish is when it's rainin' and when it ain't.
~ PATRICK F. McMANUS

There is no greater fan of fly-fishing than the worm.
~ PATRICK F. McMANUS

What a tourist terms a plague of insects, the fly-fisher calls a great hatch.
~ PATRICK F. McMANUS

Scholars have long known that fishing eventually turns men into philosophers. Unfortunately, it is almost impossible to buy decent tackle on a philosopher's salary.
~ PATRICK F. McMANUS

Fishermen and hypochondriacs have one thing in common – they don't have to catch anything to be happy.
~ ROBERT ORBEN

A trout is a fish mainly known by hearsay. It lives on anything not included in a fisherman's equipment.
~ H.I. PHILIPS

Give a man a fish and he has food for a day; teach him how to fish and you can get rid of him for the entire weekend.
~ ZENNA SCHAFFER

Calling fishing a hobby is like calling brain surgery a job. ~ PAUL SCHULLERY

It has always been my private conviction that any man who pits his intelligence against a fish and loses has it coming. ~ JOHN STEINBECK

There is no use in walking five miles to fish when you can depend on being just as unsuccessful near home. ~ MARK TWAIN

Fishing is such great fun, I have often felt that it really ought to be done in bed. ~ JOHN VOELKER

There's a fine line between fishing and just standing on the shore like an idiot. ~ STEVEN WRIGHT

Last year I went fishing with Salvador Dali. He was using a dotted line. He caught every other fish. ~ STEVEN WRIGHT

The chief difference between big-game fishing and weightlifting is that weightlifters never clutter up their library walls with stuffed barbells. ~ ED ZERN

Fly-fishermen are born honest, but they get over it. ~ ED ZERN

BAT AND BALL

Baseball

Fred Patek was so small when he was born that his father passed out cigar butts.

~ JOEY ADAMS ON THE 5FT 5IN PLAYER

If horses can't eat it, I won't play on it. ~ DICK ALLEN

When we played softball, I'd steal second base, feel guilty and go back.

~ WOODY ALLEN

Me carrying a briefcase is like a hotdog wearing earrings. ~ SPARKY ANDERSON

I only had a high-school education and believe me, I had to cheat to get that.

~ SPARKY ANDERSON

Choo Choo Coleman is quick on the bases, but this is an attribute that is about as essential for catchers as neat handwriting. ~ ROGER ANGELL

Orel Hershiser is the only Major League pitcher to have two consecutive pronouns in his surname. ~ ROGER ANGELL

Confucius say, baseball wrong – man with four balls cannot walk. ~ ANON

If at first you don't succeed, try playing second base. ~ ANON

I like my players to be married and in debt. That's the way you motivate them.

~ ERNIE BANKS

If a woman has to choose between catching a fly ball and saving an infant's life, she will choose to save the infant's life without even considering if there is a man on base. ~ DAVE BARRY ON THE DIFFERENCE BETWEEN MEN AND WOMEN

Right now I feel that I've got my feet on the ground as far as my head is concerned. ~ BO BELINSKY

Slumps are like a soft bed. They're easy to get into and hard to get out of.

~ JOHNNY BENCH

I was thinking about making a comeback, until I pulled a muscle vacuuming.

~ JOHNNY BENCH

England and America should scrap cricket and baseball and come up with a new game that they both can play. Like baseball, for example.   ~ ROBERT BENCHLEY

One of the chief duties of the fan is to engage in arguments with the man behind him. This department of the game has been allowed to run down fearfully.   ~ ROBERT BENCHLEY

The only thing my father and I have in common is that our similarities are different.   ~ DALE BERRA

It seems like déjà vu all over again.   ~ YOGI BERRA

Baseball is 90 per cent mental; the other half is physical.   ~ YOGI BERRA

We made too many wrong mistakes.   ~ YOGI BERRA

You've got to be very careful if you don't know where you're going, because you might not get there.

~ YOGI BERRA

If the people don't want to come out to the park, nobody's going to stop 'em.

~ YOGI BERRA

You've known me all these years, Jack, and you still don't know how to spell my name.   ~ YOGI BERRA, RECEIVING A CHEQUE THAT SAID 'PAYABLE TO BEARER'

I always thought that record would stand until it was broken.   ~ YOGI BERRA

You can observe a lot just by watching.   ~ YOGI BERRA

Slump? I ain't in no slump. I just ain't hittin'.   ~ YOGI BERRA

Better make it four.
I don't think I can eat eight.
~ YOGI BERRA, ASKED IF HE WANTED HIS PIZZA CUT INTO FOUR OR EIGHT SLICES

I usually take a two-hour nap from one to four.   ~ YOGI BERRA

It ain't the heat, it's the humility.   ~ YOGI BERRA

Never answer an anonymous letter.   ~ YOGI BERRA

The Mets are overwhelming underdogs.   ~ YOGI BERRA

No one goes to that restaurant any more. It's too crowded. ~ YOGI BERRA

There's one word that describes baseball: you never know.   ~ YOGI BERRA

When you come to a fork in the road, take it.   ~ YOGI BERRA

I really didn't say everything I said.   ~ YOGI BERRA

—Reporter: Has first baseman Don Mattingly exceeded expectations?
—Yogi Berra: I'd say he's done more than that.

—Fan: What time is it?
—Yogi Berra: You mean now?

More than any other American sport, baseball creates the magnetic, addictive
illusion that it can almost be understood.   ~ THOMAS BOSWELL

Baseball is not necessarily an obsessive-compulsive disorder, like washing your hands 100 times a day, but it's beginning to seem that way. We're reaching the point where you can be a truly dedicated state-of-the-art fan or you can have a life. Take your pick.
~ THOMAS BOSWELL

He should be nicknamed 'Chicken'. Get it? Chicken Catcher Torre.
~ BOBBY BRAGAN ON JOE TORRE

If a tie is like kissing your sister, losing is like kissing your grandmother with her teeth out.
~ GEORGE BRETT

There was never any question about his courage. He proved it by getting married four times.
~ JACK BRICKHOUSE ON ENOS SLAUGHTER

It's a good thing I stayed in Cincinnati for four years – it took me that long to learn how to spell it.
~ ROCKY BRIDGES

There'll be two buses leaving the hotel for the park tomorrow. The two o'clock bus will be for those of you who need a little extra work. The empty bus will be leaving at five o'clock.
~ DAVE BRISTOL, MANAGER OF SAN FRANCISCO GIANTS, TO HIS STRUGGLING TEAM

The clock doesn't matter in baseball. Time stands still or moves backward. Theoretically, one game could go on for ever. Some seem to.
~ HERB CAEN

What does a mama bear on the pill have in common with the World Series? No Cubs.
~ HARRY CARAY ON CHICAGO'S LACK OF SUCCESS

Montreal Expos fans discovered 'boo' is pronounced the same in French as it is in English.
~ HARRY CARAY

It's a partial sellout.

~ SKIP CARAY

How can we keep the [Atlanta] Braves on their toes? Raise the urinals.

~ DARREL CHANEY

When we [England] have a World Series, we ask other countries to participate.

~ JOHN CLEESE

Last night's homer was Willie Stengell's 399th home run, leaving him one shy of 500.

~ JERRY COLEMAN

Hi folks! I'm Gerry Gross.

~ JERRY COLEMAN CONFUSING HIMSELF WITH ANOTHER
SPORTS ANNOUNCER TO LISTENERS OF A SAN DIEGO RADIO SHOW

Baseball fans love numbers. They love to swirl them around their mouths like Bordeaux wine.

~ PAT CONROY

A baseball fan has the digestive apparatus of a billy goat. He can, and does, devour any set of diamond statistics with insatiable appetite and then nuzzles hungrily for more.

~ ARTHUR DALEY

I want all the kids to do what I do, to look up to me. I want all the kids to copulate me.

~ ANDRE DAWSON

The doctors X-rayed my head and found nothing.

~ DIZZY DEAN

Fans, don't fail to miss tomorrow's game.

~ DIZZY DEAN

The runners have returned to their respectable bases.

~ DIZZY DEAN

There is a commotion in the stands. I think it has something to do with a fat lady… I've just been informed that the fat lady is the Queen of Holland.

~ DIZZY DEAN

Could be that Bill Terry's a nice guy when you get to know him, but why bother?

~ DIZZY DEAN

Sure I eat what I advertise. Sure I eat Wheaties for breakfast. A good bowl of Wheaties with Bourbon can't be beat.

~ DIZZY DEAN

Ballplayers and deer hunters are alike. They both want the big bucks.

~ LARRY DOUGHTY

We used to pray the White Sox and the Cubs would merge so Chicago would only have one bad team.

~ TOM DREESEN

What are we at the park for except to win? I'd trip my mother. I'd help her up, brush her off, tell her I'm sorry. But Mother don't make it to third.

~ LEO DUROCHER

I made a game effort to argue but two things were against me: the umpires and the rules.

~ LEO DUROCHER

I never questioned the integrity of an umpire. Their eyesight, yes. ~ LEO DUROCHER

I believe in rules. Sure I do. If there weren't any rules, how could you break them?

~ LEO DUROCHER

If you don't win, you're going to be fired. If you do win, you've only put off the day you're going to be fired.

~ LEO DUROCHER

I've seen better hands on a clock.

~ MEL DURSLAG ON ERROR-PRONE SHORTSTOP BILL RUSSELL

I told Roland Hemond to go out and get me a big-name pitcher. He said, 'Dave Wehrmeister's got 11 letters. Is that a big enough name for you?' ~ EDDIE EICHORN

Bruce Sutter has been around a while, and he's pretty old. He's 35 years old. That will give you an idea of how old he is.   ~ RON FAIRLY

He couldn't hit a curveball with an ironing board.

~ BOB FELLER ON MICHAEL JORDAN'S PLANS TO TAKE UP BASEBALL

Congress today conducted an undercover investigation of steroids in baseball. Their conclusion: the Chicago Cubs are just months away from getting nuclear weapons.   ~ CRAIG FERGUSON

I watch a lot of baseball on the radio.

~ GERALD FORD

I occasionally get birthday cards from fans. But it's often the same message: they hope it's my last.   ~ EX-UMPIRE AL FORMAN

A baseball park is the one place where a man's wife doesn't mind his getting excited over somebody else's curves.   ~ BRENDAN FRANCIS

I don't put any foreign substances on the baseball. Everything I use is from the good old USA.   ~ GEORGE FRAZIER

I can see the sun OK, and that's 93 million miles away.

~ UMPIRE BRUCE FROEMMING, AFTER HAVING HIS EYESIGHT QUESTIONED

They shouldn't throw at me. I'm the father of five or six kids.   ~ TITO FUENTES

Rick Burleson is even-tempered. He comes to the ballpark mad and stays that way.   ~ JOE GARAGIOLA

Billy Loes was the only player in the majors who could lose a ground ball in the sun.   ~ JOE GARAGIOLA

Nolan Ryan is pitching much better now that he has his curveball straightened out.   ~ JOE GARAGIOLA

I went through baseball as 'a player to be named later'. ~ JOE GARAGIOLA

A great catch is like watching girls go by – the last one you see is always the prettiest. ~ BOB GIBSON

I'm throwing twice as hard as I ever did. It's just not getting there as fast. ~ LEFTY GOMEZ

When Neil Armstrong first set foot on the moon, he and all the space scientists were puzzled by an unidentifiable white object. I knew immediately what it was. That was a home run hit off me in 1937 by Jimmy Foxx. ~ LEFTY GOMEZ

I'm a four-wheel-drive pickup type of guy. So is my wife. ~ MIKE GREENWELL

Baseball is very big with my people. It figures. It's the only time we can get to shake a bat at a white man without starting a riot. ~ DICK GREGORY

Sometimes they [journalists] write what I say and not what I mean. ~ PEDRO GUERRERO

If it turns out that Barry Bonds used steroids to bulk up and add muscle mass, he could get four to eight years as governor of California. ~ ARGUS HAMILTON

Lew Burdette would make coffee nervous. ~ FRED HANEY

Crowd? This isn't a crowd. It's a focus group!
~ FRAN HEALY DISAPPOINTED BY THE POOR ATTENDANCE AT A GAME IN MONTREAL

I wish I could play Little League now. I'd be way better than before.
~ MITCH HEDBERG

Don't forget to swing hard, in case you hit the ball. ~ WOODIE HELD

All I'm asking for is what I want.

~ RICKEY HENDERSON

I shall tell my doctors that baseball has more curative powers than all their medicine.

~ HERBERT HOOVER

I don't want to play golf. When I hit a ball, I want somebody else to go chase it.

~ ROGERS HORNSBY

People ask me what I do in winter when there's no baseball. I'll tell you what I do. I stare out the window and wait for spring.

~ ROGERS HORNSBY

The only reason I don't like playing in the World Series is I can't watch myself.

~ REGGIE JACKSON

He's not going to get sick. Germs are scared of him.

~ REGGIE JACKSON ON A BURLY TEAM-MATE

I hate baseball. It's dull. Nothing happens. It's like watching grass – no, Astroturf – grow.

~ JEFF JARVIS

Gary Maddox has turned his life around. He used to be depressed and miserable. Now he's miserable and depressed.

~ HARRY KALAS

It's permanent, for now.

~ ROBERTO KELLY

Two-thirds of the earth is covered by water, the other one-third is covered by Gary Maddox.

~ RALPH KINER

This time he grounds it on the ground.

~ RALPH KINER

Some guys are inwardly outgoing.

~ RALPH KINER

The Hall of Fame ceremonies are on the 31st and 32nd of July.

~ RALPH KINER

Half of Jeff King's extra-base hits last year were extra-base hits. ~ RALPH KINER

The reason the Mets have played so well at Shea this year is they have the best home record in baseball. ~ RALPH KINER

Chuck Hiller was a helluva hitter, but he had iron hands. You couldn't play him on rainy days; his hands would rust. ~ ED KRANEPOOL

You can be stupid once, but idiotic to do it again. I'll settle for being stupid.
~ ST LOUIS CARDINALS MANAGER TONY LA RUSSA, REFUSING TO MAKE
ANY MORE PREDICTIONS THAT HIS TEAM WOULD LIFT THE TITLE

If Mike Scioscia raced his pregnant wife he'd finish third. ~ TOMMY LASORDA

There goes Rick Monday. He and Manny Mota are so old, they were waiters at the Last Supper. ~ TOMMY LASORDA

The average age of our bench is deceased. ~ TOMMY LASORDA ON VETERANS
VIC DAVALILLO AND MANNY MOTA

By the time he gets a sign from his brain to scratch his groin, he's made $1,600.
~ JAY LENO ON KEN GRIFFEY JR'S $8.5 MILLION-A-YEAR CONTRACT

Major League baseball has asked its players to stop tossing baseballs into the stands during games, because they say fans fight over them and they get hurt. In fact, the Florida Marlins said that's why they never hit any home runs. It's a safety issue. ~ JAY LENO

Do you know what I love most about baseball? The pine tar, the resin, the grass, the dirt – and that's just in the hot dogs. ~ DAVID LETTERMAN

Most of the time you send them a bottle of Dom Perignon when they win their first game. But our kids are so young, you send them a can of Ovaltine.

~ FLORIDA MARLINS' JIM LEYLAND

I'm not going to panic about results – I'll panic if my kid flunks math.

~ JIM LEYLAND

Tonight, we're honouring one of the all-time greats in baseball, Stan Musial. He's immoral.

~ JOHNNY LOGAN

The secret to keeping winning streaks going is to maximise the victories while at the same time minimising the defeats.

~ JOHN LOWENSTEIN

Umpiring is best described as the profession of standing between two seven-year-olds with one ice-cream cone.

~ RON LUCIANO

If it's true you learn by your mistakes, Jim Frey will be the best manager ever.

~ RON LUCIANO

Pudge [Fisk] is so old, they didn't have history class when he went to school.

~ STEVE LYONS

He could speak in eight languages, but he couldn't hit in any of them.

~ TED LYONS ON MOE BERG

Stan Musial's batting stance looks like a small boy looking around a corner to see if the cops are coming.

~ TED LYONS

I hated to bat against [Don] Drysdale. After he hit you he'd come around, look at the bruise on your arm and say, 'Do you want me to sign it?' ~ MICKEY MANTLE

It's not that he's a bad outfielder. He just has trouble judging the ball and picking it up.

~ BILLY MARTIN

The rule book is only good for you when you go deer hunting and run out of toilet paper.
~ BILLY MARTIN

I'm one of those people who's not really turned on by baseball. My idea of a relief pitcher is one that's filled with martinis.
~ DEAN MARTIN

Many fans look upon an umpire as a necessary evil to the luxury of baseball, like the odour that follows an automobile.
~ CHRISTY MATTHEWSON

His reputation preceded him before he got here.
~ DON MATTINGLY

When owner Charlie Finley had his heart operation, it took eight hours – seven just to find his heart.
~ STEVE McCATTY

Always root for the winner. That way you won't be disappointed.
~ TUG McGRAW

My best advice to any player? Don't park in the spaces marked 'Reserved for Umpires'.
~ JOHN McSHERRY

Statistics are like loose women: once you get them, you can do anything you want with them.
~ WALT MICHAELS

Trying to hit Phil Niekro was like trying to eat Jell-O with chopsticks.
~ BOBBY MURCER

Baseball is a game where a curve is an optical illusion, a screwball can be a pitch or a person, stealing is legal and you can spit anywhere you like except in the umpire's eye or on the ball.
~ JIM MURRAY

Sandy Koufax's fastball was so fast, some batters would start to swing as he was on his way to the mound.
~ JIM MURRAY

The only difference between the Mets and the *Titanic* is that the Mets have a better organist.

~ JIM MURRAY

When I was a little boy, I wanted to be a baseball player and join the circus. With the Yankees, I've accomplished both.

~ GRAIG NETTLES

The club didn't mind the added weight, but it gave him two weeks to get down to his playing height.

~ SCOTT OSTLER, AFTER KEN GRIFFEY JR TURNED UP FOR PRE-SEASON TRAINING 20 POUNDS HEAVIER AND TWO INCHES TALLER

Contrary to popular belief, I have always had a wonderful repertoire with my players.

~ DANNY OZARK

Even Napoleon had his Watergate.

~ DANNY OZARK

It is beyond my apprehension.

~ DANNY OZARK

How is our morale? Morality at this point isn't a factor.

~ DANNY OZARK

His limitations are limitless.

~ DANNY OZARK ON MIKE ANDERSON

There's nothing wrong with the Little League World Series that locking out the adults couldn't cure.

~ MIKE PENNER

I seldom refused autograph seekers unless they were old enough to look like collection agents.

~ JOE PEPITONE

The last time I smiled so much was for a jury. ~ PASQUEL PEREZ, AFTER A RUN OF SUCCESS

When you win you eat better, sleep better and your beer tastes better. And your wife looks like Gina Lollobrigida.

~ JOHNNY PESKY

Would the lady who left her nine kids at Wrigley Field please pick them up immediately? They are beating the Chicago Cubs 4-0 in the seventh inning.

~ RADIO DJ

Statistics are to baseball what a flaky crust is to Mom's apple pie.   ~ HARRY REASONER

He's the world's quietest person. The night he broke Lou Gehrig's record, he went out and painted the town beige.   ~ BILLY RIPKEN ON BROTHER CAL

Dan Napoleon is so ugly, when you walked by him your pants would wrinkle.

~ MICKEY RIVERS

Me and George [Steinbrenner] and Billy [Martin] are two of a kind.

~ MICKEY RIVERS

The wind was blowing about 100 degrees.   ~ MICKEY RIVERS

Imagine having to tell a salesgirl that you're buying them for a wife who is six foot two and weighs over 200 pounds.

~ BILL ROBINSON, BUYING LADIES' TIGHTS FOR HIMSELF FOLLOWING A PULLED MUSCLE

Therapy can be a good thing; it can be therapeutic.   ~ ALEX RODRIGUEZ

How can anyone as slow as you pull a muscle?   ~ PETE ROSE TO TONY PEREZ

It's a round ball and a round bat, and you got to hit it square.   ~ PETE ROSE

I'd walk through hell in a gasoline suit to play baseball.   ~ PETE ROSE

If you slid into bases head first for 20 years, you'd be ugly too!   ~ PETE ROSE

Hating the New York Yankees is as American as apple pie, unwed mothers and cheating on your income tax.   ~ MIKE ROYKO

Bobby Bonilla looks less comfortable donning a glove than anyone since O.J.

~ STEVE RUSHIN

All ballplayers should quit when it starts to feel as if all the baselines run uphill.

~ BABE RUTH

I had only one superstition. I made sure to touch all the bases when I hit a home run.

~ BABE RUTH

We were given a choice. We could either run around the field three times or around Tommy Lasorda once.

~ STEVE SAX

He's one of the hardest workers on this team. He's had his ear to the grindstone all season.

~ MIKE SHANNON

Defensively the Red Sox are a lot like Stonehenge. They are old, they don't move, and no one is certain why they are positioned the way they are.

~ DAN SHAUGHNESSY

Baseball has the great advantage over cricket of being sooner ended.

~ GEORGE BERNARD SHAW

Trying to throw a fastball past Hank Aaron is like trying to sneak sunrise past a rooster.

~ CURT SIMMONS

I'm not blind to hearing what everybody else hears.

~ ZANE SMITH

Anything that goes that far ought to have a stewardess on it.

~ PAUL SPLITORFF, ON A GEORGE BRETT HOME RUN

David Cone is in a class by himself with three or four other players.

~ GEORGE STEINBRENNER

I'm not a win-at-all-costs guy. Winning isn't everything. It's second to breathing.

~ GEORGE STEINBRENNER

I got a kid, Greg Goosen, he's 19 years old and in ten years he's got a chance to be 29.

~ CASEY STENGEL

Look at him. He doesn't drink, he doesn't smoke, he doesn't chew, he doesn't stay out late, and he still can't hit 250.

~ CASEY STENGEL

This has been a team effort. No one or two guys could have done all this.

~ CASEY STENGEL AFTER THE METS LOST 120 GAMES IN A SEASON

The secret of managing is to keep the guys who hate you away from the guys who are undecided.

~ CASEY STENGEL

They're very much alike in a lot of similarities.

~ CASEY STENGEL

A lot of people my age are dead at the present time.

~ CASEY STENGEL

I am the most loyal player money can buy.

~ DON SUTTON

As a teenager, Gonzo [Luis Gonzalez] was so skinny he had to take steroids just to be on the chess team.

~ GREG SWINDELL

Toronto pitcher David Wells was so disgusted with the *Sports Illustrated* cover depicting him as a big fat slob that he ate the first 50,000 copies.

~ TERRY TOLL

I call my hairstyle the 'Watergate'. I cover up everything I can.

~ JOE TORRE

The last time the Chicago Cubs won a World Series was in 1908. The last time they were in one was 1945. Hey, any team can have a bad century.

~ TOM TREBELHORN

Nick Etten's glove fields better with Nick Etten out of it. ~ JOE TRIMBLE

What have they lost, nine of their last eight? ~ TED TURNER

My doctor tells me to drink lemon juice after a hot bath, but I can never finish the bath. ~ BOB UECKER

I've never criticised my players in public, and I'll never do it again.

~ BOBBY VALENTINE

The Pittsburgh Pirates have a worse defence than Pearl Harbor. ~ ANDY VAN SLYKE

As an umpire, you're expected to be perfect the day you start – and then improve. ~ ED VARGO

Baseball is the only thing beside the paper clip that hasn't changed. ~ BILL VEECK

Baseball is the only game left for people. To play basketball, you have to be seven foot six. To play football, you have to be the same width. ~ BILL VEECK

Baseball is almost the only orderly thing in a very unorderly world. If you get three strikes, even the best lawyer in the world can't get you off. ~ BILL VEECK

I have discovered in 20 years of moving around a ball park that the knowledge of the game is usually in inverse proportion to the price of the seats. ~ BILL VEECK

I was a victim of circumcision. ~ PETE VUKOVICH

Steve Carlton: one of the all-time greatest players of all time. ~ BOB WALK

I see three baseballs, but I only swing at the middle one.

~ PAUL WANER ON THE PERILS OF DRINKING

Baseball is like church. Many attend, but few understand.

~ WES WESTRUM

Baseball, it is said, is only a game. True. And the Grand Canyon is only a hole in Arizona.

~ GEORGE WILL

Baseball is the only field of endeavour where a man can succeed three times out of ten and be considered a good performer.

~ TED WILLIAMS

For the parents of a Little Leaguer, a baseball game is simply a nervous breakdown in innings.

~ EARL WILSON

Why did I get married in a ballpark? My wife wanted a big diamond.

~ MOOKIE WILSON

It went quickly, but it was like an eternity.

~ DAVE WINFIELD

You don't get your first home run too often.

~ RICK WRONA

You don't want to have to walk back to the dugout with your head between your legs.

~ DMITRI YOUNG

Cricket

A very small crowd here today. I can count the people on one hand. Can't be more than 30.

~ MICHAEL ABRAHAMSON

Strangely, in slow motion replay, the ball seemed to hang in the air for even longer.

~ DAVID ACFIELD

When you're an off-spinner there's not much point glaring at a batsman. If I glared at Vivian Richards he'd just hit me even further.

~ DAVID ACFIELD

Like an elephant trying to do the pole vault.

~ JONATHAN AGNEW AS HEAVYWEIGHT PAKISTAN CAPTAIN INZAMAM-UL-HAQ FALLS OVER HIS OWN STUMPS AT HEADINGLEY IN 2006

This has been completely and utterly limp by England. They're playing with all the intensity of my drunk aunt playing Cluedo at Christmas.   ~ JONATHAN AGNEW

Botham just couldn't quite get his leg over.

> ~ JONATHAN AGNEW AFTER IAN BOTHAM LOST HIS BALANCE WHILE ATTEMPTING
> TO HOOK CURTLY AMBROSE. AS HE TRIED TO AVOID TRAMPLING ON HIS WICKET,
> BOTHAM STEPPED OVER THE STUMPS BUT IN DOING SO FLICKED OFF THE BAIL

He [Shane Warne] really is the big bad wolf, isn't he? Even the three pigs and their brick house would have blown down with his huffing and puffing.

> ~ JONATHAN AGNEW

As I look around the ground I can see about 30 young girls all wearing Dutch caps.   ~ JONATHAN AGNEW AT A HOLLAND GAME

I've never got to the bottom of streaking.   ~ JONATHAN AGNEW

Umpire Fenwick just twitches his nose, instead of putting his finger up in the usual way.   ~ PAUL ALLOTT

Bill Lawry is a corpse with pads on.   ~ ANON

The only bowler ever to require the services of a runner.   ~ ANON, ON INJURY-PRONE CHRIS OLD

I feel I have had a very interesting life, but I am rather hoping there is still more to come. I still haven't captained the England cricket team.   ~ JEFFREY ARCHER

It is rather suitable for umpires to dress like dentists, since one of their tasks is to draw stumps.   ~ JOHN ARLOTT

What we have here is a clear case of Mann's inhumanity to Mann.

> ~ JOHN ARLOTT AT A 1948 TEST IN WHICH SOUTH AFRICAN BOWLER 'TUFTY' MANN
> WAS CAUSING PROBLEMS FOR ENGLAND BATSMAN GEORGE MANN

He approaches the wicket like Groucho Marx chasing a pretty waitress.

~ JOHN ARLOTT ON THE CROUCHING RUN-UP OF PAKISTAN'S ASIF MASOOD

Like an old lady poking with her umbrella at a wasp's nest.

~ JOHN ARLOTT ON THE BATTING OF AUSTRALIAN ERNIE TOSHACK

Ken 'Slasher' Mackay is the only athlete I have ever known who, as he walked, sagged at ankles, knees and hips. ~ JOHN ARLOTT

Clive Lloyd hits him high away over mid-wicket for four, a stroke of a man knocking a thistle top with a walking stick.

~ JOHN ARLOTT

The umpire signals a bye with the air of a weary stork. ~ JOHN ARLOTT

Bill Frindall has done a bit of mental arithmetic with a calculator. ~ JOHN ARLOTT

He played a cut so late as to be positively posthumous. ~ JOHN ARLOTT

Umpire Harold Bird, having a wonderful time, signalling everything in the world, including stopping traffic coming on from behind. ~ JOHN ARLOTT

[Ray Jennings] was to orthodoxy what King Herod was to child-minding.

~ MIKE ATHERTON ON THE SOUTH AFRICAN COACH

It looks more suitable for growing carrots.

~ ANDY ATKINSON, ICC GROUNDS INSPECTOR, ON BERMUDA'S NEW PITCH

If the Poms bat first, keep the taxi running.

~ AUSTRALIAN FANS' BANNER DURING THE 1994-95 ASHES SERIES

Tufnell! Can I borrow your brain? I'm building an idiot.

~ AUSTRALIAN FAN TO ENGLAND SPINNER PHIL TUFNELL

Leaving out Dennis Lillee against England would be as unthinkable as the Huns dropping Attila.

~ AUSTRALIAN TV COMMENTATOR, 1982

Well, Andrew Strauss is certainly an optimist – he's come out wearing sunblock!

~ AUSTRALIAN COMMENTATOR DURING THE FIFTH TEST IN ENGLAND'S 5-0 WHITEWASH, 2006-7

The first time you face up to a googly you're going to be in trouble if you've never faced one before.

~ TREVOR BAILEY

The Port Elizabeth ground is more of a circle than an oval. It is long and square.

~ TREVOR BAILEY

There are good one-day players, there are good Test players and vice versa.

~ TREVOR BAILEY

On the first day Logie decided to chance his arm and it came off. ~ TREVOR BAILEY

I don't think he expected it, and that's what caught him unawares. ~ TREVOR BAILEY

We owe some gratitude to Gatting and Lamb, who breathed some life into a corpse which had nearly expired.

~ TREVOR BAILEY

No captain with all the hindsight in the world can predict how the wicket is going to play.

~ TREVOR BAILEY

This series has been swings and pendulums all the way through.   ~ TREVOR BAILEY

Lloyd did what he achieved with that shot.

~ JACK BANNISTER

The traditional dress of the Australian cricketer is the baggy green cap on the head and the chip on the shoulder. Both are ritualistically assumed.

~ SIMON BARNES

I bowl so slowly that if I don't like a ball I can run after it and bring it back.

~ J.M. BARRIE

England trained and grass grew at the MCG yesterday, two activities virtually indistinguishable from each other in tempo.

~ GREG BAUM

It was an excellent performance in the field marred only when Harris dropped Crapp in the outfield.   ~ BBC COMMENTATOR ON A MISSED CHANCE OFF BATSMAN JACK CRAPP

Batting is a major trial before an 11-man jury.

~ RICHIE BENAUD

The hallmark of a great captain is the ability to win the toss at the right time.

~ RICHIE BENAUD

He's not quite got hold of that one. If he had, it would have gone for nine.

~ RICHIE BENAUD DESCRIBING A JUSTIN LANGER SIX

Gatting at fine leg – that's a contradiction in terms.

~ RICHIE BENAUD

Laird has been brought in to stand in the corner of the circle.

~ RICHIE BENAUD

He's usually a good puller – but he couldn't get it up that time.

~ RICHIE BENAUD

His throw went absolutely nowhere near where it was going.

~ RICHIE BENAUD

I think the batsman's strategy will be to make runs and not get out.

~ RICHIE BENAUD

This shirt is unique: there are only 200 of them.

~ RICHIE BENAUD

There were congratulations and high sixes all round.   ~ RICHIE BENAUD

That slow-motion replay doesn't show how fast the ball was travelling.
~ RICHIE BENAUD

How can you tell your wife you are just popping out to play a match and then not come back for five days?   ~ SOCCER MANAGER RAFA BENITEZ STRUGGLING
TO COME TO TERMS WITH THE CONCEPT OF TEST CRICKET

England's pace bowlers are making the helmet go out of fashion. ~ SCYLD BERRY

If they want me down to 12 stone, I would have to cut off a leg. ~ IAN BLACKWELL

In the rear, the small diminutive figure of Shoaib Mohammed, who can't be much taller than he is.   ~ HENRY BLOFELD

It's a catch he would have caught 99 times out of 1,000.   ~ HENRY BLOFELD

If the tension here was a block of Cheddar cheese, you could cut it with a knife.
~ HENRY BLOFELD

Flintoff starts in, his shadow beside him. Where else would it be? ~ HENRY BLOFELD

Ashley Giles trundles in to bowl rather like a wheelie bin.   ~ HENRY BLOFELD

I don't think I've actually drunk a beer for 15 years, except a few Guinnesses in Dublin, where it's the law.   ~ IAN BOTHAM

Pakistan is the sort of place everyone should send his mother-in-law for a month … all expenses paid.   ~ IAN BOTHAM

He arrived on earth from the Planet Loony.   ~ IAN BOTHAM ON DICKIE BIRD

I'd rather face Dennis Lillee with a stick of rhubarb than go through that again.

~ IAN BOTHAM AFTER BEING CLEARED OF ASSAULT CHARGES AT GRIMSBY CROWN COURT

I don't ask my wife Kathy to face Michael Holding, so there's no reason why I should be changing nappies.

~ IAN BOTHAM

It couldn't have been Gatt. Anything he takes up to his room after nine o'clock, he eats.

~ IAN BOTHAM ON THE MIKE GATTING BARMAID SCANDAL

This can only help England's cause. ~ IAN BOTHAM ON HEARING THAT GEOFFREY BOYCOTT IS TO COACH THE PAKISTAN BATSMEN BEFORE THEIR 2001 TOUR OF ENGLAND

A few years ago England would have struggled to beat the Eskimos.

~ IAN BOTHAM, 2005

[Ian] Chappell was a coward. He needed a crowd around him before he would say anything. He was sour like milk that had been sitting in the sun for a week.

~ IAN BOTHAM

I've had about ten operations. I'm a bit like a battered old Escort. You might find one panel left that's original.

~ IAN BOTHAM

If I'd done a quarter of the things of which I'm accused, I'd be pickled in alcohol. I'd be a registered drug addict and would have sired half the children in the world's cricket-playing countries.

~ IAN BOTHAM

After their 60 overs, West Indies have scored 244 for 7, all out.

~ FRANK BOUGH

Life without sport is like life without underpants.

~ BILLY BOWDEN

Get a single down the other end and watch someone else play him.

~ GEOFFREY BOYCOTT, ASKED HOW BEST TO HANDLE GLENN MCGRATH

The face of a choirboy, the demeanour of a civil servant and the ruthlessness of a rat catcher.   ~ GEOFFREY BOYCOTT ON DEREK UNDERWOOD

On present form Waqar [Younis] and Wasim [Akram] could bowl out the England team with an orange.   ~ GEOFFREY BOYCOTT

I reckon my mum could have caught that in her pinny!
~ GEOFFREY BOYCOTT ON A DROPPED CATCH

He could have caught that between the cheeks of his backside.
~ GEOFFREY BOYCOTT ON ANOTHER DROPPED CATCH

He carried on like a small child whose mother would have smacked him.
~ GEOFFREY BOYCOTT ON SHANE WARNE'S TANTRUM AFTER AN APPEAL WAS REJECTED

I feel so bad about mine now I am going to tie it around the cat.
~ GEOFFREY BOYCOTT, DISMAYED AT THE AWARD OF AN MBE TO
PAUL COLLINGWOOD FOR SCORING 17 RUNS IN THE 2005 ASHES SERIES

I'm glad two sides of the cherry have been put forward.   ~ GEOFFREY BOYCOTT

Richie Benaud simply says 'out' with the grisly finality of the hangman.
~ TONY BRACE

Playing against a team with Ian Chappell as captain turns a cricket match into gang warfare.   ~ MIKE BREARLEY

Why is Tufnell the most popular man in the team? Is it the Manuel factor, in which the most helpless member of the cast is most affectionately identified with?   ~ MIKE BREARLEY

The prospect of staging an Ashes Test in Wales may be slightly less appropriate than holding an eisteddfod in Bulgaria.   ~ STEPHEN BRENKLEY

[Geoffrey] Boycott and controversy have shared the longest opening partnership in the game. ~ TERRY BRINDLE

Merv Hughes always appeared to be wearing a tumble-dried ferret on his top lip.

~ RICK BROADBENT

[Kevin] Pietersen is big and brash and as subtle as colonic irrigation.

~ RICK BROADBENT

Too high? If the ball had hit his head it would have hit the bloody wickets!

~ ALAN BROWN, DENIED AN LBW APPEAL AGAINST 5FT 3IN HARRY PILLING

After years of patient study I have decided that there is nothing wrong with the game that the introduction of golf carts wouldn't fix in a hurry.

~ BILL BRYSON, *DOWN UNDER*

It [cricket] is the only competitive activity of any type, other than perhaps baking, in which you can dress in white from head to toe and be as clean at the end of the day as you were at the beginning. ~ BILL BRYSON, *DOWN UNDER*

I am quite certain that if the rest of the world vanished overnight and the development of cricket was left in Australian hands, within a generation the players would be wearing shorts and using the bats to hit each other.

~ BILL BRYSON, *DOWN UNDER*

We had one or two disagreements but once he realised that he was wrong and I was right we moved on. ~ SURREY COACH ALAN BUTCHER ON WORKING WITH SON MARK

Ed Smith has been an endless source of amusement, especially for the Yorkshire boys. They have never heard anybody speak like Ed. At the crease he looks a million dollars, which is probably what he has got tucked away somewhere.

~ MARK BUTCHER

Billy Bowden should be in a circus and not the Elite umpires' panel.

~ *CALCUTTA TELEGRAPH*

I am more inclined to believe that the Pope is guilty of multiple bigamy than to believe Hansie [Cronje] is guilty of being involved in bribery and corruption.

~ CALLER TO A SOUTH AFRICAN RADIO SHOW

A snick by Jack Hobbs is a sort of disturbance of a cosmic orderliness.

~ NEVILLE CARDUS

A Yorkshire cricketer is one born within the sound of Bill Bowes.

~ MICHAEL CAREY

I once delivered a simple ball, which I was told, had it gone far enough, would have been considered a wide.

~ LEWIS CARROLL

I can't really say I'm batting badly. I'm not batting long enough to be batting badly.

~ GREG CHAPPELL

A Test match is like a painting. A one-day match is like a Rolf Harris painting.

~ IAN CHAPPELL

The other advantage England have got when Phil Tufnell is bowling is that he isn't fielding.

~ IAN CHAPPELL

In my day 58 beers between London and Sydney would have virtually classified you as a teetotaller.

~ IAN CHAPPELL, AFTER BATSMAN DAVID BOON DRANK 58 CANS OF BEER ON THE FLIGHT FROM AUSTRALIA TO ENGLAND

It's tough for a natural hooker to give it up.

~ IAN CHAPPELL

Three bad days does not mean you're a bad team overnight.

~ PAUL COLLINGWOOD

—David Gower: Do you want Gatt [Mike Gatting] a foot wider?
—Chris Cowdrey: No, he'd burst!

The Queen's Park Oval, exactly as its name suggests – absolutely round.
~ TONY COZIER

Now Botham, with a chance to put everything that's gone before behind him.
~ TONY COZIER

Angus Fraser's bowling is like shooting down F-16 aeroplanes with sling shots. Even if they hit, no damage would be done. Like an old horse, he should be put out to pasture. ~ COLIN CROFT

The ball came back, literally cutting Graham Thorpe in half. ~ COLIN CROFT

Who could forget Malcolm Devon?
~ TED DEXTER, COMPLETELY FORGETTING DEVON MALCOLM

Cricket is the only game that you can actually put on weight while playing.
~ TOMMY DOCHERTY

My wife had an uncle who could never walk down the nave of an abbey without wondering whether it would take spin. ~ ALEC DOUGLAS-HOME

Oh God! If there be cricket in heaven, let there also be rain. ~ ALEC DOUGLAS-HOME

He would lumber up to the wicket and toss up the ball in a take-it-or-leave-it style, as if he cared little whether it pitched between the wickets or in the next parish. ~ ARTHUR CONAN DOYLE ON W.G. GRACE'S BOWLING ACTION

We used to eat so many salads there was a danger of contracting myxomatosis.
~ RAY EAST ON A COUNTY CRICKETER'S LIFE

I can't bat, can't bowl and can't field these days. I've every chance of being picked for England.   ~ RAY EAST

He could do all the right things superbly, but when he broke all the rules the ball still ended up at the fence.   ~ BASIL EASTERBROOK ON DENIS COMPTON

It's difficult to be more laid back than David Gower without actually being comatose.   ~ FRANCES EDMONDS

Ian Botham is in no way inhibited by a capacity to over-intellectualise.
                                                          ~ FRANCES EDMONDS

He's got a reputation for being awkward and arrogant, probably because he is awkward and arrogant.   ~ FRANCES EDMONDS ON HUSBAND PHIL

—Reporter: What are you looking forward to most when you get home from India?
—Phil Edmonds: A dry fart!

You should play every game as if it's your last, but make sure you perform well enough to ensure that it's not.   ~ JOHN EMBUREY

Dickie Bird was the first umpire to combine the distinct roles of top-flight umpire and music-hall comedian.   ~ MATTHEW ENGEL

Derek Randall bats like an octopus with piles.   ~ MATTHEW ENGEL

We sometimes argue about the cricketer we would choose to bat for one's life (consensus answer: Don Bradman for your life, Geoff Boycott for his own).
                                                          ~ MATTHEW ENGEL

Another day, another dolour. ~ MATTHEW ENGEL, AS ENGLAND STRUGGLE IN THE WEST INDIES

Waugh! What is he good for? Absolutely nothing!

~ ENGLAND FANS' SONG DURING THE 1993 ASHES SERIES

I've not been to bed yet. Behind these sunglasses there's a thousand stories.

~ BLEARY-EYED ANDREW FLINTOFF AFTER THE 2005 ASHES TRIUMPH

It means I can drive a flock of sheep through the town centre, drink for free in no less than 64 pubs and get a lift home with the police when I become inebriated. What more could you want?

~ ANDREW FLINTOFF ON BEING GRANTED THE FREEDOM OF PRESTON

I'm completely different from Pietersen. He would turn up to the opening of an envelope.   ~ ANDREW FLINTOFF

It's far more daunting than bowling to Ricky Ponting or facing Shane Warne.

~ ANDREW FLINTOFF ON NEWS THAT HE WAS TO DUET WITH ELTON JOHN

I'm ugly, I'm overweight, but I'm happy.   ~ ANDREW FLINTOFF

In the past five weeks I have trained hard, trying to get my ankle back to where I want it to be.   ~ ANDREW FLINTOFF

Lady, if I were built in proportion, I'd be eight foot ten!

~ JOEL GARNER

—Interviewer: Do you feel that the selectors and yourself have been vindicated by the result?
—Mike Gatting: I don't think the Press are vindictive. They can write what they want.

Srikkanth is a vegetarian. If he swallows a fly, he will be in trouble.

~ SUNIL GAVASKAR

Glenn McGrath joins Craig McDermott and Paul Reiffel in a three-ponged prace attack.

~ TIM GAVEL

This is Cunis at the Vauxhall End. Cunis – a funny sort of name. Neither one thing nor the other.

~ ALAN GIBSON

It's typical of English cricket. A tree gets in the way for 200 years and, when it falls down, instead of cheering they plant a new one.

~ DAVID GILBERT ON KENT'S NEW LIME TREE AT CANTERBURY

I don't think my bum can twitch any more than it did last Sunday.

~ ASHLEY GILES, HERO OF TRENT BRIDGE, PREPARES FOR THE 2005 ASHES DECIDER AT THE OVAL

It was a mixture of bad bowling, good shots and arse.

~ JASON GILLESPIE REFLECTING ON HIS 2005 ASHES SERIES

Hansel and Gretel and Dizzy's double hundred – they're one and the same. An absolute fairytale.

~ JASON 'DIZZY' GILLESPIE ON HIS 200 AGAINST BANGLADESH

I've been copping the calls for so long now, I've felt like putting a sign out saying, 'The caravan's in for repairs.'

~ JASON GILLESPIE AFTER YEARS OF 'WHERE'S YOUR CARAVAN?' TAUNTS FROM ENGLAND FANS

The only thing Ian Botham knows about dawn runs is coming back from parties.

~ GRAHAM GOOCH

A fart competing with thunder.

~ GRAHAM GOOCH, ASSESSING ENGLAND IN AUSTRALIA, 1990-91

If it had been a cheese roll, it would never have got past him.

~ GRAHAM GOOCH AFTER MIKE GATTING WAS BOWLED BY SHANE WARNE'S 'BALL OF THE CENTURY'

Illy [Ray Illingworth] had the man-management skills of Basil Fawlty.

~ DARREN GOUGH

I don't know an England player who could fix a light bulb, let alone a match.

~ DARREN GOUGH

It's hard work making batting look effortless.
~ DAVID GOWER

When you win the toss, bat. If you are in doubt, think about it, then bat. If you have very big doubts, consult a colleague – then bat.

~ W.G. GRACE

I don't like defensive shots – you can only get threes.

~ W.G. GRACE

They came to see me bat, not you umpiring.

~ W.G. GRACE, REFUSING TO LEAVE THE CREASE AFTER BEING BOWLED OUT FIRST BALL

Cricket shouldn't be used as a political football.

~ DAVID GRAVENEY

As far as Flintoff's shoulder is concerned, he is going to be OK. He didn't have any trouble lifting up a can of beer anyway.

~ DAVID GRAVENEY

Clearly the West Indies are going to play their normal game, which is what they normally do.

~ TONY GREIG

What a magnificent shot! No, he's out.

~ TONY GREIG

In the back of Hughes' mind must be the thought that he will dance down the piss and mitch one.

~ TONY GREIG

Being the manager of a touring team is rather like being in charge of a cemetery – lots of people underneath you, but no one listening.

~ WES HALL

If Mike Gatting had sworn at the barmaid and shagged the Pakistan umpire, he'd probably be Chairman of Selectors now.

~ NICK HANCOCK

Ashley Giles made a simple attempt at a top-edged hook by Mahela Jayawardene look like a Mr Bean Christmas special.

~ PETER HAYTER, LAMENTING THE STANDARD OF ENGLAND'S FIELDING IN SRI LANKA, 2003

Shane Warne's idea of a balanced diet is a cheeseburger in each hand. ~ IAN HEALY

Professional cricket coaching for women is a man trying to get you to keep your legs close together when other men had spent a lifetime trying to get them apart.

~ RACHEL HEYHOE-FLINT

I'd like to think that I haven't got any weaknesses except chocolate. ~ GRAEME HICK

Cricket needs brightening up a bit. My solution is to let players drink at the beginning of the game, not after. It always works in our picnic matches.

~ PAUL HOGAN

Cricket corruption is a rolling stone – it's gathering moss all the time.

~ OLIVER HOLT

It's obviously a great occasion for all the players. It's a moment they will always forget.

~ RAY HUDSON

Mate, if you just turn the bat over, you'll find the instructions on the other side.

~ AUSTRALIAN FAST BOWLER MERV HUGHES TO ROBIN SMITH
AFTER THE ENGLAND BATSMAN REPEATEDLY PLAYED AND MISSED

[Mike]Atherton gave as good as he got. His sledging was always more subtle and intelligent than my basic stuff. It would often take me three overs to understand what he meant.

~ MERV HUGHES

The sight of Imran [Khan] tearing fearsomely down the hill and the baying of the crowd made me realise for the first time that adrenalin was sometimes brown.   ~ SIMON HUGHES, *A LOT OF HARD YAKKA*

Dermot Reeve was so self-obsessed that even on the local nudist beach he only admired himself.   ~ SIMON HUGHES

You don't need a helmet facing Waqar so much as a steel toe cap.
~ SIMON HUGHES ON WAQAR YOUNIS'S SWINGING YORKER

Clinching the [County] Championship is a strange sensation… There's more atmosphere in a doctor's waiting room.   ~ SIMON HUGHES, *A LOT OF HARD YAKKA*

Angus Fraser never looks over-lively and once or twice in the West Indies we thought he might not make it back to the end of his run.   ~ RAY ILLINGWORTH

I absolutely insist that all my boys should be in bed before breakfast.
~ COLIN INGLEBY-MACKENZIE EXPLAINING HOW HAMPSHIRE
WON THE COUNTY CHAMPIONSHIP UNDER HIS CAPTAINCY

Cricket makes no sense to me. I find it very beautiful to watch and I like that they break for tea. That is very cool.   ~ JIM JARMUSCH

Ilott is out of this game with a groin strain and thus joins Darren Gough, Chris Lewis and Andrew Caddick on the list of those more in line for a trip to Lourdes rather than Lord's.   ~ MARTIN JOHNSON, *THE INDEPENDENT*

[Angus] Fraser's approach to the wicket currently resembles someone who has his braces caught in the sightscreen.   ~ MARTIN JOHNSON

Peter Willey is one of the few men you would back to get past a Lord's gateman with nothing more than an icy stare.   ~ MARTIN JOHNSON

His mincing approach resembled someone in high heels and a panty-girdle running after a bus.   ~ MARTIN JOHNSON ON MERV HUGHES' RUN-UP

At least we are safe from an intoxicated rendition of 'There's only one Graeme Hick'. There are, quite clearly, two of them. The first one turns out for teams like Worcestershire and New Zealand's Northern Districts and plays like a god. The second one pulls on an England cap and plays like the anagram of a god.
                                                                    ~ MARTIN JOHNSON

Michael Atherton is one of the few people capable of looking more dishevelled at the start of a six-hour century than at the end of it.

                                                                    ~ MARTIN JOHNSON

The most charismatic cricketer of his generation, who used to roar through the Lord's gates on a 1,000cc motorbike, will phut-phut his way back out of them on a metaphorical moped, his public persona having altered – in the space of four and a half years – from a latter-day Lawrence of Arabia into something closer to Mr Magoo.
                ~ MARTIN JOHNSON ON FORMER ENGLAND CHAIRMAN OF SELECTORS TED DEXTER

It would be a surprise if the mirrors in [Kevin] Pietersen's house totalled anything less than the entire stock at one of the larger branches of B&Q.
                                                                    ~ MARTIN JOHNSON

As a preparation for a Test match, the domestic game is the equivalent of training for the Olympic marathon by taking the dog for a walk.
                                                                    ~ MARTIN JOHNSON

Javed Miandad is lightning fast, and if he got rid of the extra ballast by removing the gold nuggets draped around his neck, he could look for two to short leg.
                                            ~ MARTIN JOHNSON ON THE PAKISTAN BATSMAN

Merv [Hughes] was a hard man to lip-read as his words were delivered through a moustache large enough to house a colony of koalas.   ~ MARTIN JOHNSON

How anyone can spin a ball the width of Gatting boggles the mind.

~ MARTIN JOHNSON ON SHANE WARNE'S FAMOUS 1993 DELIVERY

On the subject of skin care, James Anderson says: 'I always use a daily moisturiser.' It's one of the great tragedies that Fred Trueman is no longer on *Test Match Special*, because Jonathan Agnew asking Fred what type of moisturiser he used in his day could have produced one of sport's truly great radio moments.   ~ MARTIN JOHNSON

The open-topped bus ride around Trafalgar Square was a joyous moment in history, but if these things are graded by magnitude of achievement, England's reward for beating Sri Lanka will be a gentle spin in a milk float down Marylebone Road.   ~ MARTIN JOHNSON

If he's not talking about the flipper it's the zooter, the slider, or the wrong 'un. He'll shortly start working on a ball that loops the loop, disappears down his trouser leg, and whistles 'Waltzing Matilda' before rattling into the stumps.

~ MARTIN JOHNSON ON SHANE WARNE

There are two ways to play Warne, and somewhere between their two innings England decided to abandon the Fred Astaire routine which had served them so well for the first two days, and switch to the kind of footwork that would have embarrassed a boxful of battery hens.   ~ MARTIN JOHNSON, *DAILY TELEGRAPH*

Welcome to Worcester where you've just missed Barry Richards hitting one of Basil D'Oliveira's balls clean out of the ground.   ~ BRIAN JOHNSTON

Henry Horton has a funny stance. It looks as if he's shitting on a sooting stick.

~ BRIAN JOHNSTON

Welcome to Leicester where the captain Ray Illingworth has just relieved himself at the Pavilion End.
~ BRIAN JOHNSTON

The bowler's Holding, the batsman's Willey.

~ BRIAN JOHNSTON AS PETER WILLEY FACES UP TO MICHAEL HOLDING

As he comes in to bowl, Freddie Titmus has got two short legs, one of them square.
~ BRIAN JOHNSTON

[Glenn] Turner looks a bit shaky and unsteady, but I think he's going to bat on … one ball left.
~ BRIAN JOHNSTON AFTER TURNER WAS HIT IN THE BOX AREA BY THE PENULTIMATE BALL OF THE OVER

Neil Harvey's at slip, with his legs wide apart, waiting for a tickle.
~ BRIAN JOHNSTON

Bill [Frindall] needs a small ruler. How about the Sultan of Brunei? I hear he is only four foot ten.
~ BRIAN JOHNSTON

Batsmen wear so much protection these days that I mostly identify them from their posteriors.
~ BRIAN JOHNSTON

This bowler's like my dog: three short legs and balls that swing each way.

~ BRIAN JOHNSTON

I haven't noticed too many comments about my Aussie background out in the middle, but that's probably because I haven't been batting for long enough to notice!
~ GERAINT JONES

Don't bowl him bad balls, he hits the good ones for fours.

~ MICHAEL KASPROWICZ ON SACHIN TENDULKAR

A 1914 biplane tied up with elastic bands trying vainly to take off.

~ FRANK KEATING ON BOB WILLIS'S RUN-UP

Ian Botham plays a net as if he is on Weston-super-Mare beach and the tide is coming in fast.

~ FRANK KEATING

The programme implied that...he made love like he played cricket: slowly, methodically, but with the very real possibility that he might stay in all day.

~ MARTIN KELNER, REVIEWING A TV DOCUMENTARY ABOUT GEOFFREY BOYCOTT

An interesting morning, full of interest.

~ JIM LAKER

And Ian Greig's on eight, including two fours.

~ JIM LAKER

It's a unique occasion really – a repeat of Melbourne 1977.

~ JIM LAKER

Phil Edmonds needs two more field changes to get his 1,000 for the season.

~ JIM LAKER

Watching [Peter] Roebuck was like being at a requiem mass.

~ JIM LAKER ON A PAINFULLY SLOW INNINGS

I condone anyone who tampers with the ball.

~ ALLAN LAMB, WHO MAY HAVE MEANT 'CONDEMN'

Sometimes people think it's like polo, played on horseback, and I remember one guy thought it was a game involving insects.

~ CLAYTON LAMBERT ON EXPLAINING CRICKET TO AMERICANS

A cricket tour in Australia would be the most delightful period in your life – if you were deaf.

~ HAROLD LARWOOD

England have no McGrathish bowlers, there are hardly any McGrathish bowlers, except for McGrath.

~ STUART LAW

There's nothing like the sound of flesh on leather to get a cricket match going.

~ GEOFF LAWSON

Basically cricket is just a whole bunch of blokes standing around scratching themselves.

~ KATHY LETTE

The first time two batsmen have ever crossed in the toilet.

~ TONY LEWIS AS GLAMORGAN FACED WEST INDIES FAST BOWLER WES HALL

For any budding cricketers listening, do you have any superstitious routines before an innings, like putting one pad on first and then the other one?

~ TONY LEWIS

If I've to bowl to Sachin [Tendulkar], I'll bowl with my helmet on. He hits the ball so hard.

~ DENNIS LILLEE

Geoffrey [Boycott] is the only fellow I've met who fell in love with himself at a young age and has remained faithful ever since.

~ DENNIS LILLEE

I hate bowling at you. I'm not as good at hitting a moving target.

~ DENNIS LILLEE TO DEREK RANDALL

They've got to swing like a 70s disco to get anywhere near from here.

~ DAVID LLOYD ON AN ESSEX TWENTY20 RUN CHASE

If this bloke's a Test match bowler, then my backside is a fire engine.

~ DAVID LLOYD ON FIRST SEEING NATHAN ASTLE

What do I think of the reverse sweep? It's like Manchester United getting a penalty and Bryan Robson taking it with his head. ~ DAVID LLOYD

England have nothing to lose here, apart from this Test match. ~ DAVID LLOYD

She was a lovely mature lady and quite ample. In fact, Muttiah Muralitharan would have had plenty of room to sign his name.
~ DAVID LLOYD, ASKED TO SIGN A WOMAN'S CLEAVAGE

—Ian Botham: Where were you last night?
—David Lloyd: An oyster bar – apparently it puts lead in your pencil. I don't know about that. I think it only matters if you have got someone to write to.

It was rather a pity Ellis got run out at 1107, because I was just striking a length.
~ ARTHUR MAILEY WHO TOOK FOUR FOR 362 DURING VICTORIA'S RECORD SCORE

Cricket – a game which the English, not being a spiritual people, have invented in order to give themselves some conception of eternity. ~ LORD MANCROFT

The enigma with no variation. ~ VIC MARKS ON CHRIS LEWIS

So how's your wife and my kids?
~ ROD MARSH, AUSTRALIAN WICKET-KEEPER, WELCOMING IAN BOTHAM TO THE CREASE

As far as farewells go, this was like Dame Nellie Melba getting a frog in her throat. Then falling into the orchestra pit.
~ TREVOR MARSHALLSEA ON STEVE WAUGH'S DISAPPOINTING FINALE

And we don't need a calculator to tell us that the run-rate required is 4.5454 per over. ~ CHRISTOPHER MARTIN-JENKINS

Gul has another ball in his hand and bowls to Bell who has two.

~ CHRISTOPHER MARTIN-JENKINS

It's a perfect day here in Australia, glorious blue sunshine.

~ CHRISTOPHER MARTIN-JENKINS

It is extremely cold here. The England fielders are keeping their hands in pockets between balls.

~ CHRISTOPHER MARTIN-JENKINS

When's the game itself going to begin?

~ GROUCHO MARX, WATCHING A CRICKET MATCH AT LORD'S

If you go in with two fast bowlers and one breaks down, you're left two short.

~ BOB MASSIE

I doubt if many of my contemporaries, especially the older ones, did many exercises. I have often tried to picture [Godfrey] Evans and [Denis] Compton doing press-ups in the outfield before the day's play, but so far have failed miserably.

~ PETER MAY

Off the field, Bill O'Reilly could be your life-long buddy, but out in the middle, he had all the loveable qualities of a demented rhinoceros.

~ COLIN McCOOL

This game will be over any time from now.

~ ALAN McGILVRAY

It's been a weekend of delight and disappointment for [Kim] Hughes. His wife presented him with twins yesterday…and a duck today.

~ ALAN McGILVRAY

Freddie Flintoff's sparkling earring looks utterly ridiculous – like an Old Etonian tie on an orang-utan.

~ PETER McKAY

Many continentals think life is a game; the English think cricket is a game.

~ GEORGE MIKES

I'll tell you what pressure is. Pressure is a Messerschmitt up your arse. Playing cricket is not. ~ KEITH MILLER

I've seen batting all over the world. And in other countries too. ~ KEITH MILLER

I'm confident they play the game in heaven. Wouldn't be heaven otherwise, would it? ~ PATRICK MOORE

Are you aware that the last time I saw anything like that on a top lip, the whole herd had to be destroyed? ~ ERIC MORECAMBE TO THE MOUSTACHIOED DENNIS LILLEE

I would rather watch a man at his toilet than on a cricket field. ~ ROBERT MORLEY

Boycott, somewhat a creature of habit, likes exactly the sort of food he himself prefers. ~ DON MOSEY

Well, everyone is enjoying this except Vic Marks, and I think he's enjoying himself. ~ DON MOSEY

I am to cricket what Dame Sybil Thorndike is to non-ferrous welding. ~ FRANK MUIR

I suppose I can gain some consolation from the fact that my name will be permanently in the record books.

~ MALCOLM NASH, AFTER BEING HIT FOR SIX SIXES IN AN OVER BY GARY SOBERS IN 1968

His claim of being an all-rounder is clearly more a reflection of his physique than abilities in Test cricket. ~ *NEW AGE*, BANGLADESH NEWSPAPER, ON THE NATIONAL TEAM'S CAPTAIN KHALED MAHMUD

One of the Kiwi girls has been fingered by officials. ~ NEW ZEALAND BROADCASTER

Australians Have An Underarm Problem ~ NEW ZEALAND FANS' BANNER AFTER TREVOR
CHAPPELL'S UNDERHAND DELIVERY STOPPED NEW ZEALAND WINNING A ONE-DAY GAME IN 1981

Michael Vaughan has a long history in the game ahead of him. ~ MARK NICHOLAS

It's a funny kind of month, October. For the really keen cricket fan, it's when
you realise that your wife left you in May. ~ DENIS NORDEN

Mark Nicholas simpers to camera in the self-besotted manner of one who's been
told he has bedroom eyes. ~ MATTHEW NORMAN

If my grandfather was alive, he would have slaughtered a cow.
~ SOUTH AFRICA'S MAKHAYA NTINI AFTER TAKING 5 FOR 75 AGAINST ENGLAND AT LORD'S

Boy George would be considered straight at the University of Western Australia.
~ KERRY O'KEEFE, CASTING DOUBTS ABOUT THE TESTS DONE BY THE UNIVERSITY
ON MUTTIAH MURALITHARAN'S CONTROVERSIAL BOWLING ACTION

God had given him everything required of a bowler, except a brain-box. He was
definitely a screw loose.
~ BILL O'REILLY ON AUSTRALIAN SPINNER 'CHUCK' FLEETWOOD-SMITH
WHO USED TO DO BIRD IMPRESSIONS AS HE CAME IN TO BOWL

Have nothing to do with coaches. In fact, if you should see one coming, go and hide behind the pavilion until he goes away. ~ BILL O'REILLY

One good bit of news for England is that Ian Botham's groin is back to full
strength. ~ ELEANOR OLDROYD

I have prepared for the worst case scenario, but it could be even worse than that.
~ MONTY PANESAR, READY TO FACE ABUSE IN AUSTRALIA

Aussie sledging? I'm just glad they've heard of me! ~ MONTY PANESAR

At best, his action is suspicious. At worst, it belongs in a darts tournament.
~ MICHAEL PARKINSON ON MUTTIAH MURALITHARAN

The physique of a hat-pin and the only geriatric stoop I have ever seen on a 15-year-old. ~ MICHAEL PARKINSON ON A YOUNG DICKIE BIRD

Andre Nel is big and raw-boned and I suspect he has the IQ of an empty swimming pool.

~ ADAM PARORE

Sorry, skipper, a leopard can't change his stripes. ~ LENNIE PASCOE

Botham? I could have bowled him out with a cabbage, with the outside leaves still on. ~ CEC PEPPER

It's a Catch-21 situation. ~ KEVIN PIETERSEN

Only his mother would describe him as an athlete. ~ DEREK PRINGLE ON ASHLEY GILES

And there's the George Headley Stand, named after George Headley.
~ TREVOR QUIRK

When I first joined Middlesex there was a big card school, which would start up when it rained, with quite a lot of money going down. Now with all the public schoolboys in the Middlesex team, they play Scrabble. ~ MARK RAMPRAKASH

No good hitting me there, mate, there's nothing to damage.
~ DEREK RANDALL TO DENNIS LILLEE AFTER BEING HIT ON THE HEAD BY A BOUNCER

The blackcurrant jam tastes of fish to me.
~ DEREK RANDALL, TASTING CAVIAR FOR THE FIRST TIME ON AN MCC TOUR TO INDIA

There is, of course, a world of difference between cricket and the movie business. I suppose doing a love scene with Raquel Welch roughly corresponds to scoring a century before lunch.

~ OLIVER REED

There's only one man made more appeals than you, George, and that was Dr Barnardo.

~ UMPIRE BILL REEVE TO GEORGE MACAULEY

The only time an Australian walks is when his car runs out of petrol.

~ BARRY RICHARDS

Australia 602 for 3 declared, England 20 for 3. And in the Sixth Test, victory is slipping away from England.

~ STEVE RIDER

What [John] Buchanan knows about coaching you could write on the back of a dinner plate.

~ GREG RITCHIE

The gum-chewing habit is very catching, and you will sometimes see a whole fielding team resembling a herd of cows at pasture.

~ R.C. ROBERTSON-GLASGOW

Stuart MacGill's googly remains as hard to read as James Joyce.

~ PETER ROEBUCK

Richard Hadlee has the appearance of a rickety church steeple and a severe manner which suggests that women are not likely to be ordained yet.

~ PETER ROEBUCK

Allan Border is a walnut, hard to crack and without much to please the eye.

~ PETER ROEBUCK

David Gower never moves, he drifts.

~ PETER ROEBUCK

An ordinary bloke trying to make good without ever losing the air of a fellow with a hangover.

~ PETER ROEBUCK ON MERV HUGHES

Telling dear old Devon Malcolm to bowl down the corridor of uncertainty is like asking bombers to demolish a city without hurting any civilians. ~ PETER ROEBUCK

When Justin Langer finds his off stump akimbo he leaves the crease only after asking the Met Office whether any earthquakes have been recorded in the region.
~ PETER ROEBUCK

I thought if Rembrandt can do it, why can't I?
~ JACK RUSSELL ON HIS NEW CAREER AS AN ARTIST

I'm very concerned for New Zealand's middle order. We've already called on the immediate next people down, so who do you go to next? I've got a four-year-old son who might like a go. ~ KEN RUTHERFORD

We have had exceptionally wet weather in Derby – everywhere in the county is in the same boat. ~ TOM SEARS

Angus Fraser is like Eeyore without the joie de vivre. ~ MIKE SELVEY

He looks and bats like a librarian: a prodder and nudger with a virile bottom hand that works the ball to the on side and a top hand for keeping the other glove on. ~ MIKE SELVEY ON BERT VANCE

Devon Malcolm is the scattergun of Test cricket, capable on his worst days of putting the fear of God into short leg and second slip rather than the batsman. But sometimes, when the force is with him and he puts his contact lenses in the correct eyes, he can be devastating. ~ MIKE SELVEY

There was a time when a batsman had more chance of being hit by space debris than being done in the flight by Ashley Giles. ~ MIKE SELVEY

Inzamam-ul-Haq's languid batting can make Marcus Trescothick's footwork seem like a qualification for a starring role in *Riverdance*. ~ MIKE SELVEY

This ground is surprising. It holds about 60,000 but when there are around 30,000 in, you get the feeling that it is half empty. ~ RAVI SHASTRI

A brain scan revealed that Andrew Caddick is not suffering from a stress fracture of the shin.
~ JO SHELDON

Cricket needs umpires who grace the general scene with sartorial sharpness, instead of resembling a pair of Balkan refugees clad by Oxfam. ~ JOHN SHEPHERD

If one-day cricket was pyjama cricket, then Twenty20 is underwear cricket.
~ NAVJOT SIDHU

Wickets are like wives – you never know which way they will turn. ~ NAVJOT SIDHU

Deep Dasgupta is as confused as a child in a topless bar. ~ NAVJOT SIDHU

Umpire Eddie Nichols is a man who cannot find his own buttocks with his two hands.
~ NAVJOT SIDHU

Statistics are just like mini-skirts. They give you good ideas but hide the most important thing.
~ NAVJOT SIDHU

The third umpires should be changed as often as nappies … and for the same reason.
~ NAVJOT SIDHU

The only thing you get in life without trying is dandruff.
~ NAVJOT SIDHU

The Sri Lankan score is running like an Indian taxi meter.
~ NAVJOT SIDHU

He played that like a dwarf at a urinal.

~ NAVJOT SIDHU AS SACHIN TENDULKAR STANDS ON HIS TOES TO PLAY A SHOT

With his lovely soft hands he just tossed it off.

~ BOBBY SIMPSON ON A NEIL FAIRBROTHER STROKE AGAINST DURHAM

I just want to get into the middle and get the right sort of runs.

~ ROBIN SMITH, SUFFERING FROM DIARRHOEA ON AN ENGLAND TOUR OF INDIA

Yorkshire were 232 all out, Hutton ill. No, I'm sorry, Hutton 111.   ~ JOHN SNAGGE

You can't consider yourself a county cricketer until you've eaten half a ton
of lettuce.   ~ GARY SOBERS

We've won one on the trot.   ~ ALEC STEWART, CAPTAINING ENGLAND

Sometimes it takes him a fortnight to put on his socks.

~ MICKY STEWART ON THE LAID-BACK DEVON MALCOLM

I prefer cricket to baseball; I don't think I can be expected to take seriously any
game which takes less than three days to reach its conclusion.   ~ TOM STOPPARD

Mr Gower is the most disastrous leader since Ethelred the Unready. Beyond
question he should now stand down in favour of Ken Dodd.   ~ SUN, 1990

Not Over Till The Fat Laddie Spins

~ SUN HEADLINE ON SHANE WARNE

Martin McCague will go down as the rat who joined a sinking ship.

~ SYDNEY TELEGRAPH, AFTER THE FORMER AUSTRALIAN
YOUTH PLAYER ELECTED TO PLAY FOR ENGLAND

One day we'll lose the Ashes and it will be as horrific as waking up after a night
on the drink in a room full of images of Camilla Parker Bowles.

~ SYDNEY TELEGRAPH BEFORE THE 2005 SERIES

I still have the butterflies, but I now have them flying in formation.   ~ MARK TAYLOR

Personally, I have always looked on cricket as organised loafing. ~ WILLIAM TEMPLE

I get a few strange looks when I use the hotel laundry. They're used to washing shirts and socks, but not too many have been asked to clean a panther's head.
~ BARMY ARMY MEMBER KEVIN THAME, WHO WORE A
PINK PANTHER COSTUME TO WATCH ENGLAND IN BANGLADESH

It's not even as cold as this in my fridge back at Brisbane.
~ JEFF THOMSON ON AN ENGLISH SUMMER

Who's this then? Father Bloody Christmas?
~ JEFF THOMSON AS GREY-HAIRED DAVID STEELE ARRIVED AT THE CREASE

I thought, 'Stuff that stiff upper lip crap. Let's see how stiff it is when it's split.'
~ JEFF THOMSON ON ENGLAND

As a Pom, he'd make a great Aussie.   ~ JEFF THOMSON ON IAN BOTHAM

England's batsmen seem to get whipped more often than a saucepan full of spuds these days.   ~ JEFF THOMSON

The only change England would propose might be to replace Derek Pringle, who remains troubled by no balls.   ~ *THE TIMES*

With regard to the broken finger, when batting I'll just have to play it by ear.
~ MARCUS TRESCOTHICK

Unless something happens that we can't predict, I don't think a lot will happen.
~ FRED TRUEMAN

People only called me 'Fiery' because it rhymes with Fred, just like 'Typhoon' rhymes with Tyson.   ~ FRED TRUEMAN

I'd have looked even faster in colour.   ~ FRED TRUEMAN

There's only one head bigger than Tony Greig's – and that's Birkenhead.
                                                              ~ FRED TRUEMAN

I know why Boycott's bought a house by the sea – so he'll be able to go for a walk on the water.   ~ FRED TRUEMAN

Pitch saboteurs? I'd throw them off the top of the pavilion. Mind, I'm a fair man. I'd give them a 50-50 chance: I'd have Keith Fletcher underneath trying to catch them.   ~ FRED TRUEMAN

Kid yourself it's Sunday, Rev, and keep your hands together!
           ~ FRED TRUEMAN AFTER REVD DAVID SHEPPARD SPILLED A SUCCESSION OF CATCHES

I'm all right when his arm comes over, but I'm out of form by the time the bloody ball gets here. ~ FRED TRUEMAN, BAFFLED BY THE SLOW BOWLING OF PETER SAINSBURY

They must have fallen asleep in a greenhouse with their feet in a growbag.
                       ~ FRED TRUEMAN ON WEST INDIAN FAST BOWLERS

The game's a little bit wide open again.   ~ FRED TRUEMAN

That's what cricket is all about: two batsmen pitting their wits against one another.   ~ FRED TRUEMAN

That was a tremendous six: the ball was still in the air as it went over the boundary.   ~ FRED TRUEMAN

We didn't have metaphors in our day. We didn't beat about the bush.

~ FRED TRUEMAN

England's always expecting. No wonder they call her the Mother Country.

~ FRED TRUEMAN

Women are for batsmen, beer is for bowlers. God help the all-rounders!

~ FRED TRUEMAN

Anyone foolish enough to predict the outcome of this match is a fool.

~ FRED TRUEMAN

My main aim as far as practice went was to turn up on time in order to avoid another fine from the management. ~ PHIL TUFNELL

You can't smoke 20 a day and bowl fast. ~ PHIL TUFNELL ON WHY HE BECAME A SPINNER

I've done the elephant, I've done the poverty – I might as well go home.

~ PHIL TUFNELL ON TOUR IN INDIA

I remember when someone asked for my autograph and when I went over they slapped a minced beef and onion pie on my head. ~ PHIL TUFNELL ON AUSTRALIAN FANS

I have always imagined cricket as a game invented by roughnecks in a moment of idleness by casually throwing an unexploded bomb at one another. The game was observed by some officer with a twisted and ingenious mind who devoted his life to inventing impossible rules for it. ~ PETER USTINOV

I felt I was batting with a straw for the first 20 balls.

~ MICHAEL VAUGHAN, AFTER HIS MATCH-WINNING 86 AGAINST
AUSTRALIA IN THE 2004 CHAMPIONS TROPHY SEMI-FINAL

If I were Freddie [Flintoff], I would try to get a few of the Aussies out drinking with him because it will put them off their games. None of the Aussies could live with him. ~ MICHAEL VAUGHAN

My knee is fine but my neck hurts from watching all the sixes hit by Australia.

~ MICHAEL VAUGHAN, RETURNING TO LEAD ENGLAND FOR THE 2007 TWENTY20 SERIES

Richie Benaud eyes the camera lens with the manner of a disdainful lizard.

~ BRIAN VINER

We were brought up watching opening batsmen score nine before lunch. If Geoffrey Boycott flashed at a ball outside off stump in the first over of a Test match, questions were asked in Parliament. If he flashed at two, the ravens abandoned the Tower of London. ~ BRIAN VINER

It is important for Pakistan to take wickets if they are going to make big inroads into this Australian batting line-up. ~ MAX WALKER

He has got perfect control over the ball right up to the minute he lets it go.

~ PETER WALKER

With the possible exception of Rolf Harris, no other Australian has inflicted more pain and grief on Englishmen since Don Bradman.

~ MIKE WALTERS ON STEVE WAUGH'S RETIREMENT

My diet is still pizzas, chips, toasted cheese sandwiches and milkshakes. I have the occasional six-week burst where I stick to fruit and cereal: it bloody kills me.

~ SHANE WARNE

To break the world record, not in Australia but in India, would probably be my second choice. I'd like to think I'll do it in this Test match. If I don't, I'll probably be carrying drinks in the next one.

~ SHANE WARNE BEFORE BECOMING THE WORLD'S HIGHEST WICKET TAKER

We slept under the stars in sleeping bags – it was wonderful getting bitten by the mozzies – I'm still covered in bites. We went orienteering in the middle of the night with six-foot kangaroos jumping around. It was just a wonderful time!

~ SHANE WARNE, LESS THAN IMPRESSED BY COACH JOHN BUCHANAN'S 'BOOT CAMP'

I'm a big believer that the coach is something you travel in to get to and from the game. ~ SHANE WARNE HAVING ANOTHER DIG AT JOHN BUCHANAN

Denis Compton was the only player to call his partner for a run and wish him good luck at the same time. ~ JOHN WARR

And we have just heard, although this is not the latest score from Bournemouth, that Hampshire have beaten Nottinghamshire by nine wickets. ~ PETER WEST

So dull is he, tapes of the Willis delivery should be sold in Mothercare as a sleeping aid for fractious toddlers. ~ JIM WHITE ON BOB WILLIS'S STYLE OF COMMENTARY

I cannot for the life of me see why the umpires, the only two people on a cricket field who are not going to get grass stains on their knees, are the only two people allowed to wear dark trousers. ~ KATHARINE WHITEHORN

I never play cricket. It requires one to assume such indecent postures.

~ OSCAR WILDE

Kevin Pietersen would be deemed brash by a Texan assertiveness coach.

~ SIMON WILDE

Cricket is basically baseball on valium. ~ ROBIN WILLIAMS

I guess some guys are just naturally built for comfort rather than cricket.

~ BOB WILLIS ON ROBERT KEY

Steve Bucknor has completely lost the plot. He should take his pension back and sail off to the sunset. ~ BOB WILLIS

I was once offered a Foster's from someone over the fence, but it was warmer and frothier than a Foster's. ~ BOB WILLIS

Go on, Hedley, you've got him in two minds. He doesn't know whether to hit you for four or six. ~ ARTHUR WOOD TO HEDLEY VERITY

Most teams you know, only the next player to bat puts pads on. With Zimbabwe, everyone puts pads on! ~ ZIMBABWE SUPPORTER

BOATS

Powerboat Racing

Driving a powerboat is a bit like having one person throw a bucket of water over you while another hits you with a baseball bat.   ~ STEVE CURTIS

Rowing

Show me a crazy rower who has fallen out of a one-man boating race, and I'll show you a man who is out of his scull.   ~ ANON

And later we will have action from the men's cockless pairs.   ~ SUE BARKER

The Oxford rowing crew: eight minds with but a single thought, if that.   ~ MAX BEERBOHM

Ah! Isn't that nice – the wife of the Cambridge President is kissing the cox of the Oxford crew.   ~ HARRY CARPENTER

In water like that it's difficult to pick up much ground.   ~ TONY JOHNSON

The only Oxford and Cambridge Boat Races ever remembered are those in which one side has gratifyingly sunk.   ~ MILES KINGTON

The Boat Race: an activity that might have been designed for insomniacs with sleeping-pill allergies.   ~ MATTHEW NORMAN

I haven't stopped smiling since we won and even if I found out that my house had burned down when I got home, I would still be smiling.
~ MATTHEW PINSENT AFTER WINNING HIS FOURTH OLYMPIC GOLD MEDAL

I can't see myself racing competitively because that would really wind me up, facing old-aged, hair-coming-out-of-their-ears type people who you should be beating but you're not.   ~ MATTHEW PINSENT

There has been lots written in the last few weeks about my career, most of it inflated or wrong. As a friend said to me, 'At the rate they're going, leave it a few more days and you'll be Pope!' ~ MATTHEW PINSENT

She made it clear that if I carry on in a boat we won't have a marriage. I'll give it some thought. ~ STEVE REDGRAVE ON HIS WIFE'S VIEWS ABOUT HIS RETIREMENT

I'm not sure who's in the lead – it's either Oxford or Cambridge.
~ JOHN SNAGGE COMMENTATING ON THE BOAT RACE

Rowing seemed to me a monotonous pursuit, and somehow wasteful to be making all that effort to be going in the wrong direction. ~ PETER USTINOV, *DEAR ME*

Sailing

They're at each other the whole time. I refer to them as two randy bulls in a very small paddock. ~ DAVID ADAMS ON RIVALS ALEX THOMSON AND MIKE GOLDING

There isn't a record in existence that hasn't been broken. ~ CHAY BLYTH

The best thing about sailing on TV? No slow-motion replays. ~ NORMAN CHAD

Valencia will be hosting the next America's Cup – this is because Switzerland, who won it last time, has no sea around its coastline. ~ TIM DURRANT

A coarse sailor is one who in a crisis forgets nautical language and shouts, 'For God's sake, turn left!' ~ MICHAEL GREEN

I have no interest in sailing around the world. Not that there is any lack of requests for me to do so. ~ EDWARD HEATH

He did it alone, too. At an age when most boys believe they have been on an arduous trip if they drag themselves from the PlayStation to the fridge.
~ DES KELLY ON MICHAEL PERHAM, THE 14-YEAR-OLD WHO
SAILED SINGLE-HANDEDLY ACROSS THE ATLANTIC IN 2006

BODY SPORTS

Athletics

Running is an unnatural act, except from enemies and to the bathroom. ~ ANON

Race walking is arguably the most unnatural act that remains legal. To see a male Olympic walker in full cry is to be reminded of Barbara Windsor in a *Carry On* film, wiggling down the road in a tight skirt hoping to catch Sid James's eye.

~ ANON

Ian Mackie is here to prove his back injury is behind him. ~ ANON

I just want to get back to the shape I'm in now. ~ JAMIE BAULCH

Don't talk about Michael Johnson's style. Look, if that guy ran with his fingers up his bum he could still run the 400 in 42 seconds. ~ ROGER BLACK

What will my country give me if I win 100 metres gold in Sydney? Tobago probably. ~ ATO BOLDON, TRINIDAD AND TOBAGO SPRINTER

The only reason I would take up jogging is so that I could hear heavy breathing again.

~ ERMA BOMBECK

I held the record for the 100 metres at school. I was having a fag behind the bike shed when the dinner bell went. ~ JO BRAND

I am still looking for shoes that will make running on streets seem like running barefoot across the bosoms of maidens. ~ DAVE BROSNAN

The 880-yard heel and toe walk is the closest a man can come to experiencing the pangs of childbirth. ~ AVERY BRUNDAGE

She hasn't run faster than herself before. ~ ZOLA BUDD

My first 18-foot pole vault wasn't any more of a thrill than my first clearance at 15, 16 or 17 feet. I just had more time to enjoy it on the way down.

~ ROLAND CARTER

Is there something that sticks out that makes you an exceptional pole vaulter?

~ ADRIAN CHILES

I became a great runner because if you're a kid in Leeds and your name is Sebastian, you've got to become a great runner.

~ SEBASTIAN COE

And here's Moses Kiptanui – the 19-year-old Kenyan who turned 20 a few weeks ago.

~ DAVID COLEMAN

He just can't believe what's not happening to him.

~ DAVID COLEMAN

Bradford, who had gone up from 200 metres to 400, found it hard-going and for the last 100 was always going backwards.

~ DAVID COLEMAN

Morcelli has the four fastest 1,500-metre times ever. And all those times are at 1,500 metres.

~ DAVID COLEMAN

As they come through absolutely together with Wells in first place.

~ DAVID COLEMAN

There you can see her parents. Her father died some time ago.

~ DAVID COLEMAN

In a moment we hope to see the pole vault over the satellite.

~ DAVID COLEMAN

He is even smaller in real life than he is on the track.

~ DAVID COLEMAN

Her time is about 4:33, which she's capable of.

~ DAVID COLEMAN

One of the great unknown champions, because very little is known about him.

~ DAVID COLEMAN

And the line-up for the final of the women's 400 metres hurdles includes three Russians, two East Germans, a Pole, a Swede, and a Frenchman. ~ DAVID COLEMAN

It's gold or nothing ... and it's nothing. He comes away with a silver medal.
~ DAVID COLEMAN

And there's no 'I love you' message because Steve Ovett has married the girl.

~ DAVID COLEMAN

Linford Christie's got a habit of pulling it out when it matters most.

~ DAVID COLEMAN

It's a battle with himself and the ticking fingers of the clock.   ~ DAVID COLEMAN

A fascinating duel between three men…   ~ DAVID COLEMAN

This could be a repeat of what will happen in the European games next week.

~ DAVID COLEMAN

He's 31 this year. Last year he was 30.   ~ DAVID COLEMAN

Here are some names to look forward to, perhaps in the future. ~ DAVID COLEMAN

That's the fastest time ever run, but it's not as fast as the world record.

~ DAVID COLEMAN

Ingrid Kristiansen, then, has smashed the world record, running the 5,000 metres in 14:58:09. Truly amazing. Incidentally, this is a personal best for Ingrid Kristiansen.   ~ DAVID COLEMAN

There is Brendan Foster, by himself with 20,000 people. ~ DAVID COLEMAN

The Republic of China – back in the Olympic Games for the first time.
~ DAVID COLEMAN

We estimate, and this isn't an estimation, that Greta Waitz is 80 seconds behind.
~ DAVID COLEMAN

He is accelerating all the time. That last lap was run in 64 seconds and the one before in 62. ~ DAVID COLEMAN

It's a great advantage to be able to hurdle with both legs. ~ DAVID COLEMAN

A truly international field, no Britons involved. ~ DAVID COLEMAN

There's going to be a real ding-dong when the bell goes. ~ DAVID COLEMAN

I started running in high school. I found out if you run fast then you can get girls. ~ KIM COLLINS

From what I understand, these drugs shrink your nuts. I can't have my thingy shrunk. I can't afford that!
~ KIM COLLINS ON WHY HE WOULD NEVER TAKE BANNED DRUGS

I wasn't a very athletic boy. I was once lapped in the long jump. ~ RONNIE CORBETT

This is speed, power, grace – use whatever adjective you like about this woman.
~ STEVE CRAM

We do not have cross-country and we do not have pole-vaulting.
~ GERALD CURTIN ON SING SING PRISON'S ATHLETICS DAY

When I run marathons, my goal isn't to win or to place, or even to finish it under a certain time. It's to catch that cute guy with the nice butt in the little shorts running in front of me.

~ ANN DANTSUKA

Plainly no way has yet been found to stop long-jump commentaries sounding like naughty stories after lights-out in the dorm – 'Oooooh! It's enormous. It was long!'

~ RUSSELL DAVIES

The 400-metres boys have been supportive, although I'm still trying to remember everyone's name.

~ US-BORN MALACHI DAVIS AFTER BEING FAST-TRACKED INTO THE BRITISH OLYMPIC TRIALS

For Linford Christie to get the job he'll have to prove whiter than white.

~ VICTORIA DERBYSHIRE

Why am I returning to Brooklyn? Because I love to wake up to garbage trucks and gunshots.

~ DIANE DIXON

And finally she tastes the sweet smell of success.

~ IAN EDWARDS

The Kenyans haven't done much in the last two Games. In fact, they haven't competed since 1972.

~ BRENDAN FOSTER

I don't really understand miles – I didn't actually know how far it was going to be.

~ JADE GOODY, FAILING TO COMPLETE THE 2006 LONDON MARATHON

Born in America, John returned to his native Japan.

~ MIKE GRATTON

My roommate from Algeria checked in at 1.30am and began praying while watching porn. I told him he had to pick one or the other.

~ BREAUX GREER, OLYMPIC JAVELIN THROWER

The girls are all very tired. They have had six big events between their legs already.
~ SALLY GUNNELL

There's nothing new you can say about Linford Christie – except he's slow and has got a small penis.
~ NICK HANCOCK

Here's a good trick: get a job as a judge at the Olympics. Then, if some guy sets a world record, pretend that you didn't see it and go, 'OK, is everybody ready to start now?'
~ JACK HANDEY

If God wanted us to run, instead of a belly button, He'd have given us a fast-forward button.
~ JOE HICKMAN

You have to be suspicious when you line up against girls with moustaches.
~ MAREE HOLLAND

I'm becoming a bit familiar here, I'll need an apartment next. I'm a bit under-dressed from last time but the Queen did say, 'You've got more comfortable shoes on today.'
~ KELLY HOLMES GOES TO BUCKINGHAM PALACE TO PROMOTE THE 2006 COMMONWEALTH GAMES BATON RELAY, JUST WEEKS AFTER BEING MADE A DAME

I still think I could be the best pole vaulter in Britain, but I'm in danger of falling between two stools.
~ BRIAN HOOPER ON HIS SUCCESS IN TV'S SUPERSTARS

If Diane Modahl was 40 times over the testosterone limit, she'd have a deep voice and we'd all be calling her Barry White.
~ TONY JARRETT ON THE MODAHL DRUG ALLEGATIONS

The trouble with jogging is that by the time you realise you're not in shape for it, it's too far to walk back.
~ FRANKLIN JONES

When you go into an indoor championships like this, it's different to the outdoors.
~ MAX JONES

A muscle is like a car. If you want it to run well early in the morning, you have to warm it up.

~ FLORENCE GRIFFITH JOYNER

Derek, tell us about your amazing third leg.

~ ROSS KING TO RELAY RUNNER DEREK REDMOND

Ben Johnson must still be the fastest human in the world. He served a lifetime sentence in only two years.

~ MIKE LITTWIN, WHEN JOHNSON'S LIFE BAN WAS LIFTED AFTER TWO YEARS

My dad nearly strangled me. I didn't want to cry and look like a jessie but I couldn't help it.

~ DEAN MACEY WINNING THE DECATHLON AT THE 2006 COMMONWEALTH GAMES

The only thing that is amateur about track and field is its organisation.

~ CRAIG MASBACK

This is a double disaster, because the last thing anyone wants to see is Irina Korzhanenko stripped.

~ GAVIN McDOUGALD, AFTER THE RUSSIAN SHOT PUTTER WAS STRIPPED OF HER OLYMPIC GOLD MEDAL

To describe some of these substances as performance-enhancing is pushing at the boundaries of credibility. How much coffee do you have to drink to shave a hundredth of a second off your 100 metres time?

~ KEVIN MITCHELL

She's really tough; she's remorseful.

~ DAVID MOORCROFT

I don't think the discus will ever attract any interest until we start throwing them at each other.

~ AL OERTER

The decathlon is nine Mickey Mouse events and the 1,500 metres. ~ STEVE OVETT

Zola Budd: so small, so waif-like, you literally can't see her. But there she is.

~ ALAN PARRY

A very powerful set of lungs, very much hidden by that chest of his.   ~ ALAN PASCOE

I ran three miles today. Finally I said, 'Lady, take your purse.'   ~ EMO PHILIPS

Watch the time – it gives you an indication of how fast they are running.
~ RON PICKERING

Mary Decker, the world's greatest front-runner. I shouldn't be surprised to see her at the front.   ~ RON PICKERING

And Brian Hooper will have that recurring dream again and again.
~ RON PICKERING

Henry Rono, the man with those tremendous asbestos lungs.   ~ RON PICKERING

The Americans' heads are on their chins a little bit at the moment.
~· RON PICKERING

And the hush of anticipation is rising to a crescendo.   ~ RON PICKERING

He is going up and down like a metronome.   ~ RON PICKERING

And there goes Juantorena down the back straight, opening his legs and showing his class.   ~ RON PICKERING

And the mile once again becomes the focal point where it's always been.
~ RON PICKERING

I just wanted to win the race and I had to go. I haven't heard from Andrex, though.
~ PAULA RADCLIFFE ON HER UNSCHEDULED TOILET BREAK DURING THE 2005 LONDON MARATHON

I thought I should say, 'Move out of the way – mother and baby coming through!' ~ PREGNANT PAULA RADCLIFFE ON HER RACE TACTICS FOR THE 2006 HYDE PARK RUN

He's a well-balanced athlete; he has a chip on both shoulders.

~ DEREK REDMOND ON LINFORD CHRISTIE

Exactly how intricate a sport is jogging? You were two years old. You ran after the cat. You pretty much had it mastered. ~ RICK REILLY

The first time I see a jogger smiling, I'll consider it.

~ JOAN RIVERS, ASKED WHEN SHE WILL START JOGGING

We can't all be heroes because someone has to sit on the kerb and clap as they go by. ~ WILL ROGERS

I thought, 'You lazy cow.' I was going to turn off but the remote control was on the coffee table.

~ JONATHAN ROSS AFTER PAULA RADCLIFFE DROPS OUT OF THE 2004 OLYMPIC MARATHON

If you make one mistake, it can result in a vasectomy.

~ STEEPLECHASER MARK ROWLAND

I'm absolutely thrilled and over the world about it. ~ TESSA SANDERSON

If you want to know what you'll look like in ten years, look in the mirror after you've run a marathon. ~ JEFF SCAFF

In Russia, if a male athlete loses, he becomes a female athlete. ~ YAKOV SMIRNOFF

Somewhere inside that flabby body was an athlete trying to get out.

~ STUART STOREY ON SHOT-PUTTER GEOFF CAPES

He's got so much potential and most of it is still to be realised. ~ STUART STOREY

I'm just a normal Aussie guy who likes a smoke and a drink. I wish they'd had the final between 2am and 4am. I might have won.

~ LONG JUMPER JAI TAURIMA AT THE 2000 OLYMPICS

As a runner Daley Thompson is excellent, as a jumper he is excellent, and as a thrower he is an excellent runner and jumper. ~ CLIFF TEMPLE

Being a decathlete is like having ten girlfriends. You have to love them all, and you can't afford losing one. ~ DALEY THOMPSON

When I lost the decathlon record, I took it like a man. I cried for a week.

~ DALEY THOMPSON

Behind every good decathlete there's a good doctor. ~ BILL TOOMEY

I wouldn't be surprised if one day Carl Lewis's halo slipped and choked him.

~ ALLAN WELLS

I know I'm no Kim Basinger, but she can't throw a javelin. ~ FATIMA WHITBREAD

Most of these athletes will have a favourite lead leg, which is either left or right.

~ MIKE WHITTINGHAM

Jogging is for people who aren't intelligent enough to watch breakfast TV.

~ VICTORIA WOOD

The original Olympics were all held in the nude. That sure changed men's hurdles. The white guys won a lot more races. ~ TIM YOUNG

Biathlon

I think my favourite sport in the Olympics is the one in which you make your way through the snow, you stop, you shoot a gun, and then you continue on. In most of the world, it is known as the biathlon, except in New York City, where it is known as winter. ~ MICHAEL VENTRE

Gymnastics

Rhythmic gymnastics: adolescent girls the size of pixies, made up like the women on department store perfume counters, grinning like corpses while they wave a ribbon or bounce a ball.　　　　　　　　　　　*~ THE GUARDIAN*

Her legs are kept tightly together: she's giving nothing away.　　*~ TV COMMENTATOR*

In Russia, show the least athletic aptitude and they've got you dangling off the parallel bars with a leotard full of hormones.　　　　　　*~ VICTORIA WOOD*

Weightlifting

The guy with the biggest butt lifts the biggest weights.　　　*~ PAUL ANDERSON*

And this is Gregoriava from Bulgaria. I saw her snatch this morning and it was amazing.　　　　　　　　　　　　　　　　　　*~ PAT GLENN*

They walk on, they lift something up, they walk off again. Why do they need to wear leotards? Removal men don't and they do exactly the same job.　　　　　　　　　　　　　　　　　　　　*~ THE GUARDIAN*

What a man, what a lift, what a jerk!　　　　　　　*~ JIMMY McGEE*

Do I lift weights? Sure. Every time I stand up.　　　　*~ DOLLY PARTON*

CUES

Pool

Dressing a pool player in a tuxedo is like putting whipped cream on a hot dog.

~ MINNESOTA FATS

Every shot in pool is like putting in golf.

~ MIKE SIGEL

Every pool player's an egotist. You get four drinks inside a guy and he's never lost a game; you get ten drinks in him and he's never missed a shot. ~ DON WILLIS

Snooker

Someone threw a petrol bomb at Alex Higgins once and he drank it.

~ FRANK CARSON

In his oversized glasses, Dennis Taylor looked like Mickey Mouse with a welding shield on.

~ EDDIE CHARLTON

Two-piece snooker cues are popular these days but Alex Higgins doesn't use one because there aren't any instructions.

~ STEVE DAVIS

What Graeme Dott likes to do is win frames.

~ STEVE DAVIS

Jimmy White has popped out to the toilet to compose himself before the final push.

~ STEVE DAVIS

I suppose the charisma bypass operation was a big disappointment in my life.

~ STEVE DAVIS

I think it's a great idea to talk during sex, as long as it's about snooker.

~ STEVE DAVIS

Perhaps I will do a Jimmy White and change my name. Maybe if I call myself Paddy Power I will play better.

~ KEN DOHERTY

Just enough points here for Tony to pull the cat out of the fire.

~ RAY EDMONDS

Stephen Hendry jumps on Steve Davis's misses every chance he gets.

~ MIKE HALLETT

Stephen Hendry is the only man with a face that comes with free garlic bread.

~ NICK HANCOCK

You're short and bald and always will be.

~ QUINTEN HANN TO ANDY HICKS

I hear Peter Ebdon swims a mile every day. That means that in a year he could be 365 miles away. That is the best that we can hope for after this.

~ BARRY HEARN, FOLLOWING THE PAINFULLY SLOW 2006
WORLD FINAL BETWEEN EBDON AND GRAEME DOTT

I like playing in Sheffield; it's full of melancholy, happy-go-lucky people.

~ ALEX HIGGINS

Maybe I should put myself forward for *I'm A Celebrity… Get Me Out Of Here!* Then again, all the other guests would leave.   ~ ALEX HIGGINS PONDERING A COMEBACK

I'm going to look like Willie Thorne!

~ THE LATE PAUL HUNTER PUTTING A BRAVE FACE ON THE
PROSPECT OF CHEMOTHERAPY TO TREAT CANCER OF THE COLON

John Spencer has won the break and will toss.

~ SIDNEY LEE

That's inches away from being millimetre perfect.

~ TED LOWE

The audience are literally electrified and glued to their seats.

~ TED LOWE

Griffiths is snookered on the brown, which, for those of you watching in black and white, is the ball directly behind the pink.

~ TED LOWE

Fred Davis, the doyen of snooker, now 67 years of age and too old to get his leg over, prefers to use his left hand.   ~ TED LOWE

Steve Davis has a tough consignment in front of him.   ~ TED LOWE

It's not easy to get a snooker when there's only one ball on the table.
~ TED LOWE

He's completely disappeared. He's gone back to his dressing room, nobody knows where he has gone.   ~ TED LOWE

There is, I believe, a time limit for playing a shot. But I think it's true to say that nobody knows what that limit is.   ~ TED LOWE

That pot puts the game beyond reproach.   ~ TED LOWE

Higgins first entered the championship ten years ago. That was for the first time, of course.   ~ TED LOWE

Alex, unlike many other professionals, adds a bit on his cue rather than put on an extension.   ~ TED LOWE

Cliff [Thorburn] has been unsettled by the erratic but consistent potting of Perrie Mans.   ~ TED LOWE

And Alex has literally come back from the dead!   ~ TED LOWE

If I had had anyone else's head on my shoulders, I would be doing fine. I definitely believe I am a top 16 player, but unfortunately my head is not in the top 16.   ~ ROBERT MILKINS

I don't know if I'm still The Rocket – perhaps I'm more like Thomas the Tank Engine these days.   ~ RONNIE O'SULLIVAN

That wasn't the real me out there. Even Stevie Wonder would have beaten me.

~ RONNIE O'SULLIVAN

Snooker's a game – balls, sticks, holes. It's not worth trying to think about it.

~ RONNIE O'SULLIVAN

When I was 5-1 down, I thought I was going to lose 18-0.   ~ RONNIE O'SULLIVAN

Well, he's conceded there, but he never gives up, does he?   ~ JOHN PARROTT

It seems as if the pockets are as big as goalposts for Willie Thorne. ~ JOHN PULLMAN

From this position you've got to fancy either your opponent or yourself winning.

~ KIRK STEVENS

I was going to buy a Ferrari but I suppose now I'll have to settle for a caravan.

~ MATTHEW STEVENS, LOSING THE 2000 WORLD CHAMPIONSHIP FINAL

I remember when Steve Davis used to take valium as a stimulant. ~ DENNIS TAYLOR

He should bring out a video called 'How To Clear Up With Nothing On'.

~ DENNIS TAYLOR, AFTER MARCO FU MAKES A 50 BREAK WITH THE PINK AND BLACK TIED UP

Those long rests are never, ever used. They haven't been used in the last five years. And Mark Williams is about to use the long rest now.   ~ WILLIE THORNE

I am speaking from a deserted and virtually empty Crucible Theatre.

~ DAVID VINE

Ray Reardon, one of the great Crucible champions – won it five times when the championship was played away from the Crucible.   ~ DAVID VINE

This match has gradually and suddenly come to a climax.   ~ DAVID VINE

Somebody said to me the other day that there were no characters in the game. I asked him who his favourite player was and he replied Terry Griffiths. That threw me completely.

~ JOHN VIRGO

At that pace he was always going to hit it or miss it.

~ JOHN VIRGO

Throw caution to the wind? It's a risky thing to do.

~ JOHN VIRGO

All the reds are in the open now, apart from the blue.

~ JOHN VIRGO

John Parrott wants a screw... with plenty of bottom.

~ JOHN VIRGO

Matthew Stevens' natural expression is that of a man who may have mislaid his winning lottery ticket.

~ PAUL WEAVER

Bill Werbeniuk was a great drinker but also a very good player. Only he could get tanked up with ten pints before a match and still win.

~ JIMMY WHITE

I wouldn't come here if I didn't think I could win it. I'd go and play bad golf in Spain instead.

~ JIMMY WHITE

They should start the matches at 8am because then you could stay up all night!

~ JIMMY WHITE, CRASHING OUT OF THE UK CHAMPIONSHIP FOLLOWING A 10AM START

COMBAT

Boxing

I'm so fast that last night I turned off the light switch in my hotel room and was in bed before the room was dark.
~ MUHAMMAD ALI

I'll beat him [Floyd Patterson] so hard he'll need a shoehorn to put his hat on.
~ MUHAMMAD ALI

Sonny Liston's so ugly that when he cries, the tears run down the *back* of his head.
~ MUHAMMAD ALI

Here I predict Sonny Liston's dismemberment, I'll hit him so hard, he'll forget where October-November went.
~ MUHAMMAD ALI

Sonny Liston would rather be dropped in the middle of Vietnam with a peashooter before he'd fight me again.
~ MUHAMMAD ALI

Joe Frazier's so ugly they ought to donate his face to the World Wildlife Fund.
~ MUHAMMAD ALI

I've seen George Foreman shadow boxing, and the shadow won. ~ MUHAMMAD ALI

Mike Tyson is too ugly to be champion. He's got gold teeth. He's got bald spots all over his head. I used to call Joe Frazier 'The Gorilla' but next to Tyson, Joe was a beautiful woman.
~ MUHAMMAD ALI

If they can make penicillin out of mouldy bread, they can sure make something out of you.
~ MUHAMMAD ALI

Journalist Howard Cosell was gonna be a boxer when he was a kid, only they couldn't find a mouthpiece big enough.
~ MUHAMMAD ALI

I'm so mean I make medicine sick.
~ MUHAMMAD ALI

I'm so fast I could hit you before God gets the news.
~ MUHAMMAD ALI

There's not a man alive who can whup me. I'm too fast. I'm too smart. I'm too pretty. I should be a postage stamp. That's the only way I'll ever get licked.

~ MUHAMMAD ALI

I said I was the greatest, not the smartest.

~ MUHAMMAD ALI, AFTER FAILING AN ARMY INTELLIGENCE TEST

Boxing's a rough sport. After every fight I rush to the mirror to make sure I'm still presentable. A lot of boxers' features change – mainly when I fight 'em.

~ MUHAMMAD ALI

If you ever dream of beating me, you'd better wake up and apologise.

~ MUHAMMAD ALI

It's just a job. Grass grows, birds fly, waves pound the sand. I beat people up.

~ MUHAMMAD ALI

It's hard to be humble when you're as great as I am.

~ MUHAMMAD ALI

I am the astronaut of boxing. Joe Louis and Dempsey were just jet pilots. I'm in a world of my own.

~ MUHAMMAD ALI

My toughest fight was with my first wife.

~ MUHAMMAD ALI

After all the years of punishment you've taken, you must be thinking about giving up pantomime.

~ CLIVE ANDERSON TO FRANK BRUNO

They shouldn't have stopped it. The fight could have gone either way: he could have killed me or crippled me.

~ ART ARAGON

My greatest virtue? I never missed a punch in my life. Every one of them landed right on my chin.

~ ART ARAGON

I'll never forget my last time at Madison Square Garden. Hundreds of people were screaming for me. I must have sold 250 hot dogs.   ~ ART ARAGON

You've got your health, you've got your money, you've even got most of your ear.
          ~ JIM ARMSTRONG ON WHY EVANDER HOLYFIELD SHOULD RETIRE FROM BOXING

I was in stitches then – although Willie was in stitches at the end!
          ~ ALEX ARTHUR RECALLS THE BANTER BEFORE A FIGHT WITH WILLIE LIMOND

Sugar Ray Leonard's retirements last about as long as Elizabeth Taylor's marriages.   ~ BOB ARUM

I've seen tougher croissants.
          ~ TEDDY ATLAS ON FRENCH CHALLENGER PATRICK CHARPENTIER

My definition of fear? Standing across the ring from Joe Louis and knowing he wants to go home early.   ~ MAX BAER

—Hotel operator: Do you want the house doctor?
—Max Baer: No, get me a people doctor.
(These were Baer's last words)

Introducing the only man to hold three titles simultaneously and at the same time…   ~ HARRY BALOGH

And now over to ringside, where Harry Commentator is your carpenter.
          ~ BBC ANNOUNCER

The British Press hate a winner who's British. They don't like any British man to have balls as big as a cow's, like I have.   ~ NIGEL BENN

I get worried when a guy goes down, in case he doesn't get up for me to hit him again.   ~ NIGEL BENN

How many fighters does it take to change a light bulb? None. The promoter will fix it. ~ MIKE BIANCHI

[Muhammad] Ali was in the Midlands on business, so I asked him if he'd pop over to open my fish and chip shop. He didn't charge me a penny, but I gave him some cod and chips. ~ JACK BODELL, FORMER EUROPEAN HEAVYWEIGHT CHAMPION

Nothing is going to stop Tyson that doesn't have a motor attached. ~ DAVID BRENNER

Boxing is just show business with blood. ~ FRANK BRUNO

That's cricket, Harry. You get these sorts of things in boxing. ~ FRANK BRUNO

I was about18 six years ago. I'm 28 now. ~ FRANK BRUNO

I'm not going to predict what I'm gonna do, but I'm gonna come out of there the winner. ~ FRANK BRUNO

I was in a no-win situation, so I'm glad that I won rather than lost. ~ FRANK BRUNO

And I want to say anything is possible. Comma. You know. ~ FRANK BRUNO

Even though I've retired from boxing, I still go to the gym to spar every day. I miss being hit on the head.
~ FRANK BRUNO

I was ranked fourth in the world and you know what that means? I was fourth in the world. ~ JOE BUGNER

I don't know what impressive is, but Joe was impressive tonight. ~ MARLENE BUGNER, JOE'S WIFE

The noise that comes from the wretched throats of a boxing crowd indicates that brain damage is also in the head of the beholder. ~ JULIE BURCHILL

They voted him the most sexy man in Wales. And I finished second, because I'm his dad. ~ ENZO CALZAGHE ON SON JOE

My girlfriend boos me when we make love because she knows it turns me on. ~ HECTOR CAMACHO

I can happily say I've made a 100-degree turn in my life. ~ HECTOR CAMACHO ON RETURNING TO THE RING

You know why Mike Tyson's eyes water when he's having sex? Mace. ~ JOHN CAPONERA

Tyson's the only guy I know who could drive a Rolls-Royce and say, 'See those licence plates? I made them myself.' ~ JOHN CAPONERA

Don't you think it's funny that all those tough-guy boxers are fighting over a purse? ~ GEORGE CARLIN

Undisputed heavyweight champion? Well, if it is undisputed, what's all the fighting about? To me, 'undisputed' means we all agree. Here you have two men beating the shit out of one another over something they apparently agree on. Makes no sense. ~ GEORGE CARLIN

He looks up at him through his blood-smeared lips. ~ HARRY CARPENTER

This boxer is doing what is expected of him, bleeding from his nose. ~ HARRY CARPENTER

The question looming over Magri is not will he keep the title, but can he? ~ HARRY CARPENTER

And Magri has to do well against this unknown Mexican who comes from a famous family of five boxing brothers.   ~ HARRY CARPENTER

Marvellous oriental pace he's got, just like a Buddhist statue.   ~ HARRY CARPENTER

It's not one of Bruno's fastest wins, but it's one of them.   ~ HARRY CARPENTER

They've given it all tonight, but there's a little bit left to give yet.
~ HARRY CARPENTER

Boxers don't have sex before a fight. Do you know why? They don't fancy each other.   ~ JIMMY CARR

When I got up I stuck to my plan – stumbling forward and getting hit in the face.   ~ RANDALL 'TEX' COBB

If I wanted to communicate with Larry during the fight, I would have had to send him a letter. Every time I wanted to say something I found it hard speaking because he kept putting his left hand in my mouth.
~ RANDALL 'TEX' COBB AFTER BEING ACCUSED OF TALKING TO LARRY HOLMES DURING AN UNSUCCESSFUL WORLD HEAVYWEIGHT TITLE CHALLENGE

I don't think his hands could take the abuse.
~ RANDALL 'TEX' COBB ON A POSSIBLE RE-MATCH WITH LARRY HOLMES

I'd love to fight Gerry Cooney. But I have my price: 25 cents and a loose woman.
~ RANDALL 'TEX' COBB

There ain't nobody as bad as Bob Arum. That New York City Jew lawyer will make you hate city folks, Jews and lawyers in the same day.   ~ RANDALL 'TEX' COBB

A fat, cocaine-snorting drunk? I'm not fat.   ~ RANDALL 'TEX' COBB

I've been knocked out once, by a Mexican bantamweight. How come? Six of my pals were swinging him around by the heels at the time. ~ RANDALL 'TEX' COBB

If you screw things up in tennis, it's 15-love. If you screw up in boxing, it's your ass. ~ RANDALL 'TEX' COBB

Was acting hard? Hell, no. Anybody who can live with the same woman for four months can act. ~ RANDALL 'TEX' COBB ON HIS MOVIE CAREER

I'm going down so often these days you'd think I was making a blue movie. ~ JOHN CONTEH

I'm hoping we can fight again or at least have a re-match. ~ JOHN CONTEH

It seems I have luck, but it's all bad. ~ GERRY COONEY

—Baroness Edith Summerskill: Mr Cooper, have you looked in the mirror lately and seen the state of your nose?
—Henry Cooper: Well, madam, have you looked in the mirror and seen the state of your nose? Boxing is my excuse. What's yours?

I got into the ring with Muhammad Ali once and I had him worried for a while. He thought he'd killed me! ~ TOMMY COOPER

George Michael does a bit of boxing. For years he's been knocked around the ring. ~ RUSSELL CROWE

When promoter Bob Arum pats you on the back, he's just looking for a spot to stick the knife. ~ CUS D'AMATO

I'm a washed-up boxer who hasn't fought for 15 years. Do you know what that makes me today? It makes me a contender. ~ TONY DANZA

John Conteh has a neck built like a stately home staircase. ~ TOM DAVIES

I was a hopeless boxer. I had handles sewn into my shorts so that they could carry me out of the ring easily. ~ LES DAWSON

Nailing Tommy Gibbons was like trying to thread a needle in a high wind. ~ JACK DEMPSEY

You only spend so much time in the spotlight before they change the bulb. ~ JACK DEMPSEY

All the time he's boxing, he's thinking. All the time he was thinking, I was hitting him. ~ JACK DEMPSEY

Honey, I just forgot to duck. ~ JACK DEMPSEY TO HIS WIFE AFTER LOSING HIS WORLD HEAVYWEIGHT TITLE

I thought, 'Hello, [Dick] Tiger looks a lot bigger than me.' But it was because I was on the floor looking up at him. ~ TERRY DOWNES

I'll shake hands with [Bob] Arum, but I'll take my ring off first. ~ MICKEY DUFF

Chris Eubank is as genuine as a three-dollar bill. ~ MICKEY DUFF

Why would anyone expect Tyson to come out smarter? He went to prison for three years, not Princeton. ~ LOU DUVA

He [Andrew Golota] is a guy who gets up at six o'clock in the morning regardless of what time it is. ~ LOU DUVA

We're having a meeting of minds, but right now only one is functioning – mine. ~ LOU DUVA ON LIVINGSTONE BRAMBLE

When George [Foreman] goes into a restaurant, he doesn't ask for a menu. He asks for an estimate.
~ LOU DUVA

Some people say George [Foreman] is fit as a fiddle, but I think he looks more like a cello.
~ LOU DUVA

Look at that. They've got the name of Evander's next opponent up already.
~ LOU DUVA, SEEING THE NAME OF 96-YEAR-OLD GEORGE BURNS ON A LAS VEGAS SIGN, AS HE ARRIVES FOR EVANDER HOLYFIELD'S TITLE BOUT AGAINST VETERAN LARRY HOLMES

—Interviewer: Have you ever thought of writing your autobiography?
—Chris Eubank: On what?

Nigel Benn is like washing-up liquid: built on hype and one day the bubble will burst.
~ CHRIS EUBANK

Every time I hear the name Joe Louis my nose starts to bleed.
~ TOMMY FARR

Ali wouldn't have hit Joe Louis on the bum with a handful of rice.
~ TOMMY FARR

I know it's said I can't punch, but you should see me putting the cat out at night.
~ CHRIS FINNEGAN

I was a schizophrenic when I met Hector Camacho. I soon found out he was a schizophrenic too. The four of us have gotten along fine ever since.
~ PATRICK FLANNERTY

He started out crazy, but he took so many punches he's now straightened out.
~ PADDY FLOOD, MANAGER OF CHUCK WEPNER

Mike Tyson's not all that bad. If you dig deep, dig real deep, go all the way to China, I'm sure you'll find there's a nice guy in there.
~ GEORGE FOREMAN

Buster Douglas is a nice guy but he's a bore. His poster could put people to sleep.   ~ GEORGE FOREMAN

Boxing is like jazz. The better it is, the less people appreciate it.   ~ GEORGE FOREMAN

How far do I run in training? Depends on how far my refrigerator is.   ~ GEORGE FOREMAN

I want to keep fighting because it is the only thing that keeps me out of the hamburger joints. If I don't fight, I'll eat this planet.   ~ GEORGE FOREMAN

I was once on a diet for two weeks running. All I lost was two weeks.
                                                          ~ GEORGE FOREMAN

He's got a nutritionist, and I've got room service.
                              ~ GEORGE FOREMAN ON EVANDER HOLYFIELD

There's more to boxing than hitting. There's not getting hit, for instance.
                                                          ~ GEORGE FOREMAN

Sure the fight was fixed. I fixed it with a right hand.
                    ~ GEORGE FOREMAN, AFTER KNOCKING OUT MICHAEL MOORER

In boxing you have to prepare for memory loss. I wanted to make sure I didn't forget anybody's name.   ~ GEORGE FOREMAN ON WHY HE NAMED ALL HIS SONS GEORGE

The referee is the most important man in the ring besides the two fighters.
                                                          ~ GEORGE FOREMAN

We have an all-American boy here, even though he is a Canadian.
                         ~ BILLY JOE FOX ON SIGNING WILLIE DE WIT

You get your brains shook, your money took, and your name in the undertaker's book.
~ JOE FRAZIER ON THE DANGERS OF BOXING

There are certain things you can't get back, like the elastic in your socks.
~ EDDIE FUTCH ON FIGHTERS WHO MAKE COMEBACKS

Shakespeare? I ain't never heard of him. He's not in no ratings. I suppose he's one of them foreign heavyweights. They're all lousy. Sure as hell I'll murder that bum.
~ TONY GALENTO

He now floats like an anchor, stings like a moth.
~ RAY GANDOLFO ON MUHAMMAD ALI AT 39

The world is full of people who will shove an umbrella up your ass. But some of the people in the WBC will shove it up and then open it just for fun.
~ RICHIE GIACHETTI

They all look better than Rocky when they're doing their job. But they don't look so good on the canvas.
~ CHARLIE GOLDMAN, REPLYING TO CRITICISM OF ROCKY MARCIANO'S STYLE

Me and Jake LaMotta grew up in the same neighbourhood. You wanna know how popular Jake was? When we played hide-and-seek, nobody ever looked for LaMotta.
~ ROCKY GRAZIANO

I quit school in the sixth grade because of pneumonia. Not because I had it, but because I couldn't spell it.
~ ROCKY GRAZIANO

And the crowd go wild as they see the shaven head of [Marvin] Hagler enter the auditorium. And there he is, hooded…
~ REG GUTTERIDGE

[Prince] Naseem Hamed is naturally fit. I've seen more fat on a butcher's apron.
~ REG GUTTERIDGE

His potatoes kept getting cut eyes!

~ REG GUTTERIDGE ON WHY HENRY COOPER QUIT AS A GREENGROCER

Congratulations. You have a great future behind you.

~ MARVIN HAGLER TO JAMES TILLIS

Chris Eubank lost his recent comeback fight on points – the main one being that he's a total git.

~ NICK HANCOCK

To me, boxing is like a ballet, except there's no music, no choreography and the dancers hit each other.

~ JACK HANDEY

I think Lewis will stop Tua somewhere between the ninth and tenth rounds.

~ AUDLEY HARRISON

Ricky can't sing but his mates are too scared to tell him.

~ RAY HATTON ON HIS SON'S LOVE OF KARAOKE

I'm going to say hello to two friends who I've shut out of my life for the past ten weeks while I trained the hardest I've ever done for a fight. So welcome back Mr Guinness and Mr Dom Perignon.

~ RICKY HATTON

Life is the best left hooker I ever saw, although some say it was Charlie White of Chicago.

~ ERNEST HEMINGWAY

Basically [Audley] Harrison's fat, can't fight and can't knock anyone out. He's not strong enough to smash an egg with a baseball bat.

~ HERBIE HIDE

Don't make me laugh! It's the WBF belt – I heard they are giving them away with five litres of petrol down at Texaco.

~ HERBIE HIDE POURS SCORN ON AUDLEY HARRISON'S WBF HEAVYWEIGHT TITLE

It will be the first time in boxing annals that the referee's instructions will be, 'Shake hands and come out breathing.'

~ EARL HOCHMAN ON THE FIGHT BETWEEN VETERANS GEORGE FOREMAN AND LARRY HOLMES

All I want is a referee who can count to ten and doesn't stutter.

~ LARRY HOLMES BEFORE A FIGHT WITH MIKE TYSON

[Gerry] Cooney can't beat me. If I was 90 years old, he couldn't beat me.

~ LARRY HOLMES

Don King doesn't care about black or white. He just cares about green.

~ LARRY HOLMES

It's hard being black. You ever been black? I was black once – when I was poor.

~ LARRY HOLMES

I don't think I could possibly be that good an actor.

~ EVANDER HOLYFIELD ON WHY HE TURNED DOWN A MOVIE SCRIPT THAT
REQUIRED HIM TO BE BEATEN BY ASPIRING HEAVYWEIGHT TOMMY MORRISON

The bell went ding and I went dong.

~ LLOYD HONEYGHAN, FLOORING JOHNNY BUMPHUS RIGHT AT THE START OF THE SECOND ROUND

I was called 'Rembrandt' Hope in my boxing days, because I spent so much time on the canvas.

~ BOB HOPE

I'll bet the hardest thing about prize fighting is picking up your teeth with a boxing glove on.

~ KIN HUBBARD

Francesco Damiani punches with all the violence and bad intentions of Mahatma Gandhi.

~ JERRY IZENBERG

The trouble with suing Bob Arum is that you have to stand in the line.

~ JIM JACOBS

I'm in the ring with this guy who's trying to take my head off, and I'm thinking of how I'm going to decorate the baby's new room. I lost my focus sometimes.

~ STEVIE JOHNSTON

The bum was up and down so many times I thought he was an Otis elevator.
~ HARRY KABAKOFF ON CHANGO CRUZ

I've only ever seen Errol Christie fight once before and that was the best I've ever seen him fight.

~ MARK KAYLOR

Frank Bruno's fall was that of a felled oak. As the dust settled there was a silence, and then followed the gentle rustle of falling leaves of greenbacks. ~ FRANK KEATING

This is America. It's different. It's not like England, where you can fight a tuna fish and get $3 million.

~ KEVIN KELLEY

I've told Chris not to worry about the final. When this Russian breaks your jaw he does it cleanly. He's decent enough that way.

~ CHARLIE KERR, ASSISTANT TRAINER TO THE BRITISH OLYMPIC TEAM, ON CHRIS FINNEGAN'S OPPONENT IN THE 1968 MIDDLEWEIGHT FINAL, ALEXEI KISELIOV

He's the man of the hour at this particular moment.

~ DON KING

He [Julio Cesar Chavez] speaks English, Spanish, and he's bilingual too.

~ DON KING

The chances of a rematch for Lewis are slim and none. And slim is out of town.

~ DON KING

When you can count your money, you ain't got none.
~ DON KING

They went down the list of every known charge conceivable to man: racketeering, skimming, kickback, ticket scalping, fixing fights, pre-ordaining fights, vitiating fights, corrupting judges, all the way down to laundering money. Everything but the Lindbergh baby.
~ DON KING, INVESTIGATED BY THE FBI

Sadly, America's oldest man has died at age 114. However, Don King is confident that he'll be able to find another opponent for George Foreman.
~ BOB LACEY

On the way here this guy steps up to us and says, 'Would you like to join Jehovah's Witnesses?' And Rocky [Graziano] says, 'I didn't see nuttin'!'
~ JAKE LaMOTTA

I fought Sugar so many times that I'm lucky I didn't get diabetes.
~ JAKE LaMOTTA ON HIS CONTESTS WITH SUGAR RAY ROBINSON

My first wife divorced me because I clashed with the drapes. My second wife used to ignore me all the time. I was in so much hot water I felt like a tea bag. My third wife divorced me because the only thing I said to her was, 'Darling, your stockings are wrinkled.' Now, how the hell did I know she wasn't wearing any?
~ JAKE LaMOTTA

He's standing there making a sitting target of himself.
~ TERRY LAWLESS

In the ring I can feel that halo over my head turn into those two little horns.
~ SUGAR RAY LEONARD

I'm undisputed and there's no disputing that.
~ LENNOX LEWIS

You've got to remember this guy's basically undefeated, except for that one loss.
~ LENNOX LEWIS ON JOE CALZAGHE

You've got to come in with more than a left hook and a bad haircut to beat Lennox Lewis.   ~ LENNOX LEWIS AFTER HIS POINTS VICTORY OVER DAVID TUA

The only way I'll ever fight again is if someone steals my last Rolo.   ~ LENNOX LEWIS

Even the push button elevators don't stop for me now.
                                ~ SONNY LISTON AFTER LOSING HIS WORLD HEAVYWEIGHT TITLE

He hasn't fought anybody yet. He's been knocking over selling platers. The wife could have knocked out the last two mugs he met.
                                                ~ STEWART LITHGO ON FRANK BRUNO

Sure, as long as he ties a 56-pound weight to each leg.
                                ~ BRIAN LONDON, ASKED IF HE WOULD FIGHT MUHAMMAD ALI AGAIN

I'm only a prawn in the game.   ~ BRIAN LONDON

I don't like money actually, but it quiets my nerves.   ~ JOE LOUIS

They say that money talks, but the only thing it ever said to me was goodbye.
                                                            ~ JOE LOUIS

Do I believe in superstitions? No. If you have superstitions, that's bad luck.
                                                            ~ ERIC LUCAS

Born in Italy, most of his fights have been in his native New York.
                                                            ~ DES LYNAM

Frank, you deserve a knighthood, or maybe even Lord of the Rings.
                                                ~ DES LYNAM TO FRANK BRUNO

People talk about the altitude, but you've got to remember he's been on American time.   ~ FRANK MALONEY

Tyson is still crazy – he bit my nipple! Good job he wasn't a midget, otherwise he'd have bitten something else!

~ KEVIN McBRIDE

Jumbo Cummings – a name that sounds like an elephant ejaculating.

~ RORY McGRATH

If they said I had to defend my title against Mahatma Gandhi, I would fight him.

~ BARRY McGUIGAN

I miss things like the camaraderie in the gym. I don't miss being smacked in the mouth every day.

~ BARRY McGUIGAN

In his prime [Joe] Bugner had the physique of a Greek statue, but he had fewer moves.

~ HUGH McILVANNEY

—Joe Bugner (annoyed by Press criticism): Get me Jesus Christ, I'll fight him tomorrow.
—Hugh McIlvanney: Ah, Joe, you're only saying that because you know He's got bad hands.

There seems only one way to beat George Foreman: shell him for three days and then send the infantry in.

~ HUGH McILVANNEY

This is an era when calling the heavyweight division a desert insults the fecundity of the Sahara.

~ HUGH McILVANNEY, 2006

George Chuvalo's best punch is a left cheek to the right glove.

~ LARRY MERCHANT

Were you as surprised as we all were when he came from behind and licked you in the ring?

~ MRS MERTON TO CHRIS EUBANK AFTER HIS DEFEAT TO STEVE COLLINS

A boxer makes a comeback for two reasons: either he's broke or he needs the money.

~ ALAN MINTER

I had Bernard Taylor five rounds ahead going into the fifth round. ~ ALAN MINTER

Sure there have been injuries and deaths in boxing – but none of them serious.

~ ALAN MINTER

I put on a video of one of his recent fights and it made my eyes water, there were so many low blows. I want a big family, so I was straight on the phone to sort out some insurance for my meat and two veg!

~ KEVIN MITCHELL BEFORE A FIGHT WITH GHANA'S GEORGE ASHIE

Why do I like speaking at prisons? Because nobody walks out in the middle of my speech.

~ ARCHIE MOORE

It pays me better to knock teeth out than put them in.

~ DENTIST-TURNED-BOXER FRANK MORAN

Joe's got the easy part: he's only got to fight Frank Bruno, but I've got to deal with Marlene.   ~ BILL MORDEY, AUSTRALIAN PROMOTER, ON JOE BUGNER'S FEARSOME WIFE

I have an advantage in this fight. I have only one chin to expose.

~ TOMMY MORRISON, PREPARING TO FACE GEORGE FOREMAN

Venezuela? Great! That's the Italian city with the guys in the boats, right?

~ MURAD MUHAMMAD

Marvellous Marvin and Sugar Ray: sounds like a pillow fight between a hairdresser and an interior decorator.   ~ JIM MURRAY ON A HAGLER-LEONARD FIGHT

One looked like a Greek god. The other looked like a Greek restaurant.

~ JIM MURRAY ON THE EVANDER HOLYFIELD-GEORGE FOREMAN FIGHT

When Mike Tyson gets mad you don't need a referee, you need a priest.

~ JIM MURRAY

They stopped it before Tyson put him in a pot.

~ JIM MURRAY ON MIKE TYSON'S ACT OF CANNIBALISM IN
BITING OFF PART OF EVANDER HOLYFIELD'S EAR

He's got more talent than I've seen in a long time, but right now he's playing with only about 50 cards in a 52-card deck.

~ PAT O'GRADY ON TROUBLED HEAVYWEIGHT JERRY HALSTEAD

He's gonna need an industrial-strength toothpick to pick the leather out of his teeth.   ~ MICHAEL OLAJIDE BEFORE BEING STOPPED IN THE FIFTH ROUND BY IRAN BARKLEY

Lennox Lewis is demanding a bonus clause to fight Mike Tyson – more money if Tyson fouls. So this could be history's first pay-per-chew fight.   ~ SCOTT OSTLER

Brian London possesses the most unbeautiful face. It looks as if it, at one time, fell apart and was reassembled by a drunken mechanic.   ~ MICHAEL PARKINSON

Terry Downes' face looked as if he had slept on it.   ~ MICHAEL PARKINSON

Do I know where I am? You're damn right I do! I'm in Madison Square Garden getting the shit knocked out of me!   ~ WILLIE PASTRANO TO THE RING DOCTOR

Fear was absolutely necessary. Without it, I would have been scared to death.

~ FLOYD PATTERSON

His legs turned to spaghetti, and I was all over him like the sauce.

~ VINNIE PAZIENZA

The worst thing that happened to managers was when boxers learned to read and write.   ~ PAUL PENDER

They call Ray Robinson the best fighter pound for pound. I'm the best fighter, ounce for ounce.   ~ FEATHERWEIGHT WILLIE PEP

Lay down so I can recognise you.

~ WILLIE PEP STRUGGLING TO REMEMBER THE NAME OF AN EX-BOXER

I've got it made. I've got a wife and a TV set – and they're both working.

~ WILLIE PEP

It's a hot night at Madison Square Garden, and at ringside I see several ladies in gownless evening straps. ~ JIMMY POWERS

Mike McCallum has one of the five great chins in the world. The other four are on Mount Rushmore. ~ PAT PUTNAM

They told me Jack Bodell was awkward and he was – he fell awkwardly.

~ JERRY QUARRY AFTER KNOCKING OUT BODELL

I don't want to tell you any half-truths unless they're completely accurate.

~ DENNIS RAPPAPORT

I'd like to introduce a man who is a legacy in his own lifetime. ~ DENNIS RAPPAPORT

[Jack] Dempsey hits people only slightly harder than a bus. ~ RICK REILLY

I can close any cut in the world in 50 seconds, so long as it ain't a total beheading. ~ ADOLPH RITACCO, TRAINER

Hear about the Tyson computer? Two bytes. No memory. ~ PHIL ROSENTHAL

Hector Camacho's great dream is to someday die in his own arms. ~ IRVING RUDD

It's strange … two guys in shorts competing for a belt. They should at least award them slacks or a shirt. ~ JERRY SEINFELD

Herol 'Bomber' Graham has turned defensive boxing into a poetic art. Trouble is, nobody ever knocked anybody out with a poem. ~ EDDIE SHAW

He has everything a boxer needs except speed, stamina, a punch, and ability to take punishment. In other words, he owns a pair of shorts.   ~ BLACKIE SHERROD

I can't wait to play the piano on his ribs.   ~ TONY SIBSON ON HEROL GRAHAM

I was once offered $300 to throw a fight in the third round but I had to turn it down because I had never made it to the third round.   ~ LON SIMMONS

I know a lot of people think I'm dumb. Well, at least I ain't no educated fool.

~ LEON SPINKS

I'll fight Lloyd Honeyghan for nothing, if the price is right.   ~ MARLON STARLING

Lennox fought the perfect fight. He just got hit on the chin.

~ MANNY STEWARD, LENNOX LEWIS'S TRAINER, AFTER
A SHOCK WORLD TITLE KNOCKOUT BY HASIM RAHMAN

—Stewardess: Mr Ali, please fasten your seat belt.
—Muhammad Ali: Superman don't need no seat belt.
—Stewardess: Superman don't need no airplane either.

Tommy Morrison proved that he is an ambidextrous fighter. He can get knocked out with either hand.   ~ BERT SUGAR

I put my suitcase down, looked up at the Sears Tower, and said, 'Chicago, I'm going to conquer you.' When I looked down, my suitcase was gone.

~ JAMES 'QUICK' TILLIS ON HIS FIRST DAY IN CHICAGO

New York Ban On Boxing After Death.

~ *TIMES* HEADLINE

Evander [Holyfield] and I are great warriors. We put blood and guts in the ring. We do not run around and hug and kiss. Well, Evander might do that, but I do not.   ~ JAMES TONEY

Which of Tyson's punches did the most damage? The one with the baseball bat.

~ TONY TUBBS

How much do you want to bet that Simpson backs out for the most obvious reason: he can't find a pair of gloves that fit?

~ RANDY TURNER ON NEWS THAT O.J. SIMPSON WAS TO TAKE PART IN A CELEBRITY BOXING MATCH

This was your first fight at 185 pounds. Did you approach the fight any differently from your other fights at this weight?

~ TV INTERVIEWER

Not to be egotistical, but I don't think there is a man on this planet who can beat me.

~ MIKE TYSON

I really dig Hannibal. Hannibal had real guts. He rode elephants into Cartilage.

~ MIKE TYSON

I guess I'm gonna fade into Bolivian.

~ MIKE TYSON

We took two different paths in life. I scramble people's brains and he fixes 'em.

~ MIKE TYSON, WHOSE BROTHER RODNEY IS A MEDIC

The bell that tolls for all in boxing belongs to a cash register.

~ BOB VERDI

The public should be paid for going to see this fight instead of the other way around.

~ FRANK WARREN ON THE PROPOSED BOUT BETWEEN AUDLEY HARRISON AND JULIUS FRANCIS

If I had bent over any further to help him [Scott Harrison], I could have got a job as an India rubber man in Gerry Cottle's circus.

~ FRANK WARREN

Scott Harrison has pissed away a career then acted as if he is the victim.
He doesn't have a chip on his shoulder, but a bag of King Edwards.

~ FRANK WARREN AFTER HARRISON PULLED OUT OF A 2006 WORLD TITLE FIGHT

Of course I don't mind the fight being at three in the morning. Everyone in
Glasgow fights at three in the morning. ~ JIM WATT

To be honest, it was a very physical fight. ~ JIM WATT

You can stop counting, I'm not getting up.

~ JIM WATT'S SUGGESTION FOR A BOXER'S EPITAPH

I was six foot one when I started fighting, but with all the uppercuts I'm up to
six foot five. ~ CHUCK WEPNER

My best three punches were the choke hold, the rabbit punch and the head butt.

~ CHUCK WEPNER

We don't want to meet this geezer Liston walking down the street, let alone in
the ring. ~ JIM WICKS, MANAGER OF HENRY COOPER

Even against blokes my granny could beat up I have been nervous.

~ DANNY WILLIAMS

I can only see it going one way, that's my way. How it's actually going to go I
can't really say. ~ NICK WILSHIRE

I started boxing to get rid of my beer belly and my tits that were hanging down to the floor. ~ CLINTON WOODS

From the first round on, Shawn [O'Sullivan] was as flat as yesterday's beer.

~ PETER WYLIE

Martial Arts

Karate is a form of martial arts in which people who have had years and years of training can, using only their hands and feet, make some of the worst movies in the history of the world.
~ DAVE BARRY

I only train on days ending in a Y.
~ NEIL OHLENKAMP

'Ouch' is not a judo term.
~ NEIL OHLENKAMP

My brother-in-law died. He was a karate expert, then joined the army. The first time he saluted, he killed himself.
~ HENNY YOUNGMAN

Wrestling

There are bears in the woods that are tamer than Stan Hansen.
~ BOB CAUDLE

Rick Steiner is so stupid, he once stayed up all night to study for a urine test.
~ JIM CORNETTE

Norman is so stupid, mind readers charge him half price.
~ JIM CORNETTE

I can beat anyone, either male, female, animal, vegetable or mineral.
~ JIM CORNETTE

I believe that professional wrestling is clean and everything else in the world is fixed.
~ FRANK DEFORD

Jackie Pallo was a terrible businessman. But I don't mean that in a derogatory way: he was just bad at business.
~ MICK McMANUS

I don't know what it is, but I can't look at Hulk Hogan and believe that he's the end result of millions and millions of years of evolution.
~ JIM MURRAY

Professional wrestling's most mysterious hold is on its audience. ~ LUKE NEELY

Ole Anderson is as strong as an ox and almost as smart. ~ RODDY PIPER

Fat binmen in leotards wrestling for small change in Rotherham Town Hall.
~ JONATHAN ROSS ON THE GOLDEN AGE OF BRITISH WRESTLING

Professional wrestling is the only sport where participants are just thrown right out into the audience, and no one in the crowd thinks anything is happening. If you're watching a golf tournament and Jack Nicklaus goes flying over your head – first of all, I would say, you're watching a very competitive tournament.
~ JERRY SEINFELD

Wrestling is ballet with violence. ~ JESSE VENTURA

If it's all-in, why do they wrestle? ~ MAE WEST

EQUINE

Horse Racing

A racehorse is an animal that can take several thousand people for a ride at the same time.

~ ANON

Riding is the art of keeping a horse between yourself and the ground.

~ ANON

The weighing room is something of a cultural desert. This is not a criticism, because the ability to recite poetry is bugger all use to you as you sail down to Becher's.

~ MARCUS ARMYTAGE

Riding a typical [Tony] McCoy race, where he literally picks up the horse and carries it over the line.

~ CLARE BALDING

I wanted to go out on a winner rather than on a stretcher.

~ RON BARRY

Horses and jockeys mature earlier than people, which is why horses are admitted to race tracks at the age of two, and jockeys before they are old enough to shave.

~ DICK BEDDOES

One way to stop a runaway horse is to bet on him.

~ JEFFREY BERNARD

Jenny Pitman reminds me of a manatee who employs a blind milliner.

~ JEFFREY BERNARD

You never see a pretty, unattached girl on a racecourse. But you often see positive gangs of rather unpretty ones. They are the owners or the owners' wives and they wear mink in all weathers and far too much make-up. For some odd reason, I can never work out why they always seem to be married to haulage contractors in the north, builders in the south and farmers in the west.

~ JEFFREY BERNARD

Am I feeling the pressure? I don't do pressure. That's for tyres.

~ JIM BOLGER

Royal Ascot celebrates the noblest English obsessions: class, animals, the monarchy, and furtive sex.   ~ TANIA BRANIGAN

The Game Spirit Chase, named after Game Spirit, a lovely horse, owned by the Queen Mother, who dropped dead here after a long and distinguished career.
                                                                        ~ PETER BROMLEY

Desert Orchid was a different class, like driving a Ferrari rather than a Cortina.
                                                                ~ COLIN BROWN, JOCKEY

Lester Piggott appeared in the Queen's role as guest of honour, thereby notching up an unlikely double, having gone on from spending time in one of her jails to acting as her stand-in.   ~ WILL BUCKLEY ON THE 2004 DERBY

Jockeys usually have four or five dreams a night about coming from different positions.   ~ WILLIE CARSON

I'm lucky because I have an athlete between my legs.   ~ WILLIE CARSON

In 1900 the owner of the Grand National winner was the then Prince of Wales, King Edward VII.   ~ DAVID COLEMAN

No horse can go as fast as the money you bet on him.   ~ NATE COLLIER

The jockeys' biggest concern: drowning.
~ GREG COTE AFTER JOCKEYS IN FLORIDA REFUSED TO RIDE BECAUSE OF FOUR INCHES OF STANDING WATER ON THE COURSE

He was going all right until he fell.
~ JOCKEY JOHN CULLEN, WHOSE MOUNT BUNNY BOILER CAME TO GRIEF AT THE FIRST FENCE IN THE 2003 GRAND NATIONAL

I don't follow particular horses, although the horses I back seem to.
                                                                ~ TOMMY DOCHERTY

Eventually the pool from which stewards were selected was extended beyond the registered blind, the chronically inbred and those whose ear trumpets or searing gout problems rendered them half-sharp or pathologically vicious.

~ ALASTAIR DOWN

Tony McCoy would rather have a finger off than a day off. ~ RICHARD EDMONDSON

Ireland: a country where the boat-race course would be considered good to firm.

~ MATTHEW ENGEL

Horse sense is the thing a horse has which keeps it from betting on people.

~ W.C. FIELDS

Bookmakers are pickpockets who allow you to use your own hands. ~ W.C. FIELDS

Remember, Lady Godiva put all she had on a horse. ~ W.C. FIELDS

Sex is an anti-climax after that! ~ MICK FITZGERALD AFTER WINNING THE GRAND NATIONAL

Danoli is too good for me to say how good he is. ~ TOM FOLEY

This racecourse is as level as a billiard ball. ~ JOHN FRANCOME

Jenny Pitman's about as cuddly as a dead hedgehog. The Alsatians in her yard go around in pairs for protection. ~ JOHN FRANCOME

You could remove the brains from 90 per cent of jockeys and they would weigh the same. ~ JOHN FRANCOME

He must have discovered euthanasia. He never seems to get any older.

~ JOHN FRANCOME

That horse stays longer than the mother-in-law. ~ JOHN FRANCOME

That is the first time she has had 14 hands between her legs. ~ JOHN FRANCOME

—Ginger McCain: Francome, you're the worst jockey in the entire world!
—John Francome: No… That's too much of a coincidence.

Mick Channon's tongue is the vocal equivalent of that windmill right arm which rotated maniacally when celebrating a goal. ~ ALAN FRASER

Orpen Wide won his third race on the trot since we had him gelded, making us wonder what to cut off next to keep him winning. ~ CLEMENT FREUD

Owning a racehorse is probably the most expensive way of getting on to a racecourse for nothing. ~ CLEMENT FREUD

My horse was in the lead coming down the home stretch, but the caddie fell off.
~ SAM GOLDWYN

The easiest owner I trained for was Elizabeth Taylor. She was so worried her horses would get injured she never wanted them to run. ~ JOHN GOSDEN

He's a real bull of a horse. ~ DARYLL HOLLAND ON FALBRAV

The only man who makes money following the races is one who does it with a broom and shovel. ~ ELBERT HUBBARD

A loose horse is any horse sensible enough to get rid of its rider at an early stage and carry on unencumbered. ~ CLIVE JAMES

Horse racing is animated roulette. ~ ROGER KAHN

I've had an interest in racing all my life, or longer really. ~ KEVIN KEEGAN

We all have our knockers, women in racing. ~ GAY KELLEWAY

Jump jockey Paul O'Neill is being investigated after television caught him butting his horse. One question: What did that horse say to provoke him?

~ DES KELLY

Desert Orchid and I have a lot in common. We are both greys, vast sums of money are riding on our performance, the Opposition hopes we will fall at the first fence, and we are both carrying too much weight.

~ NORMAN LAMONT, CHANCELLOR OF THE EXCHEQUER, IN HIS 1991 BUDGET
SPEECH AFTER A POLL REVEALED THAT WHILE 84 PER CENT OF PEOPLE HAD
HEARD OF DESERT ORCHID, ONLY 77 PER CENT HAD HEARD OF LAMONT

Lester Piggott has a face like a well-kept grave.
~ JACK LEACH

A real racehorse should have a head like a lady and a behind like a cook.

~ JACK LEACH

Coming into the Festival, I was a Cheltenham virgin. Now I'm a real slapper!

~ JOCKEY GRAHAM LEE AFTER HIS THIRD WIN AT THE 2006 CHELTENHAM FESTIVAL

Steve Cauthen, well on his way to that mythical 200 mark.   ~ JIMMY LINDLEY

These two horses have met five times this season, and they've beaten each other on each occasion.   ~ JIMMY LINDLEY

What's the secret of reaching 80? Swim, dance a little, go to Paris every August, and live within walking distance of two hospitals.   ~ TRAINER HORATIO LURO

Tony [McCoy] has a quick look between his legs and likes what he sees.

~ STEWART MACHIN

Why did I become a jockey? I was too small to become a window cleaner and too big to be a garden gnome.   ~ ADRIAN MAGUIRE

Not many people can claim to have ridden a winner on their honeymoon – at least, not on a horse.

~ CHRIS MAUDE

Other than being castrated, things have gone quite well for Funny Cide.

~ KENNY MAYNE

If Carrie Ford wins the National, I'll bare my backside to the wind and let everyone kick it.

~ GINGER McCAIN

This is the best thing that has happened to me for a long time. I never thought I would win another National. Now you can take me around the corner and shoot me.

~ GINGER McCAIN

I went over to see the horse [Amberleigh House] and the woman who was selling him had the greatest legs I'd ever seen. I'm a great legs man and I couldn't resist.

~ GINGER McCAIN

The horse sadly died this morning, so it looks like he won't be running in the Gold Cup.

~ CHARLIE McCANN

Was I nervous? Does Dolly Parton sleep on her back? ~ CHRIS McCARRON BEFORE A BIG RACE

The thing I dream about is waking up lighter than I was.

~ TONY McCOY

There should be a law against Lester Piggott.

~ DARRELL McHARGUE

People who think racing is not about gambling probably think that dancing is not about sex.

~ HUGH McILVANNEY

Peter O'Sullevan's admirers are convinced that had he been on the rails at Balaclava he would have kept pace with the Charge of the Light Brigade, listing the fallers in precise order and describing the riders' injuries before they hit the ground.

~ HUGH McILVANNEY

When interviewing Lester Piggott, an answer a third as long as the question is the standard rate of exchange.

~ HUGH McILVANNEY

I'd give him my balls if they could transplant them.

~ JOCKEY DEAN McKEOWN ON TALENTED GELDING HUGS DANCER

I bet on a horse yesterday that was so slow, the jockey kept a diary of the trip.

~ BOB MONKHOUSE

Tony [McCoy] is as tough as old nails and he'd probably ride if he had no legs and no arms.

~ COLM MURPHY

Seattle Slew was a compassionate horse. He never beat anybody more than he had to. He was like a poker player who lets you keep your watch and car fare home.

~ JIM MURRAY

I've been covering horse races for 25 years and I still can't tell a colt from a filly except under very special circumstances.

~ JIM MURRAY

This is the last evening meeting of the year at Redcar, but we're going out with a bang because this is Ladies' Night.

~ PETER NAUGHTON

There are, they say, fools, bloody fools, and men who remount in a steeplechase.

~ JOHN OAKSEY

She was the most wonderful thing for jumping.

~ JOHN OAKSEY, PAYING TRIBUTE TO THE QUEEN MOTHER'S LOVE OF STEEPLECHASING

What do they say when they geld a racehorse? 'And they're off!'   ~ CONAN O'BRIEN

If you remove the gambling, where is the fun in watching a bunch of horses being whipped by midgets?

~ IAN O'DOHERTY

My father was a great fan of the horses. His only regret was that I never ran in the Grand National.
~ STEVE OVETT

A cantankerous cross between Jimmy Edwards and a Turkish pasha, John McCririck is the reason why we had an empire – and the reason why we lost it.
~ ALLISON PEARSON

Their bottoms are the wrong shape.
~ LESTER PIGGOTT ON LADY JOCKEYS

People ask me why I ride with my bottom in the air. Well, I've got to put it somewhere.
~ LESTER PIGGOTT

—Jeremy Tree: I've got to speak to my old school, Lester, and tell them all I know about horse racing. What should I tell them?
—Lester Piggott: Tell 'em you have got the flu.

I may have got beaten by Desert Orchid at Kempton in the King George VI Chase but it was like being beaten by the Queen Mother. You didn't really mind.
~ JENNY PITMAN

I never smoked when I was riding. It was working for Mother that got me started.
~ MARK PITMAN ON THE STRESSES OF BEING JENNY PITMAN'S SON

A racehorse is not like a machine. It has to be tuned up like a racing car.
~ CHRIS POOL

I have looked at many another woman, but I have never looked at another jockey.
~ SIR MARK PRESCOTT ON HIS STABLE JOCKEY GEORGE DUFFIELD

Instead of crawling into bed from nightclubs at 6am, I had to learn to crawl out of bed at the same time.
~ FOOTBALLER-TURNED-RACEHORSE-TRAINER MICK QUINN

Red Rum is in a stable condition.
~ RADIO 5 REPORT ON THE HORSE'S ILLNESS

Pilsudski is out in front, but only by virtue of the fact that that's where he is.

~ RADIO 5 LIVE

I never realised I'd end up being the shortest knight of the year.

~ JOCKEY GORDON RICHARDS ON BEING HONOURED

If Jesus Christ rode his flaming donkey like you just rode that horse, then he deserved to be crucified.

~ FRED RIMELL TO JOCKEY JIM OLD

The race is not always to the swift, nor the battle to the strong, but that's the way to bet.

~ DAMON RUNYON

Nobody has ever bet enough on a winning horse.

~ RICHARD SASULY

This horse has had more problems in the last six months than Bill Clinton – and this fellow's a gelding!

~ JON SCARGILL, 1998

Secretariat and Riva Ridge are the most famous pair of stablemates since Joseph and Mary.

~ DICK SCHAAP

It looks as though that premature excitement may have been premature.

~ BROUGH SCOTT

And there's the unmistakable figure of Joe Mercer ... or is it Lester Piggott?

~ BROUGH SCOTT

Flat Jockey: an anorexic dwarf in bright colours who drives a large car with cushions on the seat and blocks on the pedals.

~ JULIAN SEAMAN, *TURFED OUT*

Nice little horse, gelded him, made a man out of him.

~ BRYAN SMART

Women jockeys are a pain. Jumping's a man's game. They are not built like us. Most of them are as strong as half a disprin.

~ STEVE SMITH-ECCLES

John McCririck … looking like a hedge dragged through a man backwards.

~ *SUNDAY EXPRESS*

—Brough Scott: What are your immediate thoughts, Walter?
—Walter Swinburn: I don't have any immediate thoughts at the moment.

When Arkle first came to Mr Dreaper's his action was so bad you could drive a wheelbarrow through his hind legs. ~ PAT TAAFE

A racetrack is a place where windows clean people. ~ DANNY THOMAS

If Frankie [Dettori] didn't exist, it would be necessary for the British Horseracing Board to invent him. ~ PETER THOMAS

Further Flight seems to get better and better, although he's not as good as he was. ~ DEREK THOMPSON

In the last race, favourite-backers would certainly have had their hearts in their chests. ~ DEREK THOMPSON

You must be lost for words. Tell us how it feels. ~ DEREK THOMPSON

All jockeys must pass the same rigorous medical before they're granted a licence. Thankfully, I assess whether they're fit to ride, not whether they're barmy.
~ DR MICHAEL TURNER, CHIEF MEDICAL ADVISER TO THE JOCKEY CLUB

I didn't care about going off favourite – the horse has no idea what price he is. ~ RUBY WALSH

This is really a lovely horse and I speak from personal experience since I once mounted her mother. ~ TED WALSH

The sandwiches at Teesside Park were definitely on the firm side of good.

~ IAN WATKINSON

The horse seems to have become disenfranchised with racing. ~ JAMES WILLOUGHBY

I backed a great horse the other day – it took seven horses to beat him.

~ HENNY YOUNGMAN

I backed a horse at ten to one. It came in at half past five.   ~ HENNY YOUNGMAN

I regularly give money to sick animals – every time I put on a bet.

~ HENNY YOUNGMAN

A lot of horses get distracted. It's just human nature.   ~ NICK ZITO

Polo

Swearing at the polo club? It's a load of bollocks!   ~ MAJOR RONALD FERGUSON

Playing polo is like trying to play golf during an earthquake. ~ SYLVESTER STALLONE

Show Jumping

And Harvey Smith is on the phone now and I think that means he's on the phone.   ~ RAYMOND BROOKES-WARD

John Francome knows a lot about dressage. But not nearly as much as he knows about undressage.   ~ ALASTAIR DOWN

He's obsessed with his looks and would love a diamond earring.

~ WILLIAM FOX-PITT ON HIS HORSE TAMARILLO

She never knows when she's beaten except when she actually is. ~ STEPHEN HADLEY

There's Pam [Dunning] watching anxiously. She doesn't look anxious though.

~ STEPHEN HADLEY

As you travel the world, do you do a lot of travelling? ~ HARVEY SMITH

Minchinhampton Woman Wins Award

~ *STROUD NEWS AND JOURNAL* HEADLINE AFTER ZARA PHILLIPS, DAUGHTER OF THE
PRINCESS ROYAL, IS NOMINATED EQUESTRIAN OF THE YEAR AT THE HORSE OF THE YEAR SHOW

Once he'd gone past the point of no return, there was no way back.

~ TV COMMENTATOR

He's a very competitive competitor, that's the sort of competitor he is.

~ DORIAN WILLIAMS

FOOTBALL (SOCCER)

It looks as if I am trying to stab Dave Bassett in the back but I'm not holding a gun to anyone's head.

~ MICKY ADAMS

Apparently Andrew Whing was eating a lasagne and somehow pulled a hamstring. It has to be a world first.

~ MICKY ADAMS, RUEING AN INJURY TO ONE OF HIS PLAYERS

If we go down I will feel as bad as I did when I was a child and realised Father Christmas was actually my dad.

~ MICKY ADAMS

We bought 23 single tickets at Gunnersbury station and our unsung hero was midfielder Jay Tabb who knew we had to change at Hammersmith to get to our Shepherd's Bush destination. I feel a bit sorry for him because I didn't even put him in the team.

~ MICKY ADAMS WHOSE COVENTRY PLAYERS HAD TO HOP ON THE LONDON UNDERGROUND TO GET TO QPR AFTER THE TEAM BUS WAS DELAYED IN HEAVY TRAFFIC

Dennis [Bergkamp] is such a nice man, such a tremendous gentleman with such a lovely family. It's going to be very hard for me to kick him.

~ TONY ADAMS BEFORE ENGLAND PLAYED HOLLAND AT EURO 96

Bristol Rovers were 4-0 up at half-time, with four goals in the first half.

~ TONY ADAMSON

It doesn't matter, all that's important is getting the three points.

~ GABRIEL AGBONLAHOR, AFTER ASTON VILLA WIN ... A CARLING CUP TIE

I was watching the Blackburn game on TV on Sunday when it flashed on the screen that George [Ndah] had scored in the first minute at Birmingham. My first reaction was to ring him up. Then I remembered he was out there playing!

~ ADE AKINBIYI

We normally come here and just get a cup of tea and a few sandwiches.

~ TRANMERE MANAGER JOHN ALDRIDGE HAPPY TO TAKE SOMETHING
AWAY FROM MOLINEUX AFTER A 2-1 VICTORY AT WOLVES

Four minutes to go ... four long minutes ... 360 seconds. ~ ALISTAIR ALEXANDER

There were two Second Division matches last night, both in the Second Division.

~ DOMINIC ALLEN

Our bus broke down and delayed us for three hours, so we practised on a roundabout.

~ MARTIN ALLEN, TAKING HIS MK DONS TEAM TO LINCOLN

I've served more time than Ronnie Biggs did for the Great Train Robbery.

~ MALCOLM ALLISON ON HIS TOUCHLINE BAN

John Bond has blackened my name with his insinuations about the private lives of football managers. Both my wives are upset.

~ MALCOLM ALLISON

A lot of hard work went into this defeat.

~ MALCOLM ALLISON

He's one of the greatest players in the world, if not one of the greatest anywhere.

~ SKY ANDREW

Ben Thatcher is only 20 but he's already played for the England Under-21 side.

~ ANGLIA TV PRESENTER

The question of whether Wayne [Rooney]'s foot could take a tackle became whether Ricardo Carvalho's tackle could take Wayne's foot.

~ ANON

Jean-Alain Boumsong and Titus Bramble are the Chuckle Brothers of Premiership defending.

~ ANON

A true football fan is one who knows the nationality of every player in the Republic of Ireland team.   ~ ANON

David Healy is a certifiable legend of Northern Ireland football.   ~ ANON

A bad football team is like an old bra – no cups and little support. ~ ANON

They call Phil Neville 'Jigsaw' because he falls to pieces in the box.   ~ ANON

Stan Collymore has joined Leicester City. Not to play – just to watch.   ~ ANON

I see Aldridge has kept a clean sheet again.

~ ANON, AFTER STRIKER JOHN ALDRIDGE'S 19TH GOALLESS GAME FOR THE REPUBLIC OF IRELAND

The bad news for Saddam Hussein is that he's just been sentenced to the death penalty. The good news for Saddam is that David Beckham is taking it.   ~ ANON

Being Welsh, Clive Thomas had an unfair advantage over other British referees hoping to officiate at the World Cup finals because he knew that he would always be neutral.   ~ ANON

The shit has hit the fan.

~ ANON, AFTER BRIAN CLOUGH ATTACKED A PITCH INVADER AT NOTTINGHAM FOREST

What's the difference between Fabien Barthez and a turnstile? A turnstile only lets in one at a time.   ~ ANON

You wouldn't want to meet Iain Dowie down a dark alley, or worse still in broad daylight.   ~ ANON

Only Rome has been sacked more often than Alan Ball.   ~ ANON

If you wanted somebody to take a penalty to save your life, Chris Waddle would rank slightly below Long John Silver. ~ ANON

Titus Bramble: dodgy defender who's often caught in two minds … Abbott and Costello's. ~ ANON

Glenn [Hoddle] is putting his head in the frying pan. ~ OSSIE ARDILES

The three toughest jobs are football management, lion taming and mountain rescue – in that order. ~ JIMMY ARMFIELD

I think you and the referee were in a minority of one. ~ JIMMY ARMFIELD

I'd like to have seen Tony Morley left on as a down-and-out winger. ~ JIMMY ARMFIELD

He's only a foot away from the linesman – or should I say a metre, in modern parlance. ~ JIMMY ARMFIELD

I think that their young legs would have found younger hearts inside them. ~ JIMMY ARMFIELD

With eight minutes left, the game could be won in the next five or ten minutes. ~ JIMMY ARMFIELD

I think the big guns will come to the boil. ~ JIMMY ARMFIELD

Liverpool will be without Kvarme tonight – he's illegible. ~ JIMMY ARMFIELD

They're not so different. They've got two arms and two legs and some of them even have heads. ~ AUSTRALIA BOSS FRANK AROK ON OPPONENTS SCOTLAND

He's bald, he's shit, he plays when no one's fit, Pascal Cygan, Pascal Cygan.

~ ARSENAL FANS' SONG ABOUT THEIR OWN PLAYER

Juan Pablo Angel, there's only Juan Pablo Angel!   ~ ASTON VILLA FANS' SONG

Have you ever seen a salad?

~ ASTON VILLA FANS' CHANT TO BURLY SHEFFIELD UNITED GOALKEEPER PADDY KENNY

If I was still at Ipswich, I wouldn't be where I am today.   ~ DALIAN ATKINSON

I always make sure I write Atkinson D. on the team sheet. Sometimes I wonder if I'm making a mistake.   ~ RON ATKINSON ON HIS VILLA NAMESAKE, STRIKER DALIAN

Oggy [Steve Ogrizovic] has had a bit of plastic surgery which has improved his looks – he had to get Wimpey in to do the scaffolding.   ~ RON ATKINSON

Devon Loch was a better finisher.   ~ RON ATKINSON ON CARLTON PALMER

Carlton Palmer can trap the ball further than I can kick it.   ~ RON ATKINSON

Why did I move to the dugout? I wanted to pass on some technical information to the team, like the fact the game had started.   ~ RON ATKINSON

Turned the corner? I'd be happy if we won a corner!   ~ RON ATKINSON

There's nobody fitter at his age, except maybe Raquel Welch.

~ RON ATKINSON SIGNING 39-YEAR-OLD GORDON STRACHAN FOR COVENTRY

You're welcome to my home phone number, but don't ring me during *The Sweeney*.   ~ RON ATKINSON TO REPORTERS

It's the first time that we've had to replace divots in the players!

~ RON ATKINSON AFTER HIS MANCHESTER UNITED TEAM PLAYED A PHYSICAL VALENCIA SIDE

I see Atletico Madrid just sacked another manager before the season has even started. He must have had a bad photocall. ~ RON ATKINSON

I hope you enjoyed that nine-goal thriller.
~ RON ATKINSON AS HIS NOTTINGHAM FOREST TEAM CRASHED 8-1 AT HOME TO MANCHESTER UNITED

You won't see that again, now that the Scouser's got it!
~ RON ATKINSON AS STEVE MCMANAMAN RAISES THE EUROPEAN CUP
AFTER REAL MADRID'S VICTORY OVER VALENCIA

He'll take pleasure from that, Brian Carey. He and Steve Bull have been having it off all afternoon. ~ RON ATKINSON

Liverpool are outnumbered numerically in midfield. ~ RON ATKINSON

He dribbles a lot and the opposition don't like it – you can see it all over their faces. ~ RON ATKINSON

His white boots were on fire against Arsenal, and he'll be looking for them to reproduce tonight. ~ RON ATKINSON

The action replay showed it to be worse than it actually was. ~ RON ATKINSON

You half-fancied that to go in as it was rising and dipping at the same time.
~ RON ATKINSON

They've picked their heads up off the ground and they now have a lot to carry on their shoulders. ~ RON ATKINSON

The keeper was unsighted – he still didn't see it. ~ RON ATKINSON

The Spaniards have been reduced to aiming aimless balls into the box.
~ RON ATKINSON

Well, either side could win it, or it could be a draw.

~ RON ATKINSON

Phil Neville was treading on dangerous water there.

~ RON ATKINSON

He's not only a good player, but he's spiteful – in the nicest sense of the word.

~ RON ATKINSON

When Scholes gets it [tackling] wrong, they come in so late that they arrive yesterday.

~ RON ATKINSON

Scholes is very influential for England at international level.

~ RON ATKINSON

Our fans have been branded with the same brush.

~ RON ATKINSON

He could have done a lot better there, but full marks to the lad.

~ RON ATKINSON

He had acres of time there.

~ RON ATKINSON

It's not as good as Adams' challenge, but it's on a par.

~ RON ATKINSON

Think of a number between 10 and 11.

~ RON ATKINSON

I would not say he [David Ginola] is the best left-winger in the Premiership, but there are none better.

~ RON ATKINSON

Well, Clive, it's all about the two Ms – movement and positioning.

~ RON ATKINSON

I think that was a moment of cool panic there.

~ RON ATKINSON

I know where the linesman should've stuck his flag, and he would have got plenty of help.

~ RON ATKINSON

I never comment on referees and I'm not going to break the habit of a lifetime for that prat.   ~ RON ATKINSON

If that was a penalty, I'll plait sawdust.   ~ RON ATKINSON

The only way I'd be a pin-up is if someone needed a photo to hang over the mantelpiece to keep the young 'uns away from the fire.
~ RON ATKINSON AFTER READING THAT HE WAS A SEX SYMBOL

I'm as baffled as Adam on Mother's Day.   ~ XABIER AZKARGORTA

One of the opposition coaches came on the pitch and hit me, so naturally I smacked him back. What else could I do? My son was watching on TV. I had to stand up for myself.   ~ VITTOR BAIA

We're halfway round the Grand National course with many hurdles to clear. So let's all make sure we keep our feet firmly on the ground.   ~ MIKE BAILEY

We were playing football in the garden and I took it past George Best. I stopped and screamed, 'I beat George Best, I beat George Best.' Mind you, he was holding a pint of white wine at the time.   ~ DANNY BAKER

One-nil is usually enough to win in the group games.   ~ MARCELLO BALBOA

Rumour has it that when Julian Dicks moved to Liverpool he picked up the No. 23 shirt because it said Fowler on it.   ~ KEVIN BALDWIN

Seeing 42 players coming towards me, I felt like the garrison commander at Rorke's Drift when the Zulus came pouring over the hill.
~ ALAN BALL, INHERITING A LARGE SQUAD AT MANCHESTER CITY

The important thing is he shook hands with us over the phone.   ~ ALAN BALL

We've got one point from 27, but it's not as bad as that.   ~ ALAN BALL

Keith Curle has an ankle injury but we'll have to take it on the chin.   ~ ALAN BALL

I'm not a believer in luck, although I believe you need it.

~ ALAN BALL

You can't turn a fire extinguisher on fans. It'll only inflame the situation.

~ JOHN BALL

When God gave Paul Gascoigne this enormous footballing talent, He took out his brain at the same time to equal it up.   ~ TONY BANKS

Vinnie [Jones] admits he threw a piece of toast at Gary Lineker. What he didn't say was that it was still in the toaster.   ~ TONY BANKS

When I first heard about Viagra, I thought it was a new player Chelsea had just signed.   ~ TONY BANKS

Paul Gascoigne has done more for Mars Bars than anyone since Marianne Faithfull.   ~ PATRICK BARCLAY

If Glenn Hoddle had been any other nationality, he would have had 70 or 80 caps for England.   ~ JOHN BARNES

That may have been another corner if it had come off a defender.   ~ JOHN BARNES

Rooney seems to have modelled his style of play on the baby elephant that ran amok in the *Blue Peter* studio.   ~ SIMON BARNES

If you're a manager, you don't have fitted carpets.   ~ JOHN BARNWELL

An inch or two either side of the post and that would have been a goal.

~ DAVE BASSETT

I'd like to think it's a case of crossing the i's and dotting the t's.　　~ DAVE BASSETT

It would be foolish to believe that automatic promotion is automatic in any way whatsoever.　　~ DAVE BASSETT

You weigh up the pros and cons and try to put them into chronological order.
　　~ DAVE BASSETT

You have got to miss them to score sometimes.　　~ DAVE BASSETT

At the moment we couldn't hit a cow's arse with a banjo.　　~ DAVE BASSETT

It's been two ends of the same coin.　　~ DAVE BASSETT

It would be a nice scalp for Scunthorpe to put Wimbledon on our bottoms.
　　~ DAVE BASSETT

The Sheffield United board have been loyal to me. When I came here they said there would be no money, and they've kept their promise.　　~ DAVE BASSETT

Simon Tracey has got the brains of a rocking horse.　　~ DAVE BASSETT

And I honestly believe we can go all the way to Wembley unless somebody knocks us out.　　~ DAVE BASSETT

When Charlie Cooke sold you a dummy, you had to pay to get back into the ground.　　~ JIM BAXTER

If you get a man sent off, you can be pretty certain your team is only going to have ten men.　　~ GRAHAM BEACROFT

The Sheffield United strip looks as if it was designed by Julian Clary when he had a migraine.　　~ SEAN BEAN

I could have signed for Newcastle when I was 17, but I decided I would be better off at Carlisle. I'd had a drink that night…   ~ PETER BEARDSLEY

Alan Ball and I didn't see eye to eye, and it had nothing to do with his being five foot three and me being six foot four.   ~ DAVE BEASANT

Sometimes we are predictable, but out of that predictability we are unpredictable.   ~ JOHN BECK, CAMBRIDGE UNITED MANAGER

We just went out and played the same stale cheese.   ~ FRANZ BECKENBAUER

My parents have always been there for me, ever since I was about seven.
~ DAVID BECKHAM

Alex Ferguson is the best manager I've ever had at this level. Well, he's the only manager I've actually had at this level. But he's the best manager I've ever had.
~ DAVID BECKHAM

I definitely want him to be christened, but I don't know into what religion yet.
~ DAVID BECKHAM ON SON BROOKLYN

No matter who we're playing against, or who our opponents are, we want to win the game.   ~ DAVID BECKHAM

It's going to be difficult for me: I've never had to learn a language and now I do.   ~ DAVID BECKHAM ON HIS MOVE TO SPAIN

It's not easy when someone pulls your ponytail.   ~ DAVID BECKHAM ON PROVOCATION

It was really difficult for us, playing in the midday sun with that three o'clock kick-off.
~ DAVID BECKHAM AFTER ENGLAND STRUGGLED TO BEAT PARAGUAY AT THE 2006 WORLD CUP

It's a great honour … and it's an honour to be with Her Majesty, obviously …
I'm very honoured to be given this honour. ~ DAVID BECKHAM RECEIVING THE OBE

They do not judge Pavarotti by how he sings in the shower. They wait until he is
on stage. ~ LEO BEENHAKKER, CRITICISED AFTER HIS DUTCH TEAM LOSE TO
AUSTRIA IN THE BUILD-UP TO THE 1990 WORLD CUP

A deflection, that's what changed the course of the ball. ~ JIM BEGLIN

Arsenal are streets ahead of everyone in this League and Manchester United are
up with them, obviously. ~ CRAIG BELLAMY

He [Souness] has just gone behind my back in front of my face. ~ CRAIG BELLAMY

The problem was conceding four goals in the first half.
~ RAFA BENITEZ STATING THE OBVIOUS AFTER LIVERPOOL'S 6-3
CARLING CUP DEFEAT TO ARSENAL AT ANFIELD, 2007

Teams don't lose, they 'crash' or 'slump' to defeat. Goalkeepers who don't let any
goals in have 'clean sheets', which presumably saves on detergent. And managers
do not buy players, they 'splash out' on them, although whether they do so on a
'clean sheet' is rarely specified. ~ MARCUS BERKMANN ON MEDIA COVERAGE

People think I had a square Afro, because it was so big it never fitted into photo
frames and the papers and magazines had to crop it that way. ~ GEORGE BERRY

I spent a lot of money on booze, birds and fast cars. The rest I just squandered.
~ GEORGE BEST

I used to go missing a lot – Miss Canada, Miss United Kingdom, Miss Germany.
~ GEORGE BEST

If you'd given me the choice of beating four men and smashing in a goal from
30 yards against Liverpool or going to bed with Miss World, it would have been
a difficult choice. Luckily I had both. It's just that you do one of those things in
front of 50,000 people. ~ GEORGE BEST

In 1969 I gave up women and alcohol. It was the worst 20 minutes of my life.

~ GEORGE BEST

It's a pleasure to be standing up here. In fact, it's a pleasure to be standing up.

~ GEORGE BEST

It was typical of me to be finishing a long and distinguished drinking career just as the Government is planning to open pubs 24 hours a day.

~ GEORGE BEST

Most of the things I've done are my own fault, so I can't feel guilty about them.

~ GEORGE BEST

Paul Gascoigne wears a number 10 jersey. I thought it was his position, but it turns out to be his IQ.

~ GEORGE BEST

He cannot kick with his left foot. He cannot head a ball. He cannot tackle and he doesn't score many goals. Apart from that he's all right.

~ GEORGE BEST ON DAVID BECKHAM

I sent my son to one of Bobby Charlton's schools of excellence and he came back bald.

~ GEORGE BEST

I'd be surprised if all 22 players are on the field at the end of the game – one's already been sent off.

~ GEORGE BEST

I hear Tony Adams is appealing. Apparently he wasn't pissed. He was just trying to get the wall back ten yards.

~ BOB 'THE CAT' BEVAN, AFTER ADAMS WAS JAILED FOR DRINK-DRIVING FOLLOWING A COLLISION WITH A WALL

Most managers would give their right arm for a European Cup, and Bob Paisley had three.

~ MANISH BHASIN

A man who's fulfilled every schoolboy's dream. He's won the Double, captained England, and driven a car into a brick wall at very high speed.

~ SANJEEV BHASKAR, INTRODUCING TONY ADAMS ON THE KUMARS AT NO. 42

We had to bang a few heads together, which must have been the kick up the backside we needed. ~ MARC BIRCHAM

There's more meat on a toothpick than on Robbie Savage. ~ ALAN BIRCHENALL

If brains were chocolate, Robbie Savage wouldn't have enough to fill a Smartie.

~ ALAN BIRCHENALL

He plays with his arm on his sleeve.

~ GARRY BIRTLES

Football is a fertility festival: 11 sperm trying to get into the egg. I feel sorry for the goalkeeper. ~ BJÖRK

You only have to fart in the box to concede a penalty these days.

~ KEVIN BLACKWELL

There's no doubt we'll be seen as a big fish in the First Division next year – everybody will be trying to knock us off our perch.

~ KEVIN BLACKWELL, MANAGER OF LEEDS UNITED

Everything in our favour was against us.

~ DANNY BLANCHFLOWER

Our tactics are to equalise before the other side scores. ~ DANNY BLANCHFLOWER

They've come out with all cylinders flying. ~ LUTHER BLISSETT

To a man, every Czech fan is on his or her feet. ~ GARY BLOOM

The people in the Everton executive boxes are the lucky ones. They can draw the curtains.
~ STAN BOARDMAN

I have other irons in the fire, but I'm keeping them close to my chest.
~ JOHN BOND

His strengths were my weaknesses and my weaknesses were his strengths.
~ JOHN BOND

I promise results, not promises.
~ JOHN BOND

We would get more for [Paul] Robinson if we sold him in the *Leeds Weekly News*.
~ JOHN BOOCOCK, CHAIRMAN OF THE LEEDS UNITED SUPPORTERS' TRUST, AFTER THE ENGLAND GOALKEEPER IS SOLD TO SPURS FOR £1.5 MILLION

To my mind, referees who get decisions wrong should be demoted. Possibly we should put them in the stocks and hit them with rotten tomatoes.
~ AIDY BOOTHROYD, AFTER A CONTROVERSIAL LATE PENALTY DENIES HIS WATFORD TEAM A POINT AT PORTSMOUTH

Norwich's goal was scored by Kevin Bond, who is the son of his father.
~ FRANK BOUGH

Liverpool are my nap selection – I prefer to sleep when they're on the box.
~ STAN BOWLES

Albion face their toughest task yet, in the freezing hothouse at Sunderland.
~ MALCOLM BOYDEN

He was a dead man walking – he didn't have a leg to stand on.
~ MALCOLM BOYDEN ON BRYAN ROBSON'S DEPARTURE FROM WEST BROM

Footballers are only interested in drinking, clothes, and the size of their willies.
~ KARREN BRADY

British ferries have stopped transporting live animals to the Continent. This has made it very difficult for England fans to get to away matches.   ~ JO BRAND

One moment I'm playing football and the next – whack – I wake up in hospital unconscious.   ~ ALAN BRAZIL

The tackles are coming in thick and thin.   ~ ALAN BRAZIL

The Derby fans walking home absolutely silent in their cars.   ~ ALAN BRAZIL

Our talking point this morning is George Best, his liver transplant and the booze culture in football. Don't forget, the best caller wins a crate of John Smith's.   ~ ALAN BRAZIL

Obviously Paul Ince is almost certain to get the job, but we don't know that.   ~ IAN BRIGHTWELL

I saw him kick the bucket over there, which suggests he's not going to be able to continue.   ~ TREVOR BROOKING

Merseyside derbies usually last 90 minutes and I'm sure today's won't be any different.   ~ TREVOR BROOKING

Historically, the host nations do well in Euro 2000.   ~ TREVOR BROOKING

Fortunately Paul Scholes' injury wasn't as bad as we'd hoped for.
~ TREVOR BROOKING

Unfortunately we don't get a second chance. We've already played them twice.   ~ TREVOR BROOKING

He looks as if he's been playing for England all his international career.   ~ TREVOR BROOKING

He is like an English equivalent of Teddy Sheringham.

~ TREVOR BROOKING

Martin Keown's up everybody's backside.

~ TREVOR BROOKING

He's chanced his arm with his left foot.

~ TREVOR BROOKING

Leeds are enjoying more possession now that they have the ball.

~ SIMON BROTHERTON

Liverpool goalkeeper Chris Kirkland has signed a contract which will keep him at the club until the start of the next century.

~ SIMON BROTHERTON

They had a dozen corners, maybe 12, I'm guessing.

~ CRAIG BROWN

Michael Owen – he's got the legs of a salmon.

~ CRAIG BROWN

The underdogs will start favourites for this match.

~ CRAIG BROWN

At Rangers I was third choice left-back behind an amputee and a Catholic.

~ CRAIG BROWN

It will be a shame if either side lose, and that applies to both sides.   ~ JOCK BROWN

With our luck, one of our players must be bonking a witch. ~ KEN BROWN

The players have got to know that we are not firing by the seat of our pants.

~ PHIL BROWN

That's a lot of hard work gone under the water, under the bridge.   ~ PHIL BROWN

The walking wounded are starting to walk.

~ PHIL BROWN

You have to take it on the chin – or in my case, chins!

~ STEVE BRUCE

Paul Scholes is a fantastic midfielder. There's not a weakness that he hasn't got.

~ STEVE BRUCE

The boys' feet have been up in the clouds since the win. ~ ALAN BUCKLEY

We didn't look like scoring, although we looked like we were going to get a goal.

~ ALAN BUCKLEY

Spurs will play either Eintracht or Frankfurt. ~ ALASTAIR BURNET

Are you Tamworth in disguise? ~ BURTON ALBION FANS TAUNT MANCHESTER UNITED
AFTER THE TEAMS' GOALLESS DRAW IN THE FA CUP, 2006

He's never hurt anyone. Mind you, he's frightened a few. ~ MATT BUSBY ON NOBBY STILES

George Best was able to use either foot. Sometimes he seemed to have six.

~ MATT BUSBY

The beauty of Cup football is that Jack always has a chance of beating Goliath.

~ TERRY BUTCHER

I said to them last week that I'd like them to win ugly and they certainly won ugly today. That was the ugliest thing I've seen since the ugly sisters fell out of the ugly tree. ~ MOTHERWELL BOSS TERRY BUTCHER

There were more formations out there than in a ballroom dancing team.

~ TERRY BUTCHER

He's been in a different class in training and on the pitch. He's a lovely guy and if I had a daughter, I'd let him marry her. But I haven't got a daughter and he's already married, so there you go.

~ TERRY BUTCHER ON SYDNEY FC MIDFIELDER ROBBIE MIDDLEBY

Tottenham in the last two years have never left London, but now they've been drawn away from home to meet Chelsea.

~ BRYON BUTLER

Butcher goes forward as Ipswich throw their last trump card into the fire.

~ BRYON BUTLER

What a goal from Trevor Francis. That was $1,000,000, let alone £1,000,000.

~ BRYON BUTLER

And Keegan was there like a surgeon's knife – bang!

~ BRYON BUTLER

You can't really call yourself giant-killers any more, as you kill giants so often.

~ BRYON BUTLER

The second goal was a blueprint of the first.

~ BRYON BUTLER

Terry Venables could do a Barcelona at Leeds, like he did at Barcelona.

~ TED BUXTON

Apparently if the BBC broadcast more than three minutes of your game on *Match of the Day*, they have to pay you. So we might do all right out of this because it's going to take longer than that to show all the goals.

~ LEAMINGTON BOSS JASON CADDEN AFTER A 9-1 CUP DEFEAT BY COLCHESTER

And he [Zidane] will have a private pool, with a gardener thrown in. ~ DES CAHILL

So far Villa have only troubled Bradshaw twice with shots that did not trouble him.

~ LARRY CANNING

What a goal! One for the puritans.

~ CAPITAL GOLD RADIO COMMENTATOR

David Blunkett can hold on to a lead better than AC Milan.

~ JASPER CARROTT, AFTER MILAN LET A THREE-GOAL ADVANTAGE SLIP
AGAINST LIVERPOOL IN THE 2005 CHAMPIONS' LEAGUE FINAL

Being a Birmingham City supporter, it's a case of some you lose, some you draw.
~ JASPER CARROTT

Birmingham City, the only team never to have scored during a reign of the Pope. ~ JASPER CARROTT, FOLLOWING THE DEATH OF POPE JOHN PAUL I

What's the difference between Birmingham City and a teabag?
A teabag stays in the cup longer. ~ JASPER CARROTT

David Icke says he is here to save the world. Well, he saved bugger all when he played in goal for Coventry. ~ JASPER CARROTT

I hear Glenn Hoddle's found God. That must have been one hell of a pass.
~ JASPER CARROTT

They've taken the horns by the scruff of the neck. ~ TONY CASCARINO

There's a rat in the camp throwing a spanner in the works. ~ CHRIS CATTLIN

Two Andy Gorams, there's only two Andy Gorams.
~ CELTIC FANS TAUNT RANGERS' KEEPER ANDY GORAM OVER RUMOURS
ABOUT HIM SUFFERING FROM MILD SCHIZOPHRENIA

They seem to be in total, if not complete, control. ~ JON CHAMPION

A full-blooded encounter for a number of reasons, many of them illegitimate.
~ JON CHAMPION

Victor Hernandez, like an orchestral conductor directing his troops.
~ JON CHAMPION

Andy Cole has at last broken his goal glut with his first goal for England.
~ CHANNEL 5 NEWSREADER

Believe it or not, goals can change a game. ~ MIKE CHANNON

It was a fair decision, the penalty, even though it was debatable whether it was inside or outside the box. ~ BOBBY CHARLTON

I've seen them on television on a Sunday morning most days of the week. ~ JACK CHARLTON

It was a game we should have won. We lost it because we thought we were going to win it. But then again, I thought that there was no way we were going to get a result there. ~ JACK CHARLTON

The players with the wind will have to control it a lot more. ~ JACK CHARLTON

We probably got on better with the likes of Holland, Belgium, Norway and Sweden, some of whom are not even European. ~ JACK CHARLTON

It was a definite penalty but Wright made a right swan song of it. ~ JACK CHARLTON

The Arsenal defence is skating close to the wind. ~ JACK CHARLTON

I suppose I'll only know how the fans feel when I return on Thursday and if I have to pay for my own Guinness.
~ JACK CHARLTON AFTER IRELAND'S EXIT AT THE 1994 WORLD CUP

Come on, Bury fans – you've got your night in the sun. ~ ADRIAN CHILES

Someone said you could write Barry Fry's knowledge of tactics on a stamp. You'd need to fold the stamp in half. ~ STEVE CLARIDGE

They've forced them into a lot of unforced errors. ~ STEVE CLARIDGE

We lost seven goals and yet I can't remember the keeper making a save.

~ FRANK CLARK

I had to go. Towards the end I felt like a turkey waiting for Christmas.

~ FRANK CLARK, LEAVING AS MANAGER OF NOTTINGHAM FOREST

—Rob McLean: John Hartson is playing superbly today.
—Sandy Clark: Yes, Rob, there's no one better today.
—McLean: So, Sandy, who is your man of the match?
—Clark: Alan Thompson.

This is an unusual Scotland side because they have good players. ~ JAVIER CLEMENTE

If you come any closer to me, we might as well get into the same pair of shorts
and save a few bob on laundry.

~ BRIAN CLOUGH AS A PLAYER TO DONCASTER DEFENDER CHARLIE WILLIAMS

Trevor Brooking floats like a butterfly, and stings like one.   ~ BRIAN CLOUGH

Gary Megson couldn't trap a landmine.   ~ BRIAN CLOUGH

If you were a horse, you'd have been shot. ~ BRIAN CLOUGH TO INJURY-PRONE LEEDS WINGER EDDIE GRAY

He didn't look anything like a professional athlete when I first clapped eyes on
him. In fact, there were times when he barely resembled a member of the
human race.   ~ BRIAN CLOUGH ON JOHN ROBERTSON

Whenever I felt off-colour, I'd sit next to John Robertson because then I looked
like Errol Flynn.   ~ BRIAN CLOUGH

If Jimmy Hill can find a ground where he scored a League goal, I'll meet
him there.   ~ BRIAN CLOUGH RESPONDING TO HILL'S DEMAND FOR A DEBATE

When Larry Lloyd finished playing he went into the licensed trade and became the only landlord I know who was bigger and wider than his own pub.

~ BRIAN CLOUGH

The only person certain of boarding the coach for the Littlewoods Cup Final is Albert Kershaw, and he'll be driving it. ~ BRIAN CLOUGH

Kenny Dalglish wasn't that big but he had a huge arse. It came down below his knees and that's where he got his strength from. ~ BRIAN CLOUGH

I only ever hit Roy [Keane] the once. He got up, so I couldn't have hit him very hard. ~ BRIAN CLOUGH

He's had more holidays than Judith Chalmers.

~ BRIAN CLOUGH ON ROY KEANE'S SERIES OF SUSPENSIONS

My wife said to me in bed, 'God, your feet are cold.' I said, 'You can call me Brian in bed, dear.' ~ BRIAN CLOUGH

It's easy enough to get to Ireland. It's just a straight walk across the Irish Sea as far as I'm concerned. ~ BRIAN CLOUGH

If God wanted the game played in the air, why did he put grass on the floor?

~ BRIAN CLOUGH

I'll invite him in, we'll sit down and talk about it for 20 minutes, and then we'll decide that I was right.

~ BRIAN CLOUGH ON HIS METHOD OF DEALING WITH ANY DISSENT IN THE DRESSING ROOM

I wouldn't say I was the best manager in the business, but I was in the top one.

~ BRIAN CLOUGH

He's not going to join Pisa for the simple and most important reason that his mother decided that days ago. ~ BRIAN CLOUGH ON SON NIGEL

Players lose you games, not tactics. There's so much crap talked about tactics by people who barely know how to win at dominoes. ~ BRIAN CLOUGH

Arsenal caress a football the way I dreamed of caressing Marilyn Monroe.
~ BRIAN CLOUGH

That Seaman is a handsome young man but he spends too much time looking in his mirror rather than at the ball. You can't keep goal with hair like that. ~ BRIAN CLOUGH

At last England have appointed a manager who speaks English better than the players. ~ BRIAN CLOUGH ON SVEN-GORAN ERIKSSON

Anybody who can do anything in Leicester but make a jumper has got to be a genius. ~ BRIAN CLOUGH ON MARTIN O'NEILL

Football hooligans? Well, there are 92 club chairmen for a start. ~ BRIAN CLOUGH

It has been suggested that we'll squander the sponsors' money on wine, women and song. That is not true. We don't do a lot of singing here at Portman Road. ~ FORMER IPSWICH CHAIRMAN JOHN COBBOLD

I'll take any goal, any time, any place, anywhere – you can call me the Martini striker. ~ CARLTON COLE

Tottenham have joined the quartet of five teams. ~ JOE COLE

Let's say I play 4-4-2 at home against Portsmouth and we lose 0-3. Do I then start booing the fans? ~ CHRIS COLEMAN AFTER FULHAM FANS CHANT FOR HIM TO ABANDON THE 4-5-1 FORMATION

And for those of you watching without television sets, live commentary is on Radio 2.   ~ DAVID COLEMAN

Don't tell those coming in the result of that fantastic match, but let's have another look at Italy's winning goal.   ~ DAVID COLEMAN

On this 101st FA Cup Final day, there are just two teams left. ~ DAVID COLEMAN

He is a whole-hearted player.

~ DAVID COLEMAN ON HOLE-IN-THE-HEART FOOTBALLER ASA HARTFORD

I enjoy playing against the big men and I will just have to get the stepladder out and get on with it.   ~ WALES DEFENDER JAMES COLLINS ON THE PROSPECT
OF MARKING 6FT 7IN CZECH REPUBLIC STRIKER JAN KOLLER

The simplest solution is to stop the ball getting to Ronaldo in the first place. If the ball does get to him, we have to make sure he has no space to turn or knock the ball into. And if that doesn't work, we'll have to tie his shoelaces together.

~ SCOTLAND'S JOHN COLLINS BEFORE A 1998 WORLD CUP CLASH WITH BRAZIL

[Jose] Mourinho is to flouncing what Tiger Woods is to short-iron play; it's what he does best.   ~ PATRICK COLLINS, *MAIL ON SUNDAY*

Didier Drogba tumbles as readily as a drunk on an ice-rink.   ~ PATRICK COLLINS

When McClaren could have done with a touch of public support, Tel [Terry Venables] was nowhere to be seen. We were reminded of the satellite reruns of *Minder* when the Winchester Club is raided and Arthur Daley departs on his toes, leaving a whiff of cigar smoke and a half-finished vodka and tonic.

~ PATRICK COLLINS, AFTER ENGLAND'S DEFEAT IN CROATIA, 2006

For years I thought the club's name was Partick Thistle Nil.   ~ BILLY CONNOLLY

Ally MacLeod thinks tactics are a new kind of mint.   ~ BILLY CONNOLLY

Kenny [Gilbert] is a wonderful asset to the club. I've talked about him so much this season, the players are beginning to wonder if I've got a thing for him!
~ NEALE COOPER AT ROSS COUNTY

—Tommy Cooper: Your Majesty, may I ask you a personal question?
—The Queen: As personal as I'll allow.
—Tommy Cooper: Do you like football?
—The Queen: Not particularly.
—Tommy Cooper: Well, could I have your tickets for the Cup Final?

I walked behind Peter Schmeichel off the pitch at the end. Put it this way, there was not a lot of sunlight coming my way!   ~ STEVE COPPELL

Attilio Lombardo is starting to pick up a bit of English on the training ground. The first word he learned was 'wanker'.   ~ STEVE COPPELL AT CRYSTAL PALACE

It will be difficult to get the player I want because Posh doesn't want to move to Reading!   ~ STEVE COPPELL

Glen Little dropped out at 1pm when we discovered he had tweaked a hamstring walking upstairs at home. We're now asking for him to move to a bungalow.
~ STEVE COPPELL

I'm a man of few words, but most of the ones I said to the players began with F.   ~ STEVE COPPELL

The lad got over-excited when he saw the whites of the goalpost's eyes.
~ STEVE COPPELL

He's carrying his left leg, which, to be honest, is his only leg.   ~ STEVE COPPELL

We wanted to keep it quiet, and didn't make an issue of it. We went through the proper channels and hoped it would die a death.

~ STEVE COPPELL, PLAYING DOWN DEATH THREATS TO TWO OF HIS READING PLAYERS

I'm not going to make it a target but it's something to aim for.   ~ STEVE COPPELL

At the end of the day, it's all about what's on the shelf at the end of the year.

~ STEVE COPPELL

According to legend, Eskimos have over 100 words to describe snow. Significantly, the Scots have more than 100 words to describe someone who's crap at football.   ~ STUART COSGROVE

Gobsmacked is too small a word. You don't even get a plot like this in *Star Wars*.

~ SOUTHAMPTON DIRECTOR ANDREW COWEN ON HARRY REDKNAPP'S
DEPARTURE FROM ST MARY'S TO RETURN TO RIVALS PORTSMOUTH

You sometimes open your mouth and it punches you straight between the eyes.

~ PAT CRERAND

Matt [Busby] always believed Manchester United would be one of the greatest clubs in the world. He was the eternal optimist. In 1968, he still hoped Glenn Miller was just missing.   ~ PAT CRERAND

If George [Best] had been born ugly, he probably would have played till he was 40 – just look at Peter Beardsley.

~ PAT CRERAND AS BEARDSLEY SIGNS FOR AUSTRALIAN CLUB MELBOURNE KNIGHTS

That goal surprised most people, least of all myself.   ~ GARTH CROOKS

Football's football. If that weren't the case, it wouldn't be the game that it is.

~ GARTH CROOKS

If I played for Scotland, my grandma would be the proudest woman in the country if she wasn't dead. ~ MARK CROSSLEY

I wouldn't say it's a must-win game, but it's definitely a game we need to win.
~ PETER CROUCH

It was a worry to pick up a booking, but I'm not going to change my game, although I may have to adapt it a bit. ~ PETER CROUCH

I felt sorry for the match ball – it came off the pitch crying. ~ JOHAN CRUYFF

Most bosses get kicked out the back door – I got clapped out of the front door. ~ ALAN CURBISHLEY LEAVING CHARLTON

The likes of Manchester United and Chelsea would definitely have problems fitting their squads into our away changing room. As for our pitch, most of the Premier big names have bigger back gardens. ~ COLCHESTER'S JAMIE CURETON

Liverpool's best chance ended when Beardsley shot himself. ~ *DAILY EXPRESS*

Jose Mourinho's oversight in not having cover for every position came back to haunt Chelsea last night when they revealed Stamford the Lion mascot had been kidnapped. ~ *DAILY MIRROR*

Frog On The Tyne ~ *DAILY STAR* HEADLINE AFTER NEWCASTLE SIGN FRENCHMAN DAVID GINOLA

David Ginola has just handed in a written transfer request. The handwriting was beautiful. ~ KENNY DALGLISH

Temuri Ketsbaia does more in celebrations than he does in a week's training. ~ KENNY DALGLISH

I'll expect nine out of ten in the *People*.

~ KENNY DALGLISH, COMING ON AS AN 87TH-MINUTE SUBSTITUTE

The Brazilians aren't as good as they used to be, or as they are now.

~ KENNY DALGLISH

As I've said before and I've said it in the past...   ~ KENNY DALGLISH

I refereed Croatia against Bosnia at a time when they were at war with each other and it was an easier game to handle than the Old Firm.   ~ HUGH DALLAS

And with just four minutes gone, the score is already 0-0.   ~ IAN DARKE

Billy Gilbert hit a kamikaze back pass, which Justin Fashanu pounced on like a black Frank Bruno.   ~ IAN DARKE

The Austrians are wearing the dark black socks.   ~ BARRY DAVIES

It's Brazil 2 Scotland 1, so Scotland are back where they were at the start of the match.   ~ BARRY DAVIES

The crowd think that Todd handled the ball – they must have seen something that nobody else did.   ~ BARRY DAVIES

He must be feeling on cloud seven.   ~ BARRY DAVIES

Nicky Butt, he's another aptly named player. He joins things, brings one sentence to an end and starts another.   ~ BARRY DAVIES

Poland nil, England nil, though England are now looking the better value for their nil.   ~ BARRY DAVIES

Those Dutch fans look rather like a huge jar of marmalade.   ~ BARRY DAVIES

You can imagine how they feel … surrounded by their manager Ron
Greenwood.

~ DICKIE DAVIES

White Hart Lane is a great place. The only thing wrong is the seats face
the pitch.

~ LES DAWSON

David Beckham has had his eyebrows plucked, so now he's got nothing in front
of his eyes either.

~ JACK DEE

—Bryan Hamilton: I think in the end it will be down to Manchester United and
Arsenal.
—Victoria Derbyshire: So you clearly haven't ruled out Liverpool then?

If football were meant to be art, God wouldn't have invented Carlton Palmer.

~ DOMINIK DIAMOND

He loved sex but he always checked the football scores on Teletext first.

~ MODEL EVA DIJKSTRA ON LES FERDINAND

The rest of the team are very large – they dwarf above you. ~ FRED DINENAGE

To be 13 points behind Manchester United after four games would have been
a disaster.

~ LEE DIXON

The nearest player offside was at White Hart Lane.

~ JOHN DOCHERTY ON A DISALLOWED GOAL FOR MILLWALL AT HIGHBURY

He can't run, can't tackle and can't head a ball. The only time he goes forward is
to toss the coin.

~ TOMMY DOCHERTY ON RAY WILKINS

John Barnes's problem is that he gets injured appearing on *A Question of Sport*.

~ TOMMY DOCHERTY

We put bells on a football so he would know where it was. We had complaints from morris dancers saying he was kicking them all over the place.

~ TOMMY DOCHERTY ON BIG JIM HOLTON

If Mourinho was made of chocolate, he would lick himself. ~ TOMMY DOCHERTY

There are three types of Oxo cubes. Light brown for chicken stock, dark brown for beef stock, and light blue for laughing stock.

~ TOMMY DOCHERTY BAITING MANCHESTER CITY

They offered me a handshake of £10,000 to settle amicably. I told them they would have to be a lot more amicable than that.

~ TOMMY DOCHERTY AFTER BEING SACKED BY PRESTON

Doug Ellis said he was right behind me. I told him I'd sooner have him in front of me where I could see him. ~ TOMMY DOCHERTY ON THE ASTON VILLA CHAIRMAN

Peter Swales likes publicity. He wears a card round his neck saying: 'In case of heart attack call a press conference.' ~ TOMMY DOCHERTY

We don't use a stopwatch to judge our golden goal competition now, we use a calendar. ~ TOMMY DOCHERTY AT WOLVES

I just opened the trophy cabinet. Two Japanese prisoners of war came out.

~ TOMMY DOCHERTY

We can only go up. If we get any lower, we'll fall off the pools coupons.

~ TOMMY DOCHERTY

I made a promise to the chairman that I would take Rotherham out of the Second Division. I did. I took them straight into the Third. ~ TOMMY DOCHERTY

I've had more clubs than Jack Nicklaus. ~ TOMMY DOCHERTY

I can't watch Wimbledon, Watford or Sheffield Wednesday. Football wasn't meant to be run by two linesmen and air traffic control.   ~ TOMMY DOCHERTY, 1988

I hear Elton John's made a bid for an Italian club ... AC/DC Milan.

~ TOMMY DOCHERTY

Somebody compared Lorenzo Amoruso to Billy McNeill, but I don't remember Billy being crap.   ~ TOMMY DOCHERTY

They'll be home before the postcards.

~ TOMMY DOCHERTY ON SCOTLAND'S PROSPECTS AT THE 1998 WORLD CUP IN FRANCE

The ideal board of directors should be made up of three men: two dead and the other dying.   ~ TOMMY DOCHERTY

Some teams are so negative they could be sponsored by Kodak.~ TOMMY DOCHERTY

I've always said there's a place for the Press, but they haven't dug it yet.

~ TOMMY DOCHERTY

I have no interest in gardening. If I did I would probably plant my flowers in a 4-4-2 formation.   ~ TOMMY DOCHERTY

This would cut hooliganism in half by 75 per cent.   ~ TOMMY DOCHERTY

I was disappointed with the attitude of the boy balls who slowed the game down whenever the ball went out of play.   ~ RAYMOND DOMENECH, FRENCH COACH

Alan Hansen looks like a pissed vampire.   ~ CHRIS DONALD

I'll stay in football. I don't mind if they stand me up and use me as a corner flag.

~ DEREK DOOLEY, SHEFFIELD WEDNESDAY STRIKER, AFTER HAVING A LEG AMPUTATED

Is he entitled to go dance with his wife at a do? Yes he is. Does he need some help with his dance moves? Obviously he does. We will do some more movement to music in training.   ~ IAIN DOWIE DEFENDS STRIKER ANDREW JOHNSON
AFTER TABLOID PHOTOGRAPHERS SNAP HIM ON A NIGHT OUT

I would have to have been blind or deaf not to have read the speculation.

~ BOBBY DOWNES

Wimbledon will take to Wembley. Once you've tried to get a decent bath at Hartlepool, you can handle anything.   ~ WALLY DOWNES, BEFORE THE 1988 CUP FINAL

I'd like to play for an Italian club, like Barcelona.   ~ MARK DRAPER

The crowd … a cacophony of colour.   ~ PETER DRURY

Bergkamp's been on another plane.   ~ PETER DRURY ON THE NON-FLYING DUTCHMAN

Van Persie, adjusting his undershorts, and now perhaps with Van Nistelrooy in his sights.   ~ PETER DRURY

When Dusan Vrto came to Dundee, all he could say in English was 'yes', 'no' and 'morning'. A week later he'd added 'thank you' and 'Budweiser'.   ~ JIM DUFFY

Most people who can remember when [Notts] County were a great club are dead.   ~ JACK DUNNETT

The overwhelming view of the listeners is that they are split down the middle.   ~ EAMON DUNPHY

Kilbane's head is better than his feet. If only he had three heads, one on the end of each leg.   ~ EAMON DUNPHY

An absolute waster. He should have been yanked off at half-time and put in the bath. A scalding hot bath … and left there for a long time.

~ EAMON DUNPHY ON HARRY KEWELL

The first time I've seen two men have sex on the BBC.

~ EAMON DUNPHY ON GARTH CROOKS' TAME INTERVIEW WITH SVEN-GORAN ERIKSSON
AFTER ENGLAND'S UNINSPIRING VICTORY OVER ECUADOR AT THE 2006 WORLD CUP

The first two-syllable word I learned when I was growing up was 'discretion'.

~ EAMON DUNPHY

Brentford Reserves were involved in a nine-goal thriller when they beat Orient 4-3.

~ *EALING GAZETTE*

It's his outstanding pace that stands out.

~ ROBBIE EARLE

If you had a linesman on each side of the pitch in both halves, you'd have nearly four.

~ ROBBIE EARLE

It was a draw but it feels worse than a defeat.

~ EDMILSON

Why am I booking you? Because you're Australian and you always beat us at everything!

~ REFEREE DAVID ELLERAY TO BIRMINGHAM CITY'S STAN LAZARIDIS

When the other bidders saw Randy's helmet lying on the desk, they knew they had no chance.

~ DOUG ELLIS, ASTON VILLA CHAIRMAN, RECOUNTING HOW AMERICAN
GRIDIRON CLUB OWNER RANDY LERNER HAD PRESENTED HIM WITH A
CLEVELAND BROWNS HEADGUARD DURING THEIR TAKEOVER TALKS

If you have a fortnight's holiday in Dublin you qualify for an Eire cap.

~ MIKE ENGLAND

I am not married to David Beckham. I am not even engaged to him.

~ SVEN-GORAN ERIKSSON

—Richard Keys: Well, Roy, do you think you'll have to finish above Manchester United to win the League?
—Roy Evans: You have to finish above everyone to win the League, Richard.

Our goalkeeping coach has done a fantastic job on David James's mental side. Though you'll never get that part completely right, because all keepers are mental anyway.

~ ROY EVANS

Jermain Defoe is playing up front alongside David Owen.

~ TIM EWART

One Wigan director wanted us to sign Salford Van Hire because he thought he was a Dutch international.

~ FRED EYRE, 1981

I will have to turbo-charge my Zimmer frame.

~ OLDHAM'S 41-YEAR-OLD DAVID EYRES ON HIS PLAN TO STOP
MANCHESTER CITY WINGER SHAUN WRIGHT-PHILLIPS IN THE FA CUP

The closest I got to him was when we shook hands at the end of the game.

~ ROY FAIRFAX WHO HAD BEEN MARKING GEORGE BEST WHEN
THE LATTER SCORED SIX IN A 1970 CUP TIE AGAINST NORTHAMPTON

I know I can't go on for ever. How can I forget it when my so-called team-mates keep asking me which king was on the throne when I started.

~ LES FERDINAND

We had to come and roll our socks up.

~ LES FERDINAND

Any manager will tell you they'd rather win one and lose two than draw three, because you get more points.

~ LES FERDINAND

He needed five stitches – three in the first half and two at the interval when his brain started to seep through.

~ ALEX FERGUSON ON STEVE BRUCE

Dennis Wise could start a row in an empty house.

~ ALEX FERGUSON

Eric Cantona couldn't tackle a fish supper.   ~ ALEX FERGUSON

Wes Brown has had two cruciates and a broken ankle. It's not easy, that. Every player attached to the club is praying the boy gets a break.   ~ ALEX FERGUSON

If he [Gary Neville] was an inch taller, he'd be the best centre-half in Britain. His father is six foot two – I'd check the milkman!   ~ ALEX FERGUSON

It was a freakish incident. If I tried it 100 or a million times, it couldn't happen again. If I could, I would have carried on playing!
~ ALEX FERGUSON ON KICKING THE BOOT THAT LEFT
DAVID BECKHAM NEEDING STITCHES ABOVE THE EYE

He was towering over me and the other players were almost covering their eyes. I'm looking up and thinking, 'If he does hit me, I'm dead.'
~ ALEX FERGUSON ON A RUN-IN WITH PETER SCHMEICHEL

Nicky Butt's a real Manchester boy. He comes from Gorton where it is said they take the pavements in of a night time.   ~ ALEX FERGUSON

I remember when I first saw him. He was 13 and he just floated over the ground like a cocker spaniel chasing a piece of silver paper in the wind.
~ ALEX FERGUSON ON RYAN GIGGS

One of my players would have to be hit by an axe to get a penalty at the moment.   ~ ALEX FERGUSON

Chris Perry is like a leech, so quick.
~ ALEX FERGUSON

As with every young player, he's only 18.   ~ ALEX FERGUSON ON CRISTIANO RONALDO

Retirement? You must be joking, especially when you consider that the alternative is to stay at home with that wife of mine!   ~ ALEX FERGUSON

They called Steve Kindon 'The Horse' because of his speed. It was also because he had the brain of a clothes horse and the control of a rocking horse.

~ PAUL FLETCHER

I don't mind what they call me, as long as they don't call me late for lunch.

~ WILLIAM 'FATTY' FOULKE, 25-STONE ENGLAND GOALKEEPER

What I said to them at half-time would be unprintable on the radio.

~ GERRY FRANCIS

Klinsmann has taken to English football like a duck out of water.

~ GERRY FRANCIS

We are so high in the table our noses are bleeding.

~ GERRY FRANCIS

It's completely dead out there. I've been phoning myself up and disguising my voice just for a bit of interest.

~ QPR BOSS GERRY FRANCIS, BORED WITH THE LACK OF ACTIVITY ON TRANSFER DEADLINE DAY

There's only one thing better than getting an interview with Ron Greenwood. That's not getting one.

~ TONY FRANCIS

Barry Fry is a real kleptomaniac. He sees a player and then has to go and buy him.

~ TONY FRANCIS

When I arrived there were 47 players, and it was 49 a week later when I found two more in a cupboard.

~ TREVOR FRANCIS, SUCCEEDING BARRY FRY AS MANAGER OF BIRMINGHAM CITY

I still believe we have an outside chance of reaching the play-offs, but then again, I believe in Father Christmas.

~ TREVOR FRANCIS

He's like all great players, but he's not a great player yet.

~ TREVOR FRANCIS

Brian Clough's record speaks for itself … if it can get a word in.　~ CRIS FREDDI

I was delighted to get a point. Normally the only thing we get out of London is the train from Euston.　~ OLDHAM'S JIMMY FRIZZELL

I must admit when I came here I thought we were certs to finish bottom. Now I am very optimistic and I think we'll finish second bottom.

~ BARRY FRY AT SOUTHEND

If a jumbo jet was coming towards our area, [Liam] Daish would try to head it clear.　~ BARRY FRY

He doesn't know a goal-line from a clothes-line.

~ BARRY FRY ON BIRMINGHAM CITY OWNER DAVID SULLIVAN

If I got as many points for football as I do for driving offences, I'd be in the Premiership by now.　~ BARRY FRY

That was fantastic. In fact, the only word I can think of to describe it was awesome.　~ JIM GANNON

With that bandage around his head, Incey [Paul Ince] looked like a pint of Guinness running round in the second half.　~ PAUL GASCOIGNE

Coping with the language shouldn't prove a problem. I can't even speak English yet.

~ PAUL GASCOIGNE ON HIS MOVE TO ITALY

I've had 14 bookings this season – eight of which were my fault, but seven of which were disputable.　~ PAUL GASCOIGNE

It was a big relief off my shoulder.　~ PAUL GASCOIGNE

Because of the booking, I will miss the Holland game … if selected.

~ PAUL GASCOIGNE

I don't like being on my own because you think a lot and I don't like to think a lot.

~ PAUL GASCOIGNE

I don't make predictions and I never will.

~ PAUL GASCOIGNE

You realise we'll have to call you 15,000 Volz?

~ IVAN GASKELL, BBC REPORTER, TO FULHAM'S MORITZ VOLZ,
SCORER OF THE 15,000TH PREMIERSHIP GOAL

It's like a woman on her wedding day – nervous, out of position and hoping everything would soon be over so she could go up to the bedroom.

~ SPANISH JOURNALIST HUGO GATTI ON FABIEN BARTHEZ'S
PERFORMANCE FOR MANCHESTER UNITED AGAINST REAL MADRID

So, this movie you star in, *The Life Story of George Best*. Tell us what it's about.

~ GEORGE GAVIN

It could be bad news for Andy Sinton – his knee is locked up inside the dressing room.

~ GEORGE GAVIN

Beckham will take the free kick and he's a world-class bender.

~ GERMAN COMMENTATOR

We were told the side an hour before kick-off and the lads looked round in astonishment when we kept the same team.

~ STEVEN GERRARD , LEARNING THAT LIVERPOOL BOSS RAFA BENITEZ
WAS TO PLAY AN UNCHANGED TEAM FOR THE FIRST TIME IN 99 MATCHES

The listening bank refused to listen and the bank which likes to say yes said no.

~ HARTLEPOOL CHAIRMAN GARRY GIBSON ON HIS CLUB'S FINANCIAL PLIGHT

You should see his boots. They're like something you hang from your car mirror.
~ MIDDLESBROUGH CHAIRMAN STEVE GIBSON ON THE SIZE OF JUNINHO'S FEET

Obviously on paper, it's a very good game. Do you think, in theory, it will be one?
~ ANDREW GIDLEY

You'll be hoping that this run of injuries will stop earlier than it started.
~ ANDREW GIDLEY

Hugo Sanchez is a very dangerous man. He is about as welcome as a piranha in a bidet.
~ JESUS GIL

I'd rather play in front of a full house than an empty crowd.
~ JOHNNY GILES

We are really quite lucky this year because Christmas falls on Christmas Day.
~ BOBBY GOULD

I remember sitting in the stands watching Stuart Pearce at Wealdstone, and after a few minutes he dumped the opposing winger in my lap. I thought, he'll do for me.
~ BOBBY GOULD

It was like finding Miss World was free and asking for a date.
~ BRISTOL ROVERS MANAGER BOBBY GOULD AFTER PERSUADING DON HOWE TO BE HIS COACH

Jesus Saves, but Rooney nets the rebound
~ GRAFFITI

Wayne Rooney really has a man's body on a teenager's head.
~ GEORGE GRAHAM

There's only one person who knows how he missed that, and that's Wayne Rooney, and even he doesn't know.
~ GEORGE GRAHAM

Shay Given has shaken off a broken nose to play.
~ GRANDSTAND

It's one of the greatest goals ever, but I'm surprised that people are talking about it being the goal of the season. ~ ANDY GRAY

There's no width on the wings. ~ ANDY GRAY

There was no contact there, just a clash of bodies. ~ ANDY GRAY

I was saying the other day, how often the most vulnerable area for goalies is between their legs. ~ ANDY GRAY

For my money, Duff servicing people from the left with his balls in there is the best option. ~ ANDY GRAY

Chris Kirkland's future is definitely in front of him. ~ ANDY GRAY

It's a lot harder to play football when you haven't got the ball. ~ ANDY GRAY

Anyone who takes drugs should be hammered. ~ ANDY GRAY

Well, Kerry, you're 19 and you're a lot older than a lot of people younger than yourself. ~ MIKE GRAY

He hit the post, and after the game people will say, well, he hit the post. ~ JIMMY GREAVES

We signed to play until the day we died, and we did. ~ JIMMY GREAVES

We are really the victims of our own problems. ~ JIMMY GREAVES

Let's close our eyes and see what happens. ~ JIMMY GREAVES

I think Charlie George was one of Arsenal's all-time great players. A lot of people might not agree with that, but I personally do. ~ JIMMY GREAVES

Football tactics are rapidly becoming as complicated as the chemical formula for splitting the atom.   ~ JIMMY GREAVES

Paul Gascoigne is Tyneside's very own Renaissance Man: a man capable of breaking both leg and wind at the same time.   ~ JIMMY GREAVES

In Gazza's case, counselling clearly means a two-day bender with a couple of headbanging mates. I was obviously in counselling a lot earlier than I thought.
~ JIMMY GREAVES

As we went out on the pitch he handed me a piece of paper. It was the evening menu for the Liverpool Royal Infirmary.
~ JIMMY GREAVES ON ANFIELD HARD-MAN TOMMY SMITH

Old Sicknote should get a part on *Animal Hospital.*
~ JIMMY GREAVES ON INJURY-PLAGUED DARREN ANDERTON

He's not speaking to me yet, but I hope to be incommunicado with him in a very short space of time.   ~ JIMMY GREAVES

Tugay is writhing around all over the place as if he were dead.   ~ ALAN GREEN

This will be their 19th consecutive game without a win unless they can get an equaliser.   ~ ALAN GREEN

It was that game that put the Everton ship back on the road. ~ ALAN GREEN

Here's Brian Flynn. His official height is five feet five inches and he doesn't look much taller than that.   ~ ALAN GREEN

They care about their club, and that's why they always have something good to say, even when it is negative.   ~ ALAN GREEN

Xavier, who looks just like Zeus, not that I have any idea what Zeus looks like.

~ ALAN GREEN

You don't score 64 goals in 86 games without being able to score goals.

~ ALAN GREEN

Leicester 0, Wimbledon 1, Football minus 1.   ~ ALAN GREEN

All the Leeds team are 100 per cent behind the manager, but I can't speak for the rest of the squad.   ~ BRIAN GREENHOFF

Playing with wingers is more effective against European sides like Brazil than English sides like Wales.   ~ RON GREENWOOD

They've missed so many chances they must be wringing their heads in shame.

~ RON GREENWOOD

Glenn Hoddle hasn't been the Hoddle we know. Neither has Bryan Robson.

~ RON GREENWOOD

I don't hold water with that theory.   ~ RON GREENWOOD

To me personally, it's nothing personal to me.   ~ RON GREENWOOD

I rang Alex Ferguson to see if he'd swap Collymore for Cole. He thought for a few seconds, then said: 'How many bags?'   ~ JOHN GREGORY

He's gone in there with studs up and has cut someone in half, but I don't want to criticise him.   ~ JOHN GREGORY

Celtic manager David Hay still has a fresh pair of legs up his sleeve. ~ JOHN GREIG

I wouldn't be at all surprised if there's a shock result this afternoon. ~ JOHN GREIG

Football's not like an electric light. You can't just flick the switch and change from quick to slow.
~ JOHN GREIG

We thought we had hit the bottom but we saw today that the bottom is even lower.
~ STANISLAV GRIGA

Sing when we're fishing, we only sing when we're fishing.
~ GRIMSBY FANS' SONG

We're working on Plan B now – but just how that plan looks, I don't really know.
~ TORD GRIP, ASSISTANT TO SVEN-GORAN ERIKSSON

The fans who want to see Messi, Tevez, Saviola and Aguero all together should go out and rent *Snow White and the Seven Dwarfs*.
~ JULIO GRONDONA, PRESIDENT OF THE ARGENTINE FA, INSISTING THAT THE NATIONAL TEAM WILL NOT PLAY ALL THE PINT-SIZED PLAYMAKERS AT THE 2006 WORLD CUP

Queen In Brawl At Palace
~ *GUARDIAN* HEADLINE FROM 1970 WHEN GERRY QUEEN PLAYED FOR CRYSTAL PALACE

Arsenal are quick to credit Bergkamp with laying on 75 per cent of their nine goals.
~ TONY GUBBA

So often the pendulum continues to swing with the side that has just pulled themselves out of the hole.
~ TONY GUBBA

These two clubs had a monopoly of the domestic honours last season.
~ TONY GUBBA

He was in the right place at the right time, but he might have been elsewhere on a different afternoon.
~ TONY GUBBA

I wouldn't say the game was dead, but we killed it off in the first half.
~ EIDUR GUDJOHNSEN

In Italy I was man-marked all the time. I would go to the loo and they'd be waiting for me. I'd say, 'While you're there, hold this, will you?'   ~ RUUD GULLIT

To play Holland, you have to play the Dutch.   ~ RUUD GULLIT

We must have had 99 per cent of the match. It was the other three per cent that cost us.   ~ RUUD GULLIT

If they think they can play with two fingers up their nose and a lit cigar, it is not possible.   ~ RUUD GULLIT

A goalkeeper is a goalkeeper because he can't play football.   ~ RUUD GULLIT

I was just as disappointed as Mandela.

~ RUUD GULLIT AFTER A MEETING WITH SOUTH AFRICAN
PRESIDENT NELSON MANDELA WAS CANCELLED

I shouldn't be too upset at losing to Benfica. After all, they have the best players, the best referees and the best linesmen.   ~ VITTORIA SETUBAL MANAGER JIMMY HAGAN

The terrible thing about my job is that players get 80 per cent of my earnings.
~ AGENT ERIC HALL

I'm available 365 days a year. Only me and Father Christmas actually work on Christmas Day and he finishes early.   ~ ERIC HALL

Lee Sharpe has got dynamite in his shorts.   ~ STUART HALL

What will you do when you leave football, Jack – will you stay in football?
~ STUART HALL

Big Kyle [Lafferty] is full of energy. He'd chase paper on a windy day.
~ BILLY HAMILTON

Germany are probably, arguably, undisputed champions of Europe.

~ BRYAN HAMILTON

There's no telling what the score will be if this one goes in.
~ GEORGE HAMILTON

It flew towards the roof of the net like a Wurlitzer.

~ GEORGE HAMILTON

Madrid are like a rabbit dazed in the headlights of a car, except the rabbit has a suit of armour, in the shape of two precious away goals.

~ GEORGE HAMILTON

The Baggio brothers, of course, are not related.

~ GEORGE HAMILTON

—George Hamilton: Roy Carsley has it.
—Jim Beglin: Lee Carsley, George.
—George Hamilton: Ah yes, perhaps it's because his head reminds me of Ray Wilkins.

We play what I call 'orgy football': the other team know they're going to get it, but they don't know from whom or where from.

~ SAM HAMMAM ON CARDIFF CITY

Peter Beardsley is the only player who, when he appears on TV, Daleks hide behind the sofa.

~ NICK HANCOCK

Jimmy Greaves was controversially left out of the squad for the 1966 World Cup final. And if he ever finds out, he'll be gutted.

~ NICK HANCOCK

I have seen things on *Star Trek: The Next Generation* that I find easier to believe than the fact that Mike Duxbury was once an England regular.

~ NICK HANCOCK

According to Alex Ferguson, grey things are invisible. Apparently it's just total luck that planes manage to find aircraft carriers in the middle of the ocean.

~ NICK HANCOCK AFTER FERGUSON COMPLAINED THAT HIS MANCHESTER UNITED
PLAYERS COULDN'T SEE EACH OTHER IN THEIR NEW GREY AWAY STRIP

Alan Shearer: a man so dull he once made the papers for having a one-in-the-bed romp.

~ NICK HANCOCK

The 71-year-old thanked all the players: Him, Whassisname, Fella-me-lad, Thingy and That Bastard Alan Shearer.

~ NICK HANCOCK ON BOBBY ROBSON'S SACKING BY NEWCASTLE

Sven likes to make love like he plays football. He likes to knock it in early and then clings on desperately for 83 minutes.

~ NICK HANCOCK

And Swansea have an uphill mountain to climb.

~ JOHN HARDY

It'll never replace plastic.

~ RAY HARFORD, WHOSE LUTON TEAM PLAYED ON AN ARTIFICIAL SURFACE, DERIDES GRASS

Tony Banks described the English fans arrested in Marseille as brain-dead louts. This goes for me as well.

~ HARRIET HARMAN, MP

We are a young side that will only get younger.

~ PAUL HART

I thought from start to finish we really started well.

~ JOHN HARTSON

It felt like winning the Cup Final, if that's what it feels like.

~ GRAHAM HAWKINS

All of West Ham's away victories have come on opponents' territory this season.

~ ROB HAWTHORNE

The alarm bells are flashing.

~ ROB HAWTHORNE

The first thing I read now in the *Telegraph* is the obituaries. If I'm not in it, I have a good day.

~ JACK HAYWARD

We're coming to the end of the half and the referee is looking at his whistle.

~ JOHN HELM

We're now arithmetically, not mathematically, safe from relegation. There's neither algebra nor geometry involved in the calculations.

~ TOM HENDRIE, ST MIRREN MANAGER

The ball went over mine and Colin Calderwood's heads and who should be there at the far post but yours truly, Alan Shearer.   ~ COLIN HENDRY

When you look at other sports, like golf, the players earn a lot more money without running around. I wish I had that little cart to take me to the corner kicks.   ~ THIERRY HENRY

He had a seventh sense for soccer.

~ NANDOR HIDEGKUTI, REMEMBERING FERENC PUSKAS

What makes this game delightful is both teams are attacking their opponents' goal.   ~ JIMMY HILL

In the words of the old song, it's a long time from May to December but, you know, it's an equally long time from December to May.   ~ JIMMY HILL

Scotland were unlucky not to get another penalty like the one that wasn't given in the first half.   ~ JIMMY HILL

England now have three fresh men with three fresh legs.   ~ JIMMY HILL

It is a Cup Final and the one who wins it goes through.   ~ JIMMY HILL

Good night. And don't forget to put your cocks back.

~ JIMMY HILL, SIGNING OFF *MATCH OF THE DAY* ON THE
NIGHT BEFORE THE END OF BRITISH SUMMER TIME

Glenn Hoddle has nothing against the disabled. After all, he picked 11 of them to play for England.   ~ IAN HISLOP

When a player gets to 30, so does his body.   ~ GLENN HODDLE

I have a number of alternatives and each one gives me something different.

~ GLENN HODDLE

We are down to the barest knuckle.

~ GLENN HODDLE

OK, so we lost, but good things can come from it – negative and positive.

~ GLENN HODDLE

International football is one cog further up the football ladder.

~ GLENN HODDLE

With hindsight, it's easy to look at it with hindsight.

~ GLENN HODDLE

Robert Lee was able to do some running on his groin for the first time.

~ GLENN HODDLE

Steven Carr has hit a small blimp.

~ GLENN HODDLE

It's 60-40 against him being fit, but he's got half a chance.

~ GLENN HODDLE

Seventy-five per cent of what happens to Paul [Gascoigne] in his life is fiction.

~ GLENN HODDLE

Michael Owen is a goalscorer – not a natural born one, not yet, that takes time.

~ GLENN HODDLE

As one door shuts, another door opens – no two ways about it.

~ GLENN HODDLE

We didn't have the run of the mill.

~ GLENN HODDLE

I never heard a minute's silence like that.

~ GLENN HODDLE ON A WEMBLEY PRE-MATCH TRIBUTE FOLLOWING PRINCESS DIANA'S DEATH

I think I must have run over six black cats since I've been at Wolves.

~ GLENN HODDLE BEMOANS HIS BAD LUCK

I spent four indifferent years at Goodison Park, but they were great years.

~ MARTIN HODGE

Michael Owen is not a diver. He knows when to dive, and when not to.

~ STEVE HODGE

The problems were Friday nights and Sunday mornings – knowing we were going to lose on a Saturday and then reading about it the next day.

~ ROY HODGSON AS ASSISTANT MANAGER AT BRISTOL CITY

I can't look at Djimi Traore without seeing a new-born pony.   ~ VINCENT HOGAN

The only way we will be going to Europe is if the club splash out and take us all to EuroDisney.   ~ DEAN HOLDSWORTH AT WIMBLEDON

A contract on a piece of paper, saying you want to leave, is like a piece of paper saying you want to leave.   ~ JOHN HOLLINS

You can't get through the game without bookings, unless you don't book anyone at all.   ~ JOHN HOLLINS

I couldn't be more chuffed if I were a badger at the start of the mating season.

~ QPR MANAGER IAN HOLLOWAY AFTER HIS TEAM'S VICTORY OVER CARDIFF

It's all very well having a great pianist playing but it's no good if you haven't got anyone to get the piano on the stage in the first place, otherwise the pianist would be standing there with no bloody piano to play.

~ IAN HOLLOWAY ON DEFENSIVE MIDFIELD PLAYERS

To put it in gentlemen's terms, if you've been out for a night and you're looking for a young lady and you pull one, some weeks they're good-looking and some weeks they're not the best. Our performance today would have been not the best-looking bird but at least we got her in the taxi. She weren't the best-looking lady we ended up taking home but she was very pleasant and very nice, so thanks very much, let's have a coffee.

~ IAN HOLLOWAY AFTER AN 'UGLY' QPR VICTORY OVER CHESTERFIELD

I am a football manager, I can't see into the future. Last year I thought I was going to Cornwall on my holidays but I ended up going to Lyme Regis.

~ IAN HOLLOWAY

He's a big lad, he can clean out your guttering without standing on a ladder.

~ IAN HOLLOWAY ON GEORGE SANTOS

He can smell round corners now.

~ IAN HOLLOWAY PUTS A POSITIVE SPIN ON HASNEY ALJOFREE'S BROKEN NOSE

Everyone calls Gina Padula a gypsy, but I can assure you he doesn't live in a caravan. He has a house with foundations.

~ IAN HOLLOWAY

I'm not very happy at all; it is self-inflicted. What a complete chicken nugget with double barbecue sauce he is.

~ IAN HOLLOWAY ON PAUL CONNOLLY'S LATEST INJURY SETBACK

Paul Furlong is my vintage Rolls-Royce and he cost me nothing. We polish him, look after him, and I have him fine-tuned by my mechanics. We take good care of him because we have to drive him every day, not just save him for weddings.

~ IAN HOLLOWAY

You can say that strikers are very much like postmen: they have to get in and out as quick as they can before the dog starts to have a go.

~ IAN HOLLOWAY

Everyone was laughing because if that was not a penalty then what was? I think my wife saw that and she's down in St Albans listening to the radio!

~ IAN HOLLOWAY ON A REJECTED PENALTY AT GRIMSBY

Right now, everything is going wrong for me. If I fell in a barrel of boobs, I'd come out sucking my thumb.

~ IAN HOLLOWAY

If I had a time machine, I would go back and get a few months' worth of Lottery numbers and then buy Thierry Henry.

~ IAN HOLLOWAY

In football there is no definite lifespan or time span for a manager. After a while you start smelling of fish. The other week it looked like I was stinking of halibut!

~ IAN HOLLOWAY

If we did get in the play-offs, I'd be singing and dancing but it would be a horrible song as I can't sing a note.

~ IAN HOLLOWAY

They say that every dog has his day and today is woof day. I want to go and bark.

~ IAN HOLLOWAY

The biggest problem I've got down here in Plymouth is seagulls shitting on my car.

~ IAN HOLLOWAY

Me and my wife took in three games in two days, so she's been thoroughly spoilt.

~ IAN HOLLOWAY

I'm a Rottweiller trapped inside a terrier's body.

~ IAN HOLLOWAY

I've never written a speech in my life and I never will. I wrote one once and it was rubbish.

~ IAN HOLLOWAY

The only thing wobbling at Norwich is Delia's jelly!

~ GARY HOLT ON SUGGESTIONS THAT THE TEAM WAS LOSING ITS NERVE ON THE PROMOTION RUN-IN

The natural state of the football fan is bitter disappointment, no matter what the score. ~ NICK HORNBY, *FEVER PITCH*

Even though there is no question that sex is a nicer activity than watching football (no nil-nil draws, no offside trap, no cup upsets, *and* you're warm), in the normal run of things, the feelings it engenders are simply not as intense as those brought about by a once-in-a-lifetime last-minute Championship winner. ~ NICK HORNBY, *FEVER PITCH*

Jason Koumas is taking too few touches too many. ~ BARRY HORNE

I've taken a picture off the TV of me being ahead of Thierry [Henry] in the scoring charts and I'm going to keep it as my screensaver. ~ GEOFF HORSFIELD

It was a game of two halves and we were rubbish in both of them.

~ BRIAN HORTON

You cannot say my team aren't winners. They've proved that by finishing fourth, third, and second in the last three years. ~ GERARD HOULLIER

Hagi has got a left foot like Brian Lara's bat. ~ DON HOWE

Pat Jennings might be a bit vulnerable to a hard, low shot from the edge of the six-yard box. ~ DON HOWE

I'm finding it difficult to find a girlfriend in Barnsley or to settle into a decent way of life. The girls are far uglier than the ones back in Belgrade or Skopje and drink too much beer. ~ GEORGI HRISTOV

Trevor Francis could not spot a great footballer if the bloke's name had four letters, started with 'P' and ended in 'e'. ~ ALAN HUDSON

They call Gerard Houllier the French professor. Well, if he really is going to fork out millions on [Emile] Heskey, I can only say I'm glad he wasn't the professor who operated on me when I was rattling the pearly gates. ~ ALAN HUDSON

He is not unused to playing in midfield, but at the same time he's not used to playing there either. ~ EMLYN HUGHES

I'm not going to tell him to stop that celebration. You can tell him if you like – he's bigger than me! ~ MARK HUGHES ON STRIKER SHEFKI KUQI'S BELLY-FLOP ROUTINE

The groin's been a little sore but after the semi-final I put it to the back of my head. ~ MICHAEL HUGHES

I asked the fourth official if he was counting the time on a sundial.
~ NORWICH CARETAKER MANAGER MARTIN HUNTER AFTER
QPR SCORE AN EQUALISER DEEP INTO ADDED-ON TIME

I don't know if that result's enough to lift Birmingham off the bottom of the table, although it'll certainly take them above Sunderland. ~ MIKE INGHAM

John Bond's smile is always very, very good radio. ~ MIKE INGHAM

The Uruguayans are losing no time in making a meal around the referee.
~ MIKE INGHAM

Martin O'Neill, standing, hands on hips, stroking his chin. ~ MIKE INGHAM

And the score is 0-0, just as it was at the beginning of the game. ~ MIKE INGHAM

…Evoking memories, particularly of days gone by. ~ MIKE INGHAM

Let me fill you in on the other results so far. There are no other results so far.
~ HAZEL IRVINE

They've won the game. That's probably what they set out to do.   ~ DENIS IRWIN

Villa looking comfortable on that 1-1 lead.
                                                        ~ ANDREW JAMES

How much further down his head will Bobby Charlton have to part his hair before he faces the fact that he is bald?   ~ CLIVE JAMES

It's tough when you go to your local supermarket and the person at the checkout is thinking, 'Dodgy keeper!'   ~ DAVID JAMES

When I was growing up, he was scoring or missing penalties for England.
          ~ DAVID JAMES ON HIS NEW MANCHESTER CITY BOSS, STUART PEARCE

Andy O'Brien's got such a big hooter that some of the strikers he marks go off with broken elbows.   ~ PAUL JEWELL

When my chairman started linking me with the England job, I immediately thought he wanted to get rid of me!   ~ PAUL JEWELL

My only ambition is for us [Wigan] not to be last on *Match of the Day*. If we can do that, and if we can get more than two minutes' air time – and they even talk about our game afterwards – I'll be a happy man.   ~ PAUL JEWELL

If Brazil are the best team in the World Cup, then I am Geri Halliwell.
                                                        ~ ELTON JOHN, 2006

For a while I did unite Rangers and Celtic fans. There were people in both camps who hated me.   ~ MO JOHNSTON

He's one of those footballers whose brains are in his head.   ~ DEREK JOHNSTONE

The new West Stand casts a giant shadow over the entire pitch, even on a sunny day.   ~ CHRIS JONES

We reckon Carlton Palmer covers every blade of grass on the pitch – mainly because his first touch is terrible. ~ DAVE JONES

It's fair to say the crowd booed them off at half-time and then I booed them into the dressing room. ~ DAVE JONES

I wouldn't say I'm overweight, but I would say I'm too heavy. ~ GRAEME JONES

We got Karl Connolly from Napoli. Not the Italian club, the fish and chip shop in Liverpool. ~ JOEY JONES AT WREXHAM

Ian Rush, deadly ten times out of ten, but that wasn't one of them. ~ PETER JONES

It's Ipswich 0, Liverpool 2, and if that's the way the score stays then you've got to fancy Liverpool to win. ~ PETER JONES

It really needed the blink of an eyelid, otherwise you would have missed it. ~ PETER JONES

Leicester: runners-up at Wembley four times, never the bride, always the bridegroom. ~ PETER JONES

Sporting Lisbon in their green and white hoops, looking like a team of zebras. ~ PETER JONES

I've lost count of how many corners there have been. Lincoln have one and Crystal Palace 17. ~ RON JONES

And Rush, quick as a needle. ~ RON JONES

We say 'educated left foot', but of course there are many players with educated right foots. ~ RON JONES

A medal from Princess Di and a kiss from Sam Hammam and with no disrespect to either, you wish it could have been the other way round!

~ VINNIE JONES ON WIMBLEDON'S 1988 FA CUP TRIUMPH

Winning doesn't really matter as long as you win.

~ VINNIE JONES

The FA have given me a pat on the back. I've taken violence off the terracing and onto the pitch.

~ VINNIE JONES

I'd like to get ten goals this season, but the authorities don't normally let me play for a whole season.

~ VINNIE JONES

If all else fails, you could wait for the first corner and use his dreadlocks to tie him to a post.

~ VINNIE JONES ON RUUD GULLIT

My pot-bellied pigs don't squeal as much as him.

~ VINNIE JONES, SENT OFF FOR FOULING RUUD GULLIT

All the cul-de-sacs are closed for Scotland.

~ JOE JORDAN

These days I need ten minutes' notice to score.

~ 37-YEAR-OLD JOE JORDAN

The future's bright, the chairman's orange.

~ TITLE OF PERMATANNED CRYSTAL PALACE CHAIRMAN SIMON JORDAN'S PROGRAMME NOTES

I'd strangle him with his own tongue.

~ SIMON JORDAN ON CRAIG BELLAMY

I have no interest in schmoozing with other Premiership chairmen. I don't go to football to drink chardonnay in the boardroom with those twats. ~ SIMON JORDAN

There were times he [Ron Noades] got so far up my nose I could feel his boots on my chin.

~ SIMON JORDAN

I always find empty vessels make the most noise and, in Gordon's case, he is the size of an oil tanker. ~ SIMON JORDAN ON AGENT COLIN GORDON

I would rather gouge my eyes out with a rusty spoon than have [David] O'Leary back as manager. ~ SIMON JOSE OF THE LEEDS UNITED INDEPENDENT FANS' ASSOCIATION

Not only has he shown Junior Lewis the red card, but he's sent him off.
~ CHRIS KAMARA

Stern John had the easy task of rolling it into the net from six yards. He made it look easy, although it wasn't. ~ CHRIS KAMARA

Barnsley have started off the way they mean to begin. ~ CHRIS KAMARA

He's had three offside decisions – two right, two wrong. ~ CHRIS KAMARA

He had it on a plate – he had the sausage, bacon and eggs on it as well – but he couldn't take it. ~ CHRIS KAMARA

It's real end-to-end stuff, but unfortunately it's all up at Forest's end.
~ CHRIS KAMARA

I was at a social function with Romeo Benetti the other week, and it's the first time I've got within ten yards of him and he hasn't kicked me. Even then I kept looking over my shoulder. ~ KEVIN KEEGAN

It's like a toaster, the ref's shirt pocket. Every time there's a tackle, up pops a yellow card. ~ KEVIN KEEGAN

You can't force people to sit down, even if they have a seat. They want to sing and unless you're Val Doonican you can't do that sitting down.
~ KEVIN KEEGAN ON ALL-SEATER STADIA

Gary always weighed up his options, especially when he had no choice.

~ KEVIN KEEGAN

I'd love to be a mole on the wall in the Liverpool dressing room at half-time.

~ KEVIN KEEGAN

England have the best fans in the world and Scotland's fans are second-to-none.

~ KEVIN KEEGAN

What disappointed me was that we didn't play with any passion. I'm not disappointed, you know. I'm just disappointed.　　　~ KEVIN KEEGAN

There are two schools of thought on the way the rest of this half is going to develop; everybody's got their own opinion.　　　~ KEVIN KEEGAN

Goalkeepers aren't born today until they're in their late twenties or thirties.

~ KEVIN KEEGAN

There'll be no siestas in Madrid tonight.　　　~ KEVIN KEEGAN

Luis Figo is totally different to David Beckham and vice versa.

~ KEVIN KEEGAN

A tremendous strike which hit the defender full on the arm – and it nearly came off.　　　~ KEVIN KEEGAN

It was still moving when it hit the back of the net.　　　~ KEVIN KEEGAN

I know what is around the corner; I just don't know where the corner is.

~ KEVIN KEEGAN

I don't think they're as good as they are.　　　~ KEVIN KEEGAN

I was in Nantes two years ago. It's much the same as it is now, although now it's completely different. ~ KEVIN KEEGAN

Football's always easier when you've got the ball. ~ KEVIN KEEGAN

Shaun Wright-Phillips has got a heart as big as his size, which isn't big, but his heart's bigger than that.

~ KEVIN KEEGAN

The tide is very much in our court now. ~ KEVIN KEEGAN

In some ways, cramp is worse than having a broken leg. ~ KEVIN KEEGAN

It's understandable that people are keeping one eye on the pot and another up the chimney. ~ KEVIN KEEGAN

My father was a miner and he worked down a mine. ~ KEVIN KEEGAN

I don't think there's anyone bigger – or smaller – than Maradona. ~ KEVIN KEEGAN

Argentina are the second best side in the world – and there's no better praise than that. ~ KEVIN KEEGAN

Not many teams will come to Arsenal and get anything, home or away. ~ KEVIN KEEGAN

I would ask anyone to try to understand the world David Beckham lives in. We all have to accept that he is married to Spice Girl Victoria Adams – and I think he copes very well with it. ~ KEVIN KEEGAN

The substitute is about to come on. He's a player who was left out of the starting line-up today. ~ KEVIN KEEGAN

If we can make the rest of this tournament count, English football can end the millennium as it started – as the greatest football nation in the world.

~ KEVIN KEEGAN ON THE 1998 WORLD CUP

There's a slight doubt about only one player, and that's Tony Adams, who definitely won't be playing tomorrow. ~ KEVIN KEEGAN

We are three games without defeat is another way of looking at it. But if we are honest we have taken two points from nine. ~ KEVIN KEEGAN

We deserved to win this game after hammering them 0-0 in the first half. ~ KEVIN KEEGAN

We owe it to ourselves first and foremost, and, more importantly, to our fans.

~ KEVIN KEEGAN

The ref was vertically 15 yards away. ~ KEVIN KEEGAN

People will say that was typical City, which really annoys me. But that's typical City, I suppose. ~ KEVIN KEEGAN

Nicolas Anelka – 24 years of age, but he's been around a lot longer than that.

~ KEVIN KEEGAN

Nicolas Anelka left Arsenal for £23 million and they built a training ground on him. ~ KEVIN KEEGAN

We managed to wrong a few rights. ~ KEVIN KEEGAN

I was sitting just a few feet away from David Pleat at the World Cup. He's a nice fellow, but the man is mad: certifiably, eye-spinningly mad. ~ DANNY KELLY

The news that Sven-Goran Eriksson has a glass toilet is the stuff of nightmares. I can only assume he has a see-through lavatory for one reason. Ironically, we spent the last two years of his England reign doing the same.   ~ DES KELLY

[Didier] Drogba must be the only six foot two inches tall, 14 stone athlete cursed with the unsteady gait and low pain threshold of a toddler.   ~ DES KELLY

I wouldn't quote Kipling to the lads; they'd probably think I was talking about the cakes.   ~ LEICESTER CITY BOSS ROB KELLY

Some of our players have got no brains, so I've given them the day off tomorrow to rest them.   ~ OXFORD UNITED MANAGER DAVE KEMP

How do I view United? Preferably on television, but unfortunately we have to go down the East Lancs Road and get a bit closer.   ~ HOWARD KENDALL AT EVERTON

The biggest difference between playing for Forfar and playing for Rangers? Probably about £300 a week.
~ STEWART KENNEDY

The unthinkable is not something we're really thinking about at the moment.
~ PETER KENYON

I've always been a childhood Liverpool fan, even when I was a kid. ~ HARRY KEWELL

Jose Mourinho has got the Midas touch right now – everything he touches turns to silver.   ~ RICHARD KEYS

We pressed the self-destruct button ourselves.   ~ BRIAN KIDD

I don't know what it's like out there, but it's like an ice rink out there.
~ ANDY KILNER

We were disappointed we couldn't play on Saturday because we had supporters travelling from all over the country. There was one coming from London, one from Newcastle, one from Brighton…

~ ROCHDALE CHAIRMAN DAVID KILPATRICK AFTER THE
POSTPONEMENT OF AN FA CUP TIE AT MANCHESTER UNITED

I thought we started very, very brightly, but then the Achilles heel which has bitten us in the backside all year has stood out like a sore thumb.   ~ ANDY KING

Innovative psychologist Aidy Boothroyd has said his players should read newspapers upside-down if the League table upsets them; if television spectators do the same, maybe Watford will look like they play the ball on the ground.

~ DANIEL KING

Chelsea, led by Jose Mourinho, are a bit like global warming: everyone admits there's a big problem, no one can agree on how to combat it, and the source of the worst emissions has the least inclination to clean up its act.   ~ DANIEL KING

I can count on the fingers of one hand ten games when we've caused our own downfall.   ~ JOE KINNEAR

Sam [Hammam] told us that if we do not make Wembley he will take us to a Chekhov play every night for a week, then for another Lebanese meal. Blow that, we've got to get to Wembley now.   ~ JOE KINNEAR

The only time we [Wimbledon] have been to Europe before was to stock up on duty-free.   ~ JOE KINNEAR

John Fashanu was having karate lessons and ended up a first dan, but he was playing like Desperate Dan.   ~ JOE KINNEAR

Sam Hammam said I could bring in two new faces, so I asked him for Jack Walker and Sir John Hall.   ~ JOE KINNEAR

It's like going into a nuclear war with bows and arrows.

~ JOE KINNEAR ON THE GULF IN SPENDING POWER BETWEEN
WIMBLEDON AND THE PREMIERSHIP BIG BOYS

That's the story of my managerial life. Buy in Woolworth's, sell in Harrods.

~ JOE KINNEAR

You can't fart without Birtles' or Clough's name being mentioned.

~ JOE KINNEAR ON HISTORY-OBSESSED NOTTINGHAM FOREST

You can't always win pretty. Sometimes you have to win ugly – and I'm really ugly because I have a broken nose.

~ SHEFKI KUQI

My dad used to referee me when I was a kid. I remember him booking me – and asking my name.

~ KEVIN KYLE

He was a dedicated follower of Fashanu.

~ DAVID LACEY, AFTER QPR DEFENDER ALAN MCDONALD
CLOSE-MARKED WIMBLEDON'S JOHN FASHANU

Tell him he's Pele and get him back on.

~ PARTICK THISTLE MANAGER JOHN LAMBIE AFTER BEING TOLD THAT STRIKER
COLIN MCGLASHAN HAD CONCUSSION AND DIDN'T KNOW WHO HE WAS

I did once hit a player with a dead pigeon. His name was Declan Roche and he was talking back to me, so I got these dead pigeons out of a box and slapped him with one.

~ JOHN LAMBIE

Our first goal was pure textile.

~ JOHN LAMBIE

I thought there might be eight goals, but I never expected we'd get four of them.

~ DAVE LANCASTER AFTER CHESTERFIELD'S 4-4 DRAW AT ANFIELD IN 1992

My nine-year-old son feels more Scottish than anything else at the moment, so we have to go back to Sweden. ~ HENRIK LARSSON

Andy Gray's style is more suited to Rugby Union.
~ UDO LATTEK

I have accepted that the remainder of my career will be at smaller clubs. Aston Villa is perfect for me. ~ MARTIN LAURSEN OFFERS A BACK-HANDED COMPLIMENT

I used to say Pat Crerand was a great asset to television, because they didn't need slow motion when he was on the ball! ~ DENIS LAW

There's no way that Ryan Giggs is another George Best: he's another Ryan Giggs. ~ DENIS LAW

It was one of those goals that's invariably a goal. ~ DENIS LAW

The advantage of being at home is very much with the home side. ~ DENIS LAW

The only market I might go into would be Billingsgate. ~ LENNIE LAWRENCE AT IMPOVERISHED CHARLTON, 1989

The last time we got a penalty away from home, Christ was a carpenter. ~ LENNIE LAWRENCE

You need at least eight or nine men in a ten-man wall.
~ MARK LAWRENSON

It's slightly alarming the way Manchester United decapitated against Stuttgart. ~ MARK LAWRENSON

All strikers go through what they call a glut, where they don't score goals. ~ MARK LAWRENSON

He reminds me of a completely different version of Robbie Earle.

~ MARK LAWRENSON

These managers all know their onions and cut their cloth accordingly.

~ MARK LAWRENSON

The Republic of Ireland have just one game plan. If Plan A fails, resort to Plan A.

~ MARK LAWRENSON

Mick McCarthy will have to replace Cascarino because he's quickly running out of legs.

~ MARK LAWRENSON

Ireland will give 99 per cent – everything they've got.

~ MARK LAWRENSON

Alan Shearer's like next door's cat – always feeding off the scraps.

~ MARK LAWRENSON

For a game played in Cologne, that stunk.

~ MARK LAWRENSON

I'm sure our name's on a cup somewhere, but it will have a saucer with it.

~ BRIAN LAWS AT SCUNTHORPE

We see a lot of Ken Bates. He'll always have a laugh and a joke with you. At your expense, obviously.

~ GRAEME LE SAUX

Colin Hendry is one of those guys who isn't happy unless he's been kicked three times in the bollocks in training.

~ GRAEME LE SAUX

He's always got an Italian-English phrasebook with him. Mind you, that's for him to stand on.

~ GRAEME LE SAUX ON THE DIMINUTIVE GIANFRANCO ZOLA

When you're walking onto a bus and trying to get there before the person in front of you, that's a different level of competition to playing in front of 80,000 people.

~ GRAEME LE SAUX

The opening ceremony was good, although I missed it.

~ GRAEME LE SAUX

I'm dumbfounded, but nothing surprises me in this game.   ~ FRANCIS LEE

Even when you're dead, you shouldn't lie down and let yourself be buried.

~ GORDON LEE

Ruud Gullit's ego was as big as Amsterdam.   ~ ROB LEE

You've lost Ndlovu and Whelan.

~ LEEDS FANS TAUNT COVENTRY'S TO THE TUNE OF 'YOU'VE LOST THAT LOVING FEELING'

Since Walsall's new ground is to be built on the site of an old sewage works, may I suggest the new name of W.C. Fields?   ~ LETTER TO *BIRMINGHAM SPORTS ARGUS*, 1989

Most of the players will be wearing rubbers tonight.

~ GARY LINEKER DISCUSSING FOOTWEAR

Ronaldo must be the only man alive who can eat an apple through a tennis racket.   ~ GARY LINEKER

To be honest, it would have been better to watch them on Ceefax.

~ GARY LINEKER ON WIMBLEDON

It's amazing what you can see through Sven's specs – I must get a pair.

~ GARY LINEKER ON ERIKSSON'S POSITIVE ASSESSMENT OF A BORING ENGLAND-HOLLAND FRIENDLY

Scolari's got great credentials by winning the World Cup, but he did it with Brazil. My granny could probably have managed Brazil to World Cup success!

~ GARY LINEKER

You could say they were pulling the wool over our eyes with Lahm scoring there.

~ A SHEEPISH GARY LINEKER

An excellent player, but he [Ian Wright] does have a black side.   ~ GARY LINEKER

The World Cup is every four years, so it's going to be a perennial problem.

~ GARY LINEKER

It's a tense time for managers. They have to exhume confidence.   ~ GARY LINEKER

There's no in between, you're either good or bad. We were in between.

~ GARY LINEKER

Gordon Milne used to say to me, 'If somebody in the crowd spits at you, you've just got to swallow it.'   ~ GARY LINEKER

Football is a very simple game. For 90 minutes, 22 men go running after the ball and at the end the Germans win.   ~ GARY LINEKER

Wrighty, are you a fan of S&M?

~ GARY LINEKER, ASKING IAN WRIGHT ABOUT SERBIA & MONTENEGRO

He has had eight bookings now, which is more than Freddie Starr gets these days.   ~ COLIN LIPPIATT

He's such an honest person, it's untrue.   ~ BRIAN LITTLE

If Bill Shankly was alive, he'd be turning in his grave.

~ LIVERPOOL FAN ON A RADIO PHONE-IN

You couldn't score in a brothel.

~ LIVERPOOL FANS TAUNT WAYNE ROONEY AFTER HIS WIDELY REPORTED INDISCRETIONS

He bought three Italians – one was older than me, one was slower and the third had a heart the size of a peanut.

~ LARRY LLOYD ON DAVID PLATT'S NOTTINGHAM FOREST SIGNINGS

Germany are a very difficult team to play – they had 11 internationals out there today.   ~ STEVE LOMAS

Hodge scored for Forest after 22 seconds – totally against the run of play.

~ MATTHEW LORENZO

He didn't give the penalty, but I've seen them given for worse.   ~ ANGUS LOUGHRAN

Colin Murphy talks like a product of an unlikely liaison between Stanley Unwin and Mrs Malaprop.   ~ JOE LOVEJOY

In terms of the Richter scale, this defeat was a force eight gale.   ~ JOHN LYALL

Chesterfield 1, Chester 1. Another score draw in that local derby.   ~ DES LYNAM

He was unlucky, or was it just bad luck?   ~ DES LYNAM

If there weren't such a thing as football, we'd all be frustrated footballers.

~ MICK LYONS

Our away form this season may not be exceptional, but compared to our home form it doesn't look bad at all.   ~ GARY MABBUTT

The first half was end-to-end stuff. In contrast, in this second half it's been one end to the other.   ~ LOU MACARI

Mirandinha will have more shots this afternoon than both sides put together.

~ MALCOLM MACDONALD

Many clubs have a question mark in the shape of an axe-head hanging over them.   ~ MALCOLM MACDONALD

That's the kind he usually knocks in in his sleep – with his eyes closed.

~ ARCHIE MacPHERSON

Ardiles strokes the ball like it is part of his own anatomy.   ~ JIMMY MAGEE

Jean Tigana has spent the entire first half inside Liam Brady's shorts.

~ JIMMY MAGEE

The referee certainly isn't fond of the whistle. James Galway he ain't.

~ JIMMY MAGEE

Last week I was so low I could have walked under a door with a top hat on.

~ JIM MAGILTON

Feed the Goat and he will score.   ~ MANCHESTER CITY FANS SPUR ON SHAUN GOATER

The only Irish international who doesn't know where Dublin is.

~ *MANCHESTER EVENING NEWS* AFTER SHAY GIVEN FAILS TO SPOT A LURKING DION DUBLIN

One triple vodka, there's only one triple vodka.

~ MANCHESTER UNITED FANS' TAUNT TO TONY ADAMS

The entire contents of the Manchester City trophy room have been stolen. Police are looking for a man carrying a light blue carpet.   ~ BERNARD MANNING

A male MP was found dead in stockings and suspenders. He was also wearing a Manchester City scarf but the police kept that bit quiet so as not to embarrass the relatives.   ~ BERNARD MANNING

I don't think Lee Bowyer is racist at all. I think he would stamp on anybody's head.   ~ RODNEY MARSH

Comparing Gascoigne to Pele is like comparing Rolf Harris to Rembrandt.

~ RODNEY MARSH

They've made some signings, but it's like putting lipstick on a pig. It's still a pig.

~ RODNEY MARSH AS WEST BROM PREPARE FOR THE PREMIERSHIP

Never mind leaping like a salmon, he leaps like a goldfish. ~ RODNEY MARSH

—Alf Ramsey: If you don't work harder tonight, I'll pull you off at half-time.
—Rodney Marsh: Christ, we only get a cup of tea and an orange at City!

Kevin Keegan said that if he had a blank sheet of paper, five names would be on it. ~ ALVIN MARTIN

He's the type of player the manager's either going to keep or not keep next season. ~ ALVIN MARTIN

Steve Bruce is like a cat on hot tin bricks. ~ ALVIN MARTIN

The ball could have gone anywhere and almost did. ~ BRIAN MARWOOD

Apparently when you head a ball, you lose brain cells, but it doesn't bother me... I'm a horse. ~ DAVID MAY

I was feeling as sick as the proverbial donkey. ~ MICK McCARTHY

You want to try sitting in the dug-out when it's your arse in the bacon-slicer.
~ MICK McCARTHY TO A REPORTER WHO TOLD HIM
HE LOOKED TENSE DURING A 2002 WORLD CUP GAME

No regrets, none at all. My only regret is that we went out on penalties. That's my only regret. But no, no regrets.
~ MICK McCARTHY AFTER IRELAND GO OUT OF THE 2002 WORLD CUP

I'm thinking of sending him [Jason Beckford] to Blackheath Hospital to get 5,000 fans off his back. ~ MICK McCARTHY AT MILLWALL

I asked the players who wanted to take a penalty and there was an awful smell coming from some of them. ~ MICK McCARTHY AFTER HIS MILLWALL TEAM KNOCKED CHELSEA OUT OF THE FA CUP IN A PENALTY SHOOT-OUT

Carl Robinson has got a busted hooter and Darren Carter has got blurred vision. They were having a chat and thought they were in a crowd! ~ MICK McCARTHY

If that was intentional, I'll drop me trousers and bare me bum in Burton's window. ~ MICK McCARTHY

We should have had a penalty. But there was as much chance of us getting that as me making my way home under my own steam, flapping my arms. ~ MICK McCARTHY

My mother told me there would be days like these. She just didn't tell me when and how many.
~ MICK McCARTHY AS A 94TH-MINUTE GOAL ROBS SUNDERLAND OF A FIRST PREMIERSHIP VICTORY

It wasn't a monkey on my back, it was Planet of the Apes!
~ MICK McCARTHY AS SUNDERLAND WIN AT LAST

The goal was the deciding factor. ~ STEVE McCLAREN AFTER MIDDLESBROUGH LOSE 1-0

We conceded two quick goals over there, and we're capable of doing the same at home. ~ STEVE McCLAREN

I will never shut the door on David Beckham's international career. It will never be open, er, closed.
~ STEVE McCLAREN MAKES A FREUDIAN SLIP ON TAKING OVER AS ENGLAND MANAGER

Craig Bellamy has literally been on fire. ~ ALLY McCOIST

So correct it isn't true. ~ ALLY McCOIST

I'm on first-name terms with about half the crowd.

~ JOHN McDERMOTT, AFTER PLAYING HIS 736TH GAME FOR GRIMSBY

The best two clubs in London are Stringfellow's and The Hippodrome.

~ TERRY McDERMOTT

No one hands you cups on a plate.

~ TERRY McDERMOTT

If we get promotion, let's sit down and see where we stand.　　~ ROY McFARLAND

Vinnie Jones is as discreet as a scream in a cathedral.　　~ FRANK McGHEE

Barry Fry's management style seems to be based on the chaos theory.

~ MARK McGHEE

If Barnsley win tomorrow, we only need seven points from our last two games to pip them.　　~ MARK McGHEE

We played a 4-4-3 formation, which we have played before and never failed to win with it.　　~ MARK McGHEE

Terry Venables had his finger in more pies than Eamonn Holmes.

~ DEREK McGOVERN

I'm going to have to listen to offers for all my players – and the club cat Benny, who's pissed off because all the mice have died of starvation.

~ JOHN McGRATH AT HALIFAX TOWN

Things were so bad I received a letter from *Reader's Digest* saying I hadn't been included in their prize draw.　　~ JOHN McGRATH

My left foot is not one of my best.　　~ SAMMY McILROY

If, as every Englishman suspects, the Scots ingest a weakness for hyperbole with their mother's milk, Ally MacLeod would seem to have been breast-fed until he was 15.　　~ HUGH McILVANNEY, AFTER SCOTLAND'S DISASTROUS 1978 WORLD CUP CAMPAIGN

People talk about Newcastle as a 'sleeping giant'. They last won the championship in 1927 and the FA Cup in 1955. They already make Rip Van Winkle look like a catnapper.　　~ HUGH McILVANNEY

In any walk of life, if you get a penalty you expect to score.　　~ ALAN McINALLY

The candle is still very much in the melting pot.　　~ ALAN McINALLY

Hearts are now playing with a five-man back four.　　~ ALAN McINALLY

Wayne Rooney says he cannot get to sleep without the sound of a Hoover in the background. Maybe it's true what they say. There's a vacuum between this boy's ears.　　~ PETER McKAY

All-out attack mixed with caution.
~ JIM McLAUGHLIN, SHAMROCK ROVERS MANAGER, ON HIS TACTICS FOR A EUROPEAN TIE

I'm definitely maybe going to play Sturrock.　　~ JIM McLEAN

At the end of the day, it's not the end of the world.　　~ JIM McLEAN

Tore [Andre Flo]'s got a groin strain and he's playing with it.　　~ ALEX McLEISH

We were a little bit outnumbered there; it was two against two. ~ FRANK McLINTOCK

I don't want to be either partial or impartial.　　~ FRANK McLINTOCK

Imagine Franz Beckenbauer trying to play for Watford. He'd just be in the way.
~ FRANK McLINTOCK ON GRAHAM TAYLOR'S LONG-BALL GAME, 1982

How do I feel? Lower than a snake's belly.　　~ STEVE McMAHON

We weren't rowdy or out of order but we went to a lap-dancing bar so my mum wasn't too happy about it. It was worse facing her than it was facing the gaffer!

~ HIBS STRIKER TOM McMANUS

Some of these players never dreamed they'd be playing in a Cup Final at Wembley, but here they are today, fulfilling those dreams.   ~ LAWRIE McMENEMY

I hope Robson doesn't blow up because of the heat.   ~ LAWRIE McMENEMY

He [Stan Mortensen] had a Cup Final named after him: the Matthews Final.

~ LAWRIE McMENEMY

Southampton is a very well-run club from Monday to Friday. It's Saturdays we've got a problem with.   ~ LAWRIE McMENEMY

When the ball hits a defending player's arm or hand, it's either a penalty or it isn't.   ~ GARY MEGSON

You are talking about a man who spelt his name wrong on his transfer request.

~ GARY MEGSON ON JASON ROBERTS

That number 14 for Holland is a marvellous player ... that Johan Strauss.

~ JOE MERCER

Kevin Keegan has now tasted the other side of the fence.   ~ DAVE MERRINGTON

The manager has given us unbelievable belief.   ~ PAUL MERSON

Julian Dicks is everywhere. It's like they've got 11 Dicks on the field.

~ METRO RADIO

My wife, who was in the stand, told me that at one stage the entire row in front of her stood up and gave me the V-sign. I asked her what she did and she said she didn't want them to know who she was, so she stood up and joined in.

~ EX-REFEREE NEIL MIDGLEY

To find a way past Bobby Moore was like searching for the exit from Hampton Court maze.
~ DAVID MILLER

England bowed out of the World Cup last night with their heads held high.
~ BRUCE MILLINGTON

It's a bit like Amsterdam. They look great in the window, but it's different when you go inside.
~ BOB MILLS ON THE HAZARDS OF THE TRANSFER WINDOW

Graham Alexander had a problem at the airport – he still had Franck Ribery in his pocket and had to take him out.
~ PAUL MITCHELL AFTER SCOTLAND'S VICTORY OVER FRANCE, 2006

Football players are clever people. We have a head on the hips.
~ ALON MIZRAHI

Paul Scholes with four players in front of him – five if you count Gary Neville.
~ DARRAGH MOLONEY

Supporting Manchester United will become a criminal offence for anyone born south of Crewe.
~ MONSTER RAVING LOONY PARTY ELECTION MANIFESTO

Jim McLean, one of the few managers who can physically lift a side.
~ ARTHUR MONTFORD

History, as John Bond would agree, is all about todays and not about yesterdays.
~ BRIAN MOORE

They [Rosenborg] have won 66 games, and they've scored in all of them.
~ BRIAN MOORE

It's been an amazing year for Crystal Palace over the last 12 months.
~ BRIAN MOORE

The familiar sight of Liverpool lifting the League Cup for the first time.

~ BRIAN MOORE

The European Cup is 17 pounds of silver and is worth its weight in gold.

~ BRIAN MOORE

And their manager, Terry Neill, isn't here today, which suggests he is elsewhere.

~ BRIAN MOORE

Adams is stretching himself, looking for Seaman.

~ BRIAN MOORE

Manchester United have never beaten an Italian side on two legs in European competition.

~ BRIAN MOORE

Wayne Clarke, one of the famous Clarke family, and he's one of them, of course.

~ BRIAN MOORE

You can see how O'Leary is absolutely racked with pain, and realises it.

~ BRIAN MOORE

The news from Guadalajara, where the temperature is 96 degrees, is that Falcao is warming up.

~ BRIAN MOORE

Newcastle, of course, unbeaten in their last five wins.

~ BRIAN MOORE

Remember, postcards only, please. The winner will be the first one opened.

~ BRIAN MOORE

And now we have the formalities over, we'll have the National Anthems.

~ BRIAN MOORE

We looked like Real Madrid last week when we beat West Ham, but we looked like the Rose and Crown this week.

~ ROTHERHAM BOSS RONNIE MOORE

We can play creamy football but where are the crunchy bits and the hard bites?

~ RONNIE MOORE, IN HIS TIME AS OLDHAM MANAGER

The immortal Jackie Milburn died today.   ~ CLIFF MORGAN

I'd been ill and hadn't trained for a week and I'd been out of the team for three
weeks before that, so I wasn't sharp. I got cramp before half-time as well. But
I'm not one to make excuses.   ~ CLINTON MORRISON

Asprilla is totally unpredictable, but perfectly capable of doing the unexpected.

~ JOHN MOTSON

For those of you watching in black and white, Spurs are in the all-yellow strip.

~ JOHN MOTSON

Nearly all of the Brazilian supporters are wearing yellow shorts – it's a fabulous
kaleidoscope of colour.   ~ JOHN MOTSON

So different from the scenes in 1872, at the Cup Final none of us can remember.

~ JOHN MOTSON

The referee is wearing the same yellow-coloured top as the Slovakian goalkeeper.
I'd have thought the UEFA official would have spotted that – but perhaps he's
been deafened by the noise of the crowd.   ~ JOHN MOTSON

You couldn't count the number of moves he made. I counted four, and possibly five.

~ JOHN MOTSON

Bruce has got the taste of Wembley in his nostrils.   ~ JOHN MOTSON

And Seaman, just like a falling oak, manages to change direction.   ~ JOHN MOTSON

I can't fault Mark Palios too highly.   ~ JOHN MOTSON

Paul Gascoigne has recently become a father and has been booked for over-celebrating. ~ JOHN MOTSON

There's been a colour clash: both teams are wearing white. ~ JOHN MOTSON

And I suppose they [Spurs] are nearer to being out of the FA Cup now than any other time since the first half of this season, when they weren't ever in it anyway. ~ JOHN MOTSON

Brazil – they're so good it's like they are running around the pitch playing with themselves. ~ JOHN MOTSON

The Czech Republic are coming from behind in more than one way now. ~ JOHN MOTSON

He knows all about the Italian opposition, playing now in Turkey. ~ JOHN MOTSON

That shot might not have been as good as it might have been. ~ JOHN MOTSON

The goals made such a difference to the way the game went. ~ JOHN MOTSON

Whether that was a penalty or not, the referee thought otherwise. ~ JOHN MOTSON

The World Cup is a truly international event. ~ JOHN MOTSON

Certainly Russell Watson did very well to get through both those anthems. I suppose you could say two for a tenor really.
~ JOHN MOTSON ON THE PRE-MATCH ENTERTAINMENT BEFORE AN ENGLAND INTERNATIONAL

I think this could be our best victory over Germany since the war. ~ JOHN MOTSON

During the afternoon it rained only in this stadium – our kitman saw it. There must be a microclimate here.

~ JOSE MOURINHO BEMOANS BLACKBURN'S PITCH-WATERING TACTICS

I am in the news every day. I think they really like my overcoat, they really like my haircut, they really like my face. ~ JOSE MOURINHO

The moral of the story is not to listen to those who tell you not to play the violin but stick to the tambourine. ~ JOSE MOURINHO

As the seconds tick down, Belgium are literally playing in time that doesn't exist.

~ GUY MOWBRAY

I've just seen the replay again for the first time. ~ DAVID MOYES

Bridge has done nothing wrong, but his movement's not great and his distribution's been poor. ~ ALAN MULLERY

He has all-round, 365-degree vision. ~ ALAN MULLERY

Well, I've seen some tackles, Jonathan, but that was the ultimatum.

~ ALAN MULLERY

Roy Evans bleeds red blood. ~ ALAN MULLERY ON THE LIVERPOOL STALWART

I'd hang myself, but Hamilton Academicals cannot afford the rope. ~ IAIN MUNRO

I am in a good position at the moment because no one is running the club. I am hoping there is nobody out there to sack me.

~ WIMBLEDON MANAGER STUART MURDOCH

The local pubs aren't happy that there's 25,000 and not 48,000 in the ground. And then there's the nearby strip club and the strippers aren't too happy either. It's bad for top totty and the lap-dancing club has closed.

~ SUNDERLAND CHAIRMAN BOB MURRAY ON DECLINING ATTENDANCES
FOLLOWING THE CLUB'S RELEGATION FROM THE PREMIERSHIP

The rest of the world loves soccer. Surely we must be missing something…
Uh, isn't that what the Russians told us about communism?

~ JIM MURRAY, US SPORTSWRITER

There could be fatalities or, even worse, injuries.　　~ PHIL NEAL

The midfield picks itself: Beckham, Scholes, Gerrard and A.N. Other. ~ PHIL NEAL

We're at the top of a cliff and we can either fall off the edge or keep climbing.

~ GARY NEVILLE

He was on the six-yard line, just two yards away from the goal.　　~ PAT NEVIN

John Harkes Going To Sheffield, Wednesday.　　~ *NEW YORK POST* HEADLINE

Manchester United are breathing down the heels of Liverpool now.

~ GARY NEWBON

There's such a fine line between defeat and losing.　　~ GARY NEWBON

Borussia Moenchengladbach 5, Borussia Dortmund 1. So Moenchengladbach win the Borussia derby.　　~ GARY NEWBON

And there'll be more football in a moment. But first we've got the highlights of the Scottish League Cup Final.　　~ GARY NEWBON

Football today, it's like a game of chess. It's all about money.

~ NEWCASTLE FAN, CALLING RADIO 5 LIVE

It's imperable that they get off to a good start.　　~ CHARLIE NICHOLAS

This would bring a tear to a glass eye.

~ JIMMY NICHOLL AFTER HIS RAITH TEAM BEAT CELTIC TO LIFT THE SCOTTISH LEAGUE CUP

I'm on the transfer list and I'm going to stay on there as long as I'm on it.
~ GIFTON NOEL-WILLIAMS

A man capable of destroying the mirror because he didnae like the way the face in it was looking at him. ~ MATTHEW NORMAN, *EVENING STANDARD*, ON GRAEME SOUNESS

John Motson's career could only really be enhanced by a laryngectomy.
~ MATTHEW NORMAN

He cost his country whatever fading chance it had of a World Cup, reacting to danger with the speed and agility of Andy Fordham after 27 pints and a lamb bhuna. ~ MATTHEW NORMAN, AFTER ENGLAND'S DAVID SEAMAN WAS BEATEN BY RONALDINHO'S SEEMINGLY INNOCUOUS LOB IN THE 2002 WORLD CUP QUARTER-FINAL AGAINST BRAZIL

On transfer deadline day, it was clear that Arsenal had come out best. It was a coup more spectacular than if West Ham had signed Carlos Tevez and Javier Mascherano, then Lionel Messi to boot. The Gunners had got rid of Pascal Cygan. ~ JONATHAN NORTHCROFT

In the papers this morning they said a nation's thoughts were on Michael Owen's groin. I thought: 'Me too!' ~ GRAHAM NORTON

The Beckhams have been to Oxfam, giving away some clothes they no longer need ... like David's England shirt.

~ GRAHAM NORTON, 2006

Football Violence: Judge Hits Out ~ *NOTTINGHAM EVENING POST* HEADLINE

He's fat, he's round, he's taking Forest down, Joe Kinnear, Joe Kinnear.
~ NOTTINGHAM FOREST FANS NOT EXACTLY SINGING THE PRAISES OF THEIR MANAGER

I was a young lad when I was growing up. ~ DAVID O'LEARY

If we had taken our chances we would have won – at least. ~ DAVID O'LEARY

We feel very, very hard done by. No, make that very, very, very, very hard done by. ~ DAVID O'LEARY

Our target is to get into the play-offs. If not, we want automatic promotion. ~ DENNIS OLI

We'll still be happy if we lose. The game is on at the same time as the Beer Festival.
~ CORK CITY BOSS NOEL O'MAHONY BEFORE A EUROPEAN TIE IN MUNICH

I was both surprised and delighted to take the armband for both legs. ~ GARY O'NEIL

I tried all my career to get away crowds to give me stick and I was never good enough. I'd have loved to have 40,000 people baying for my blood, but generally they didn't even know I was playing. ~ MARTIN O'NEILL

Ian Marshall has been fantastic for us. When he's fit, he's superb. It's just that he's never fit. ~ MARTIN O'NEILL

Before the match I'd have settled for a draw, and at half-time I'd have settled for winning a corner. ~ MARTIN O'NEILL

I could have sorted out Scotland's unemployment problem if I'd signed a quarter of the players I've been linked with. ~ MARTIN O'NEILL

Anybody who is thinking of applying for the Scotland job in the next eight or nine years should go get themselves checked out by about 15 psychiatrists. ~ MARTIN O'NEILL

Graham [Poll] just said to me I should not be contesting the decisions and he was right at that stage. There is only one referee in the game and it would have been good if he'd been it. ~ MARTIN O'NEILL

I can't understand why Alf Ramsey hasn't picked Giles for England.
~ SCOTLAND BOSS WILLIE ORMOND RAVING ABOUT JOHNNY GILES, UNAWARE
THAT HE ALREADY HAD A STACK OF CAPS FOR THE REPUBLIC OF IRELAND

Watch out for the blond at corners and free kicks.
~ WILLIE ORMOND BEFORE AN INTERNATIONAL WITH SWEDEN

It is a title decider. But it's not going to decide any titles just yet. ~ MICHAEL OWEN

I was really surprised when the FA knocked on my doorbell. ~ MICHAEL OWEN

If you just came into the room and didn't know who was who, you'd obviously say Newcastle looked the most likely to score. ~ TERRY PAINE

Mind, I've been here during the bad times too. One year we came second.
~ BOB PAISLEY AT LIVERPOOL

I remember Jimmy Adamson crowing after Burnley had beaten us once that his players were in a different league. At the end of the season they were.
~ BOB PAISLEY

Everyone tries to complicate the game. Getting round the back? That's what burglars say, isn't it? ~ BOB PAISLEY

When Giggs goes at them the way he does, you don't want to be a defender. He gives them twisted blood. ~ GARY PALLISTER

There's a village somewhere that's missing a fool.
~ MILLWALL CHAIRMAN THEO PAPHITIS ON BURNLEY MANAGER STAN TERNENT

He couldn't run a kebab shop.

~ THEO PAPHITIS ON FOOTBALL LEAGUE CHIEF EXECUTIVE DAVID BURNS

Yes, we could have had a spot kick, but I don't want to say too much because, after all, the referee did give us a couple of throw-ins during the 90 minutes.

~ TONY PARKES

Premier League football is a multi-million pound industry with the aroma of a blocked toilet and the principles of a knocking shop.   ~ MICHAEL PARKINSON

And he has lit a fuse to a match that was already boiling.   ~ ALAN PARRY

Liverpool are currently halfway through an unbeaten 12-match run. ~ ALAN PARRY

Villa will probably play a lot worse than this and lose.   ~ ALAN PARRY

Within a couple of minutes he had scored two goals in a two-minute period.

~ ALAN PARRY

He will probably wake up after having sleepless nights thinking about that one.   ~ ALAN PARRY

He was the victim of his own downfall.   ~ ALAN PARRY

Ritchie has now scored 11 goals, exactly double the number he scored last season.   ~ ALAN PARRY

Lampard, as usual, arrived in the nick of time, but it wasn't quite soon enough.

~ ALAN PARRY

The Liverpool players are passing the cup down the line like a newborn baby. Although when they are back in the dressing room they will probably fill it with champagne, something you should never do to a baby.   ~ ALAN PARRY

David Beckham's wife appears to be no different from five million other girls, but she's got something that sets her apart from the other four million, nine hundred and fifty thousand and ninety-five. ~ MIKE PARRY

Aston Villa are seventh in the League – that's almost as high as you can get without being one of the top six. ~ IAN PAYNE

I wouldn't trust Newcastle's back five to protect my garden gnomes from squirrels.
~ JONATHAN PEARCE

The guy behind the goal looks as shocked as if he'd just seen his mother-in-law at seven o'clock in the morning without any make-up on. ~ JONATHAN PEARCE

When you're down, you Palace fans, the fickle finger of fate rarely smiles on you. ~ JONATHAN PEARCE

Hakan Yakin plays with Young Boys in Berne. ~ JONATHAN PEARCE

I can see the carrot at the end of the tunnel. ~ STUART PEARCE

I can't stand the thought of seeing Ron [Atkinson] beside a dugout in Barnsley. It would be like asking Frank Sinatra to play the town hall. ~ STUART PEARCE

My daughter said, 'Dad, Beanie the Horse wants to sit next to you on the touchline.' It's difficult to tell a seven-year-old that this is the Premiership and that I'm known as Psycho, I'm a hard man. So Beanie sat with me and is going with us to Everton next week.
~ STUART PEARCE ON HOW DAUGHTER CHELSEA'S FAVOURITE TOY
HELPED MANCHESTER CITY BEAT WEST HAM IN SEPTEMBER 2006

Jose Mourinho recently turned down the post of Pope when he heard it was something in the way of an assistant position. ~ HARRY PEARSON

Sadly we are back in the position we were in three years ago, but look how far we have come. ~ NIGEL PEARSON

Bobby Gould thinks I'm trying to stab him in the back. In fact, I'm right behind him. ~ STUART PEARSON

I think that France, Germany, Spain, Holland and England will join Brazil in the semi-finals. ~ PELE

It's now 4-3 to Oldham, the goals are going in like dominoes. ~ PICCADILLY RADIO

Zidane does some extraordinary things, it's true. But you have to put everything in context. What Zidane does with a ball, Maradona could do with an orange. ~ MICHEL PLATINI

How could they not know? It's not chewing gum, doping is like making love – you need two to do it, the doctor and the athlete. ~ MICHEL PLATINI ON DOPING DENIALS AT JUVENTUS

In the cold light of day you go to bed at night thinking about the chances you've missed. ~ DAVID PLATT

I can't see us getting beat now, once we get our tails in front. ~ JIM PLATT

I was looking at my watch towards the end, but not for the reason Alex Ferguson does. I was wanting to get on the bus. ~ DAVID PLEAT

We tried to redden Alex [Ferguson]'s face a bit more, but were unable to. ~ DAVID PLEAT AFTER SPURS LOSE TO MANCHESTER UNITED

The man we want has to fit a certain profile. Is he a top coach? Would the players respect him? Is he a nutcase? ~ DAVID PLEAT ASSESSING CANDIDATES FOR THE SPURS JOB

Maradona gets tremendous elevation with his balls, no matter what position he's in.
~ DAVID PLEAT

Our central defenders, Doherty and Gardner, were fantastic and I told them that when they go to bed tonight they should think of each other.
~ DAVID PLEAT

Had we not got that second goal, I think the score might have been different.
~ DAVID PLEAT

Scholes walks away a bit gingerly.
~ DAVID PLEAT

Germany benefited there from a last-gasp hand-job on the line.
~ DAVID PLEAT

We are now in the middle of the centre of the first half.
~ DAVID PLEAT

The minutes are passing faster now and the sight is in end.
~ DAVID PLEAT

And the steam has gone completely out of the Spanish sails.
~ DAVID PLEAT

There's Thierry Henry, exploding like the French train that he is.
~ DAVID PLEAT

Stoichkov is pointing at the bench with his eyes.
~ DAVID PLEAT

That is in the past, and the past has no future.
~ DAVID PLEAT

He hits it into the corner of the net as straight as a nut.
~ DAVID PLEAT

Waddle's shot onto the bar was a marvellous effort, something you can't teach anyone to do.
~ DAVID PLEAT

Michael Owen is irreplaceable, but Sven has Emile Heskey, James Beattie, Wayne Rooney and Darius Vassell, and whoever he picks can do the job.
~ DAVID PLEAT

This is a real cat and carrot situation.

~ DAVID PLEAT

Preki has literally got no right foot.

~ DAVID PLEAT

He [Charlie Nicholas] has two arms and legs, same as the rest of our players, but once he's found his feet I'm convinced he'll do well.

~ IAN PORTERFIELD

He's not like Barry Fry, that's for sure.

~ ENGLAND RECRUIT CHRIS POWELL COMPARING SVEN-GORAN ERIKSSON TO HIS OLD MANAGER AT SOUTHEND

They would be as well having Roger de Courcey and Nookie Bear for manager because Vladimir Romanov just wants a puppet he can work.

~ ALLAN PRESTON AFTER GEORGE BURLEY'S SHOCK DEPARTURE FROM HEARTS

We'll see you in the second half for the next part of the Uriah Rennie show.

~ PRESTON'S PA ANNOUNCER HAS A DIG AT THE REFEREE DURING A 2006 GAME WITH CRYSTAL PALACE

It's 50-50. It's something that, at the moment, is in the fridge.

~ REAL MADRID COACH CARLOS QUEIROZ, ASKED WHETHER PATRICK VIEIRA WOULD BE LEAVING ARSENAL

I think I'm on the side on merit – I wouldn't pick myself otherwise.

~ PLAYER-MANAGER JIMMY QUINN

He has got his tactics wrong tactically.

~ MICK QUINN

The Gillingham players have slumped to their feet.

~ MICK QUINN

The Albanians are penetrating us from all positions.

~ NIALL QUINN

He managed to make a good hash of it in the end.

~ NIALL QUINN

With eight or ten minutes to go, they were able to bring Nicky Butt back and give him 15 to 20 minutes.

~ NIALL QUINN

Keane on the ball, Butt spread wide.

~ RADIO COMMENTATOR

For those who know Selhurst Park, West Ham are playing from right to left.

~ RADIO COMMENTATOR

That's a knee in the shoulder. Let's hope it's not his kidney. ~ RADIO COMMENTATOR

Svensson was caught in two minds ... and both of them were wrong.

~ RADIO COMMENTATOR

He says that he will walk away from the game when his legs go.

~ RADIO COMMENTATOR

There is very little movement from Manchester City's midfield players. In fact, if they are planning on playing Dietmar Hamann in their next game they will have to write to the Council for planning permission. ~ RADIO COMMENTATOR

Trevor Steven, who, until recently, was a former Rangers player. ~ RADIO 5 LIVE

Their away record is instantly forgettable. The 5-1 defeat and 7-0 defeat spring to mind. ~ RADIO 5 LIVE

It's now 1-1, an exact reversal of the scoreline on Saturday. ~ RADIO 5 LIVE

Emile Zola has scored again for Chelsea. ~ RADIO 5 LIVE

Phil Neville – today he's at full-back, in the last game he took over the Butt holding role. ~ RADIO 5 LIVE

It's headed away by John Clark, using his head. ~ DEREK RAE

I am happy when our fans are happy, when our players are happy and our chairman is on the moon. ~ CLAUDIO RANIERI

It is my baby. Maybe soon it will be ready to get out of the pram. I will lead it by the hand. ~ CLAUDIO RANIERI ON CHELSEA

If you need just a first 11 and four others, why did Columbus sail to India to discover America? ~ CLAUDIO RANIERI

People have said I am a dead man walking but I am not – I am still moving.
~ CLAUDIO RANIERI

We learned a lot from United today, including how to count.
~ SHREWSBURY BOSS KEVIN RATCLIFFE, AFTER AN 8-1 PRE-SEASON DRUBBING BY MANCHESTER UNITED

Every green seat has a bottom on it, and they've made some noise in here tonight. ~ JOHN RAWLING

[John] Hartson's got more previous than Jack the Ripper. ~ HARRY REDKNAPP

A couple of wins and we could be in mid-table. Mind you, a couple of defeats and we'll be off the bottom of the page. ~ HARRY REDKNAPP

Every single morning, he [Ian Wright] is here an hour before everyone else. It's probably something to do with his wife kicking him out of the house.
~ HARRY REDKNAPP

By the look of him, he [Iain Dowie] must have headed a lot of balls.
~ HARRY REDKNAPP

At £1.5 million he is great value. What does that get you these days? For £1.5 million you're lucky if they can trap a ball. If they can tie their boots, they're worth £2 million. ~ HARRY REDKNAPP ON SIGNING PAOLO DI CANIO

I've just seen a video recording of the game, and I'm going to tape *Neighbours* over it. ~ HARRY REDKNAPP

We get carried away with coaches and coaching. I have my coaching badges, but they came out of a cornflakes packet.

~ HARRY REDKNAPP

I lay in bed the other night thinking about strikers. It's a few years ago now but I can remember there were always much better things to do in bed.

~ HARRY REDKNAPP

I'm very superstitious. I wore the same gear every Saturday when we went on that long unbeaten run at Portsmouth. It was the same shirt, tie, pants and jacket every week. The outfit used to walk itself to the ground in the end.

~ HARRY REDKNAPP

As for wages, the players have had a trim, the chairman has had a trim, and I have had a short back and sides.

~ HARRY REDKNAPP AT SOUTHAMPTON

When he picked the ball up, I'd be a liar if I said I thought he would score. I thought he was going to head it!

~ HARRY REDKNAPP AFTER PETER CROUCH'S INJURY-TIME
PENALTY WINNER FOR SOUTHAMPTON AGAINST PORTSMOUTH IN 2005

Even when they had Moore, Hurst and Peters, West Ham's average finish was about 17th. It just shows how crap the other eight of us were!

~ HARRY REDKNAPP

To be in the top four alongside teams like Chelsea, Manchester United, Liverpool and Arsenal is incredible.

~ HARRY REDKNAPP AT PORTSMOUTH, 2006

I got some girl's knickers through the post the other day but I didn't like them. To be honest, they didn't fit.

~ JAMIE REDKNAPP ON HIS FAN MAIL

I know the manager told me to play a bit deeper, but that was ridiculous.

~ KARL REED OF HERTS COUNTY LEAGUE SIDE CROXLEY GUILD OF SPORT,
AFTER FALLING DOWN A 4FT CRATER DURING A GAME AGAINST MET POLICE

When I walk around, people salute me and now I must be the only person allowed to drive in the bus lanes.

~ GREECE COACH OTTO REHHAGEL AFTER WINNING EURO 2004

At the highest level you have to score goals to win matches.   ~ PETER REID

When Eddie Gray plays on snow, he doesn't leave any footprints.   ~ DON REVIE

Maldini has really regurgitated his career at left-back.   ~ DAMIEN RICHARDSON

The match will be shown on *Match of the Day* this evening. If you don't want to know the result, look away now as we show you Tony Adams lifting the trophy for Arsenal.   ~ STEVE RIDER

We threw our dice into the ring and turned up trumps.   ~ BRUCE RIOCH

The real trouble with our national team is that in Italy we have 50 million advisers.   ~ GIANNI RIVERA

Football is a game of skill. We kicked them a bit and they kicked us a bit.

~ GRAHAM ROBERTS

Kevin Keegan is not fit to lace George Best's drinks.   ~ JOHN ROBERTS

I thought, 'That's a sweet connection, I never even felt it touch my foot.' And then I've looked round and it's in the back of the net.

~ ENGLAND GOALKEEPER PAUL ROBINSON ON HIS CALAMITOUS AIR SHOT AGAINST CROATIA IN 2006

We used to say about George Cohen: 'He's hit more photographers than Frank Sinatra.' George was quick and broke up the flanks exceptionally well, but his final ball was rarely on target. Usually he would hit his cross into the crowd or into the photographers.   ~ BOBBY ROBSON

John Cobbold's idea of a boardroom crisis was when they ran short of white wine after a game. ~ BOBBY ROBSON ON HIS OLD IPSWICH CHAIRMAN

Gascoigne in 1990 was a fantastic player. He was never going to split the atom but he had a football brain.

~ BOBBY ROBSON

Daft as a brush. ~ BOBBY ROBSON ON PAUL GASCOIGNE

In the first half he [Laurent Robert] took a corner, a poor corner which hit the first defender, and it took him 17 minutes to get back to the half-way line.
~ BOBBY ROBSON

[Laurent] Robert said I was picking the wrong team. At the time I was – because he was in it! ~ BOBBY ROBSON

Craig Bellamy is the only player I know who could start an argument with himself. ~ BOBBY ROBSON

What can I say about Peter Shilton? Peter Shilton is Peter Shilton, and he has been Peter Shilton since the year dot. ~ BOBBY ROBSON

We didn't underestimate them. They were just a lot better than we thought.
~ BOBBY ROBSON

I'd say he's the best in Europe, if you put me on the fence. ~ BOBBY ROBSON

If we start counting our chickens before they hatch, they won't lay any eggs in the basket. ~ BOBBY ROBSON

Jermaine Jenas is a fit lad. He gets from box to box in all of 90 minutes.
~ BOBBY ROBSON

I'm not going to look beyond the semi-final, but I would love to lead Newcastle out at the final. ~ BOBBY ROBSON

We're in a dog-fight, so the fight in the dog will get us through – and we'll fight. ~ BOBBY ROBSON

The first 90 minutes are the most important. ~ BOBBY ROBSON

There will be a game where somebody scores more than Brazil and that might be the game that they lose. ~ BOBBY ROBSON

Don't ask me what a typical Brazilian is because I don't know what a typical Brazilian is. But Romario was a typical Brazilian. ~ BOBBY ROBSON

He never fails to hit the target, but that was a miss. ~ BOBBY ROBSON

He's very fast and if he gets a yard ahead of himself, nobody will catch him. ~ BOBBY ROBSON

I thought that individually and as a pair, they'd do better together. ~ BOBBY ROBSON

We haven't had the rub of the dice. ~ BOBBY ROBSON

The margin is very marginal. ~ BOBBY ROBSON

Now that we've got Southgate… ~ BOBBY ROBSON, SIGNING JONATHAN WOODGATE

Gary Speed has been absolutely massive for me. His influence on the team cannot be underestimated. ~ BOBBY ROBSON

Gary Speed has never played better, never looked fitter, never been older. ~ BOBBY ROBSON

For a player to ask for a transfer has opened everybody's eyebrows.

~ BOBBY ROBSON

We had ten times as many shots on target as Bolton – and they had none at all.

~ BOBBY ROBSON

Tottenham have impressed me: they haven't thrown in the towel even though they have been under the gun.

~ BOBBY ROBSON

All right, Bellamy came on at Liverpool and did well, but everybody thinks that he's the saviour, he's Jesus Christ. He's not Jesus Christ.

~ BOBBY ROBSON

We don't want our players to be monks, we want them to be better football players because a monk doesn't play football at this level.

~ BOBBY ROBSON

We're flying on Concorde. That'll shorten the distance. That's self-explanatory.

~ BOBBY ROBSON

I would have given my right arm to be a pianist.

~ BOBBY ROBSON

Maybe not goodbye, but farewell.

~ BOBBY ROBSON

If we played like that every week, we wouldn't be so inconsistent. ~ BRYAN ROBSON

Whether Gordon Strachan is taking a sabbatical or will come back, we'll have to see.

~ BRYAN ROBSON

It wasn't going to be our day on the night.

~ BRYAN ROBSON

I'm sure sex wouldn't be as rewarding as winning the World Cup. It's not that sex isn't good, but the World Cup is every four years and sex is not. ~ RONALDO

When I score goals I am great, when I don't I am fat.

~ RONALDO ON HIS TREATMENT BY THE SPANISH MEDIA

This game is worth £12 million. And that save was priceless. ~ JIM ROSENTHAL

Peter Ward has become a new man. Just like his old self. ~ JIM ROSENTHAL

Congratulations to Wayne Rooney. He scored three times on Tuesday. He hasn't done that since he crashed a pensioners' bingo night. ~ JONATHAN ROSS

Wayne [Rooney] hasn't touched a granny for months. Apart from the blind one who dresses Colleen in the morning. ~ JONATHAN ROSS

Everyone's got an opinion on David Beckham's tackle. Didn't he think about the consequences before he slid in or is that beautician lying? ~ JONATHAN ROSS

Our guys are getting murdered twice a week. ~ ANDY ROXBURGH

The keeper was coming out in instalments. ~ JOE ROYLE

A good Cup run for us is a third-round replay. ~ JOE ROYLE AT OLDHAM

For most home games there are more scouts here than at a jamboree. ~ JOE ROYLE

It was like trying to tackle dust. ~ JOE ROYLE ON THE ELUSIVE OSSIE ARDILES

The lad was sent off for foul and abusive language but he swears blind he didn't say a word. ~ JOE ROYLE

To score four goals when you are playing like pigs in labour is fantastic.
~ JOE ROYLE AT MANCHESTER CITY

I might have been the captain when we went down, but not when we hit the iceberg. ~ MANCHESTER CITY BOSS JOE ROYLE DODGING THE BLAME FOR THE CLUB'S RELEGATION

We did not pass the ball – we could not have found our front two with radar.
~ JOE ROYLE

That was clearly a tackle aimed at getting revenge – or maybe it was just out-and-out retribution.

~ JOE ROYLE

The Italians can blame no one but themselves. They can blame the referee, but they can blame no one but themselves.

~ JOE ROYLE

I will be writing to the relevant authorities to complain, but I'm wasting my breath.

~ JOE ROYLE

Wolves beat Palace convincingly without being convincing.

~ JOE ROYLE

I don't blame individuals, I blame myself.

~ JOE ROYLE

He doesn't drink or smoke or chase women – he'll never make it in football.

~ CLYDE DIRECTOR JOHN RUDDY ON STRIKER TOM BRIGHTON

We have run a marathon and fallen just short. So we need to boost the squad to get us over that final hurdle.

~ JOHN RUDGE

I couldn't settle in Italy – it was like living in a foreign country.

~ IAN RUSH

Djimi Traore had to adapt to the English game and he did that by going out on loan to Lens last season.

~ IAN RUSH

Well, Terry, can you tell us where you are in the League, how far you are ahead of the second team?

~ IAN ST JOHN

You don't have to have been a horse to be a jockey.

~ ARRIGO SACCHI, THE FORMER MANAGER OF ITALY, WHO NEVER PLAYED PROFESSIONAL FOOTBALL HIMSELF

It's winner takes all, but a draw will do.

~ MARK SAGGERS

It's been a pretty dire year all things considered. I'd compare it to a rollercoaster ride, without the up bits. ~ JOHN SALAKO

Rooney's so strong he can do anything. He would be the ideal person to help you move house. ~ MICHEL SALGADO

It seems that they're playing with one leg tied together. ~ KENNY SANSOM

My team won't freeze in the white-hot atmosphere of Anfield. ~ RON SAUNDERS

John Toshack said it was my way or the highway – well I'm on the M56.
~ ROBBIE SAVAGE ON HIS DECISION TO QUIT INTERNATIONAL FOOTBALL WITH WALES

I got hit in the nose again – and with the size of my nose I'm surprised they didn't have to evacuate the Riverside!
~ ROBBIE SAVAGE GETS A NOSEBLEED AT MIDDLESBROUGH

It wasn't my choice to become a goalkeeper, but I was probably too violent to play outfield. ~ PETER SCHMEICHEL

Gary Neville says that Porto are a bunch of girls who go down too easily.
~ PETER SCHMEICHEL

Being a manager's a great job, apart from Saturday afternoons. ~ JOCKY SCOTT

Joe Jordan Strikes Quicker Than British Leyland
~ SCOTTISH FANS' BANNER AT WEMBLEY, 1970s

Faroes 1 Fairies 1
~ SCOTTISH NEWSPAPER HEADLINE AFTER SCOTLAND DRAW THEIR EURO 2000 QUALIFIER

The lads used to call me 'The Judge' because I sat on the bench so much.
~ LES SEALEY AT MANCHESTER UNITED

Our goalkeeper, Reg Davies, was never really tested – except of course for the five goals which passed him.

~ JIMMY SEED, MILLWALL MANAGER, AFTER A 5-2 FA CUP DEFEAT AT WORCESTER CITY, 1958

George Best without brains.

~ STAN SEYMOUR ON PAUL GASCOIGNE

Football's not a matter of life and death – it's more important than that.

~ BILL SHANKLY

[Pat] Crerand's deceptive – he's slower than you think.

~ BILL SHANKLY

With Ron Yeats at centre-half, we could play Arthur Askey in goal! ~ BILL SHANKLY

Tom Finney was so good, I would have had four men marking him when we were kicking in.

~ BILL SHANKLY

I'd have played Tom Finney in his overcoat!

~ BILL SHANKLY

George Best probably is a better player than Tom Finney. But you have to remember, Tom is 60 now...

~ BILL SHANKLY, 1970s

Brian Clough's worse than the rain in Manchester. At least God stops that occasionally.

~ BILL SHANKLY

There are two great teams in Liverpool – Liverpool and Liverpool Reserves.

~ BILL SHANKLY

If Everton were playing down at the bottom of my garden, I'd draw the curtains.

~ BILL SHANKLY

Anything off the top? Aye, Everton.

~ BILL SHANKLY TO HIS BARBER

I'm not giving away any secrets like that to Milan. If I had my way, I wouldn't even tell them the time of the kick-off. ~ BILL SHANKLY

Matt Busby has got a bad back. I tell you it's two bad backs! And not much of a midfield either. ~ BILL SHANKLY

Of course I didn't take my wife to see Rochdale as an anniversary present. It was her birthday. Would I have got married during the football season? And anyway it wasn't Rochdale, it was Rochdale Reserves. ~ BILL SHANKLY

What time will Bill be back? When he wins, of course.
~ NESSIE SHANKLY, ANSWERING THE PHONE TO A JOURNALIST WHILE HUSBAND
BILL IS OUT HAVING A KICKABOUT IN THE PARK WITH LOCAL YOUNGSTERS

You never know what could happen in a couple of one-off games like these.
~ GRAEME SHARP

I've never wanted to leave. I'm here for the rest of my life, and hopefully after that as well. ~ ALAN SHEARER

One accusation you can't throw at me is that I've always done my best.
~ ALAN SHEARER

Andy Johnson has been playing up front on his own with James Beattie all season. ~ ALAN SHEARER

Lampard picks his head up and knocks it out to the wing. ~ ALAN SHEARER

We [England] haven't been scoring goals, but football's not just about scoring goals. It's about winning. ~ ALAN SHEARER

Yes, I'm available this summer – to play golf and sit in the sun.
~ ALAN SHEARER, RULING OUT AN INTERNATIONAL COMEBACK FOR EURO 2004

He has said he will quit but, listen, I said I loved my wife when I left her this morning. Things change.   ~ NEWCASTLE CHAIRMAN FREDDY SHEPHERD ON ALAN SHEARER

You should only say good things when somebody leaves. [Laurent] Robert has gone ... good!   ~ FREDDY SHEPHERD

I didn't want to be known as the man who shot Bambi.
~ FREDDY SHEPHERD ON SACKING BOBBY ROBSON

When I joined, he came walking down the corridor and said, 'Ah, you must be Edward Sheringham.' I told him I was, but that I preferred to be called Teddy. He said, 'OK, welcome to the club, Edward.'
~ TEDDY SHERINGHAM ON SIGNING FOR BRIAN CLOUGH AT NOTTINGHAM FOREST

The sight of opposing fans walking together down Wembley Way – you won't get that anywhere other than Wembley.   ~ JOHN SILLETT

There are 0-0 draws and 0-0 draws, and this was a 0-0 draw.   ~ JOHN SILLETT

We are the Cinderellas of the World Cup. Our mission is to postpone midnight for as long as possible.   ~ RENE SIMOES, JAMAICA'S COACH

Chris Waddle is off the pitch at the moment – exactly the position he is at his most menacing.   ~ GERALD SINSTADT

From that moment the pendulum went into reverse.   ~ GERALD SINSTADT

We're like Lady Di. She's not the queen yet. She's not even married. But like us, she's nicely placed.
~ MANAGER JIMMY SIRREL ON NOTTS COUNTY'S PROMOTION PROSPECTS, 1981

The best team always wins. The rest is only gossip.   ~ JIMMY SIRREL

Did you hear about the guy who was prevented from taking his father's ashes to a game in Spain? It comes to something when you can't take a bottle of pop to a match. ~ FRANK SKINNER

I was watching Germany and I got up to make a cup of tea. I bumped into the telly and Klinsmann fell over.

~ FRANK SKINNER

So Arsenal have signed Arsene Wenger because his name sounds a bit like the club. How long before Man United sign Stefan Kuntz? ~ FRANK SKINNER

It would be great if Wimbledon got into Europe. Usually a small squad of players travels abroad, followed by several thousand wild-eyed, drunken fans. If Wimbledon got there, it'd be the other way round. ~ FRANK SKINNER

You look at Sven and you think he's a pharmacist. He should be saying, 'Here's your pile ointment.' ~ FRANK SKINNER

Danny Dichio was so slow that when he raced onto a through ball the 45-year-old linesman used to lap him. ~ FRANK SKINNER

The Premiership feels like a big party that's going on up the road but we [West Brom] are not invited. ~ FRANK SKINNER

It's a hard place to come for a southern team. You can dress well and have all the nice watches in the world but that won't buy you a result at Grimsby.

~ CRYSTAL PALACE MANAGER ALAN SMITH

When I looked down, the leg was lying one way and my ankle was pointing towards Hong Kong, so I knew I was in serious trouble.

~ MANCHESTER UNITED FORWARD ALAN SMITH

Gary Lineker is the Queen Mother of football. ~ ARTHUR SMITH

Apparently he finds the yellow and red a little too gaudy – which is pretty rich coming from someone who used to arrive on stage wearing a pink mohair jockstrap and a pair of angel's wings.

~ GILES SMITH ON ELTON JOHN'S DISTASTE FOR THE NEW WATFORD STRIP

We've got complete harmonium in the dressing room.   ~ JOE SMITH

I soon got out of the habit of studying the top end of the League table.

~ WALTER SMITH, COMPARING LIFE AT EVERTON WITH HIS PREVIOUS CLUB, RANGERS

We created four or five chances and took probably all of them.

~ OLE GUNNAR SOLSKJAER AS MANCHESTER UNITED SCORE SIX

Without picking out anyone in particular, I thought Mark Wright was tremendous.   ~ GRAEME SOUNESS

Today's top players only want to play in London or for Manchester United. That's what happened when I tried to sign Alan Shearer and he went to Blackburn.   ~ GRAEME SOUNESS

If I'm a player, I don't want to talk to anyone called Rupert, I want to speak to the manager. How many football people are called Rupert?

~ GRAEME SOUNESS, LEAVING SOUTHAMPTON AND THEIR CHAIRMAN RUPERT LOWE

It was only a matter of time before they got fit and after that it's like riding a bike – or making love to a beautiful woman – you never forget.

~ GRAEME SOUNESS ON THE FORM OF HIS BLACKBURN STRIKERS ANDY COLE AND DWIGHT YORKE

Eyal [Berkovic] is a professional and clearly wants to earn as much money as possible. But he is Jewish and I am Scottish, so it will be difficult for us to reach a financial agreement.   ~ GRAEME SOUNESS, CONTEMPLATING SIGNING THE ISRAELI MIDFIELDER

Dominate my ex-wife? A Bengal tiger could not do that!
~ GRAEME SOUNESS

If you don't believe you can win, there is no point in getting out of bed at the end of the day.

~ NEVILLE SOUTHALL

I'm not convinced that Scotland will play a typically English game.

~ GARETH SOUTHGATE

'Wait until you come to Turkey' was the shout, with fingers being passed across throats. And that was just the kit man!

~ GARETH SOUTHGATE ON THREATS MADE TO THE ENGLAND PLAYERS

He looks just like his mum has told him to come in for tea.

~ GARETH SOUTHGATE ON WAYNE ROONEY'S SULK AFTER BEING SUBSTITUTED AT THE 2006 WORLD CUP

I don't know when the manager will have told them the teams. But it will have been at quarter to two.

~ NIGEL SPACKMAN

Great striking partnerships come in pairs.

~ NIGEL SPACKMAN

What's the difference between Paul Merson and a can of Coca-Cola? One's red and white and full of coke, the other's a soft drinks container.

~ SPURS FANS' JOKE

Piss in a bottle, you couldn't piss in a bottle.

~ SPURS FANS TAUNT MANCHESTER UNITED'S RIO FERDINAND
FOLLOWING HIS LENGTHY BAN FOR MISSING A DRUG TEST

He's got a knock on his shin there; just above the knee.

~ FRANK STAPLETON

I thought their keeper Van der Sar was like a 13th man.

~ STEVE STAUNTON

Footballers have a very short career … a few seasons in the spotlight is followed by retirement, death, and then a stint on *Sky Soccer Saturday*.

~ JEFF STELLING

That's Steve Howey's third-ever League goal, and he's never scored more than two in a season before.

~ JEFF STELLING

Chris Porter scored his first League goal last week, and he's done the same this week.

~ JEFF STELLING

Brentford scored a last-minute winner four minutes from time.

~ JEFF STELLING

And they'll be dancing in the streets of Total Network Solutions tonight.

~ JEFF STELLING AS TNS LIFT THE WELSH TITLE

He [Brian Laudrup] wasn't just facing one defender – he was facing one at the front and one at the back as well.

~ TREVOR STEVEN

I've seen Shane Warne playing football before a Test match, and believe me, his second touch was always a throw-in.

~ ALEC STEWART

We can only come out of this game with egg on our faces, so it's a real banana skin.

~ STIRLING ALBION MANAGER RAY STEWART PREPARING
TO FACE NON-LEAGUE OPPONENTS IN THE SCOTTISH CUP

—Alf Ramsey: I want you to put Eusebio out of the game.
—Nobby Stiles: For tonight or for ever?

Peter Schmeichel says that the present Man United team would beat the 1968 European Cup winners. He's got a point, because we're over 50 now.

~ NOBBY STILES

Come in a taxi, you must have come in a taxi.

~ STOCKPORT FANS' CHANT TO THE SMALL TORQUAY
CONTINGENT THAT TRAVELLED TO EDGELEY PARK

Round here we threaten young Stoke fans that Alan Ball will come back and manage the club if they don't go to bed early and eat all their vegetables.

~ STOKE CITY FANZINE

It's an incredible rise to stardom. At 17 you're more likely to get a call from Michael Jackson than Sven-Goran Eriksson.   ~ GORDON STRACHAN ON WAYNE ROONEY

Dennis Wise is never involved in anything but he's always there. He's like the old lady who has been driving for 50 years and never been in an accident – but seen dozens.   ~ GORDON STRACHAN

You want a quick word? Velocity.

~ GORDON STRACHAN TO A REPORTER

What is my impression of Jermaine Pennant? I don't do impressions.

~ GORDON STRACHAN

[Neil] Lennon has a hamstring strain. Paul Telfer is injured too – why are there no rumours about Paul Telfer? The poor guy gets ignored all the time. He just wants one rumour.   ~ GORDON STRACHAN

The world looks a totally different place after two wins. I can even enjoy watching *Blind Date* or laugh at *Noel's House Party*.   ~ GORDON STRACHAN

I'm going home to get myself a Coca-Cola and a packet of crisps, sit in front of the TV and look at the League table on Teletext all night.

~ GORDON STRACHAN AS SOUTHAMPTON CLIMB TO FOURTH IN THE PREMIERSHIP

I've got more important things to think about. I've got a yoghurt to finish by today, the expiry date is today. That can be my priority rather than Agustin Delgado.   ~ GORDON STRACHAN

When he [Claus Lundekvam] was carried off at Leicester someone asked me if he was unconscious, but I didn't have a clue – that's what he's always like.

~ GORDON STRACHAN

I tried to get the disappointment out of my system by going for a walk. I ended up 17 miles from home and I had to phone my wife to come and pick me up.

~ GORDON STRACHAN

I've had better weeks. I tried to make it better by playing my dad at golf on Sunday. We played 13 holes and I got beat by a 60-year-old man with a bad limp.

~ GORDON STRACHAN

Alex McLeish and I even competed for the acne cream when we were younger. Obviously, I won that one.

~ GORDON STRACHAN

It's a tremendous honour. I'm going to have a banana to celebrate.

~ GORDON STRACHAN ON BEING NAMED FOOTBALLER OF THE YEAR FOR 1991

I still eat bananas. And seaweed. I may not be a better player, but I'm a better swimmer.

~ GORDON STRACHAN

Any changes? Naw, still five foot six, ginger hair, and a big nose.

~ GORDON STRACHAN

Reporter: So, Gordon, in what areas do you think Middlesbrough were better than you today?
—Gordon Strachan: Mainly that big green one out there.

—Reporter: Gordon, you must be delighted with that result?
—Gordon Strachan: You're spot on! You can read me like a book!

—Gary Lineker: So, Gordon, if you were English, what formation would you play?
—Gordon Strachan: If I was English, I'd top myself!

What's the definition of an atheist? Someone who goes to a Rangers-Celtic match to watch the football.

~ SANDY STRONG

And France and Romania drew 1-0. ~ MOIRA STUART

If you were in the Brondby dressing room right now, which of the Liverpool players would you be looking at? ~ RAY STUBBS

Where did you get the nickname Dickie Dosh from?
~ RAY STUBBS, ASKING THE OBVIOUS TO WALSALL MANAGER RICHARD MONEY

Although we are playing Russian roulette we are obviously playing Catch-22 at the moment and it's a difficult scenario to get my head round. ~ PAUL STURROCK

I've got too many Cavaliers in my side, and not enough Roundheads. Too many players with plumes and feathers but not enough hard workers. And the Roundheads won in the end. ~ PAUL STURROCK, SHEFFIELD WEDNESDAY MANAGER

Darren Anderton has had so many X-rays that he got radiation sickness.
~ ALAN SUGAR

I've got a gut feeling in my stomach...
~ ALAN SUGAR

I'm flabbergasted at what Simon [Jordan] has said, although I'm very impressed by his vocabulary. I've got an economics degree and I didn't understand two of the words he used. ~ DAVID SULLIVAN

I might have kicked a few full-backs in my time but I always sent them flowers afterwards. ~ MIKE SUMMERBEE

Fred [Davies] sent me to see if I could spot a weakness, and I found one. The half-time tea's too milky.
~ SHREWSBURY'S KEVIN SUMMERFIELD, ON A SPYING MISSION TO CUP OPPONENTS LIVERPOOL

Super Caley Go Ballistic – Celtic Are Atrocious
~ SUN HEADLINE AFTER INVERNESS CALEDONIAN THISTLE SHOCK CELTIC

Malice In Sunderland
~ *SUNDAY TRIBUNE* HEADLINE AFTER ROY KEANE IS SENT OFF AT SUNDERLAND

I obviously got my Angels wrong!
~ CRYSTAL PALACE'S KIT SYMONS AFTER DIVERTING A
SHOT FROM VILLA'S JUAN PABLO ANGEL INTO HIS OWN NET

If Stan Bowles could pass a betting shop like he can pass a ball, he'd have no worries at all.
~ ERNIE TAGG

Craig Mackail-Smith has the pace of a gazelle and during his fleeting time in the St Albans City first team often displayed the finishing of one.
~ DAVID TAVENER

People will look at Bowyer and Woodgate and say, 'Well, there's no mud without flames.'
~ GORDON TAYLOR

Thierry Henry has been absolutely magical and I love the way he plays the game and expresses himself. He is like Merlin the Magician and Dr Who rolled into one.
~ GORDON TAYLOR

Shearer could be at 100 per cent fitness, but not peak fitness.
~ GRAHAM TAYLOR

If it stays as it is, I can't see it altering.
~ GRAHAM TAYLOR

Footballers are no different from human beings.
~ GRAHAM TAYLOR

Very few of us have any idea whatsoever of what life is like living in a goldfish bowl – except, of course, for those of us who are goldfish.
~ GRAHAM TAYLOR

—Commentator (seeing Stuart Pearce's lucky mascot, Beanie the horse):
Did you ever have a lucky charm, Graham?
—Graham Taylor: Yes, my wife. But I never laid her on the touchline.

The manager could not even talk to us at the interval – he said we were bad.
~ JOHN TERRY

As I've grabbed Willie, the manager's there, the staff and all the players!
~ JOHN TERRY CELEBRATING A WILLIAM GALLAS GOAL

They've nicknamed me Ena Sharples because my head was never out of the net.
~ RAITH KEEPER IAN THAIN AFTER LETTING IN TEN GOALS AGAINST RANGERS

Some of our players can hardly write their own names, but you should see them add up.
~ KARL-HEINZ THIELEN

I don't mind Roy Keane making £60,000 a week. I was making the same when I was playing. The only difference was that I was printing my own.
~ MICKEY THOMAS, FORMER MANCHESTER UNITED MIDFIELDER AND CONVICTED COUNTERFEITER

We have had dozens of applications for the manager's job, ranging from the top end of the scale to an unknown 25-year-old whose only selling point is that he owns a tracksuit.
~ DUNDEE UNITED CHAIRMAN EDDIE THOMPSON

Reading just had a great five-man move that involved everyone. ~ PHIL THOMPSON

We were caviar in the first half, cabbage in the second.
~ PHIL THOMPSON

If that referee was on fire, I'd dial 998.
~ STEVE THOMPSON

If it had been the winner, I would have celebrated slightly more emphatically but I didn't think there is any point doing a Klinsmann if you have just equalised against Inverness Caley at home.
~ RANGERS' STEVEN THOMPSON

Loony Toons
~ *TIMES* HEADLINE AFTER NEWCASTLE PAIR KIERON DYER AND LEE BOWYER ARE SENT OFF FOR FIGHTING EACH OTHER

As we say in football, it'll go down to the last wire.
~ COLIN TODD

I had a reputation for being good in the air as a player but I couldn't do anything about this.
~ WALES MANAGER JOHN TOSHACK AFTER THE TEAM PLANE SUFFERED A CRACKED WINDSCREEN AT 20,000FT

He [Duncan McKenzie] is like a beautiful motor car. Six owners and been in the garage most of the time. ~ JOHN TOSHACK

Winning all the time is not necessarily good for the team. ~ JOHN TOSHACK

We can beat anyone on our day – so long as we score. ~ ALEX TOTTEN

Aston Villa began to harness the fruits of some good midfield work.

~ ALAN TOWERS

Jamie Carragher looks like he's got cramp in both groins. ~ ANDY TOWNSEND

They've tasted the other side of the coin on so many occasions. ~ ANDY TOWNSEND

There would have to be a bubonic plague for me to pick Paolo Di Canio.

~ GIOVANNI TRAPPATONI, ITALY'S COACH

We can't behave like crocodiles and cry over spilled milk and broken eggs. ~ GIOVANNI TRAPPATONI

Seen one wall, you've seen them all.

~ JOHN TREWICK, WEST BROM DEFENDER, ON A 1978 VISIT TO THE GREAT WALL OF CHINA

I've told the players we need to win so that I can have the cash to buy some new ones. ~ CHRIS TURNER, PETERBOROUGH MANAGER, BEFORE A
LEAGUE CUP QUARTER-FINAL AGAINST MIDDLESBROUGH

Football management is the only job where you can study the vacancies on Teletext as they happen. ~ GRAHAM TURNER

He's not George Best, but then again, no one is. ~ CLIVE TYLDESLEY

He is the man who has been brought on to replace Pavel Nedved. The irreplaceable Pavel Nedved. ~ CLIVE TYLDESLEY

David O'Leary's poker face betrays the emotions. ~ CLIVE TYLDESLEY

Liverpool always seem to find a boot at the right moment to keep Birmingham City at arm's length. ~ CLIVE TYLDESLEY

Gary Neville is in hospital, where Manchester United fear he may have broken his foot. ~ CLIVE TYLDESLEY

So it's Paris in the spring. The most romantic time and place in the world. And who am I here with? Ron Atkinson. ~ CLIVE TYLDESLEY

What do you say to a team that's 5-0 up at half-time … though I don't suppose you'd know? ~ COMMENTATOR CLIVE TYLDESLEY TO RON ATKINSON, HIS MATCH SUMMARISER, DURING ENGLAND'S 1999 INTERNATIONAL WITH LUXEMBOURG

He had an eternity to play that ball, but he took too long over it. ~ MARTIN TYLER

The ageless Dennis Wise, now in his thirties. ~ MARTIN TYLER

Ian Baird is dashing around like a steamroller up front. ~ MARTIN TYLER

McCarthy shakes his head in agreement with the referee. ~ MARTIN TYLER

We are about as far away from the penalty box as the penalty box is from us. ~ TOM TYRRELL

Van Nistelrooy has become a scoring phenomena. ~ TOM TYRRELL

Ferdinand, with a big long left knee, cuts that out.　　　~ TOM TYRRELL

The ball stuck to his foot like a magnet attracting a piece of steel, or metal rather.　　　~ TOM TYRRELL

Wayne Rooney can go all the way to the top if he keeps his head firmly on the ground.　　　~ DAVID UNSWORTH

It was like an episode of *M*A*S*H* in the dressing room.
　　　~ MARCO VAN BASTEN AFTER A PHYSICAL CONTEST

I can still go out as long as it's after midnight, I'm wearing dark glasses and it's a dimly lit restaurant.　　　~ TERRY VENABLES DURING A POOR RUN AT BARCELONA

Certain people are for me and certain people are pro me.　　　~ TERRY VENABLES

If you can't stand the heat in the dressing room, get out of the kitchen.
　　　~ TERRY VENABLES

Those are the sort of doors that get opened if you don't close them.
　　　~ TERRY VENABLES

If history repeats itself, I should think we can expect the same thing again.　　　~ TERRY VENABLES

There are two ways of getting the ball. One is from your own team-mates, and that's the only way.　　　~ TERRY VENABLES

That's understandable and I understand that.　　　~ TERRY VENABLES

It may have been going wide, but nevertheless it was a great shot on target.
　　　~ TERRY VENABLES

When you make a mistake, that becomes a mistake. ~ TERRY VENABLES

I felt a lump in my mouth as the ball went in.
~ TERRY VENABLES

It's like watching your mother-in-law drive over a cliff in your new car.
~ SPURS MANAGER TERRY VENABLES SEEING PAUL GASCOIGNE SOLD TO LAZIO

You would think that if anybody could put up a decent wall it would be China.
~ TERRY VENABLES, AFTER CHINA'S DEFENSIVE WALL IS BREACHED
BY A BRAZIL FREE KICK AT THE 2002 WORLD CUP

—Jimmy Hill: Don't sit on the fence, Terry. What chance do you think Germany has of getting through?
—Terry Venables: I think it's 50-50.

The Newcastle back three, back four, back five, have been at sixes and sevens.
~ BARRY VENISON

Like so many of the current Chelsea team, Zola is unique. ~ BARRY VENISON

Tempo, now there's a big word. ~ BARRY VENISON

I always used to put my right boot on first, and then obviously my right sock.
~ BARRY VENISON

You must be as strong in March, when the fish are down. ~ GIANLUCA VIALLI

I loved the physical battles in England. In Italy there are too many free kicks for small offences. I even miss Roy Keane! ~ PATRICK VIEIRA

Make love before matches? My lads can do as they like, but it's not advisable at half-time. ~ BERTI VOGTS

If I walked on water, my accusers would say it is because I can't swim.

~ FORMER SCOTLAND BOSS BERTI VOGTS

Being German, I love David Hasselhoff. It's actually the law back in the Motherland. For me the Hoff is almost like some kind of higher spirit. Hoff-ness is everywhere. The Hoff is a big inspiration – in times of trouble I often ask myself, 'How would the Hoff deal with this situation?'

~ MORITZ VOLZ, FULHAM FULL-BACK

I haven't spoken to Dick Advocaat but I know him very well – we have had the same hair transplant.

~ THEO VONK

Burnley have the potential to be a sleeping giant.

~ CHRIS WADDLE, TAKING OVER AS PLAYER-MANAGER

There's going to be four or five teams battling for the top six spots.

~ CHRIS WADDLE

The 2,000 away fans will be unhappy; in fact, half of them have gone, there's only 500 left.

~ CHRIS WADDLE

Wimbledon have changed their style. They are now kicking the ball 50 yards instead of 60.

~ MIKE WALKER

I just wonder what would have happened if the shirt had been on the other foot.

~ MIKE WALKER

Posh Spice is pregnant. At least that's one time David Beckham has stayed on long enough.

~ BRADLEY WALSH, AFTER BECKHAM'S INFAMOUS SENDING-OFF AT THE 1998 WORLD CUP FINALS

I think it's OK to get angry now. Last week I saw Barbra Streisand play in New York. Halfway through there was a guy shouting at her, a heckler. She grabbed the mike and told him to f*** off! So if she can do it then so can I.

~ NEIL WARNOCK

We couldn't pass water.

~ NEIL WARNOCK ON HIS NOTTS COUNTY SIDE

Craig Short was playing for me then and he still is. He couldn't head, tackle, or pass the ball then. Nothing's changed.

~ NEIL WARNOCK, RECALLING THE 1991-92 NOTTS COUNTY TEAM IN 2006

He never has any idea what he's going to do when he gets the ball, so how can the opposition possibly know?

~ NEIL WARNOCK ON ENIGMATIC SHEFFIELD UNITED WINGER PAUL IFILL

For me to take the manager of the month award, I would have to win nine games out of eight.

~ NEIL WARNOCK

These two ladies asked if they could have their picture taken with me in my kilt. They must have thought I was Mel Gibson in his *Braveheart* gear – I wish, and so does my wife!

~ NEIL WARNOCK

The chairman will be talking about Europe soon. In years gone by that would have meant taking on the waiters in Magalluf.

~ NEIL WARNOCK

We have to improve in two key areas: defence and attack.

~ ROBERT WASEIGE, BELGIUM NATIONAL COACH

Norman Hunter doesn't tackle opponents so much as break them down for resale as scrap.

~ JULIE WELCH

And now the goals from Carrow Road, where the game finished 0-0.

~ ELTON WELSBY

As long as no one scored it was always going to be close.

~ ARSENE WENGER

By the time you read this we'll have had a scan on Fabregas. His foot blew up after the game and that's not the best sign.

~ ARSENE WENGER

Out of nine red cards this season we probably deserved half of them.

~ ARSENE WENGER

What the national coaches are doing is like taking the car from his [the club manager's] garage without even asking his permission. They'll then use his car for ten days and abandon it in a field without any petrol left in the tank. We then have to recover it, but it is broken down. Then, a month later, they'll come to take your car again – and for good measure you're expected to be nice about it. ~ ARSENE WENGER COMPLAINING ABOUT INTERNATIONAL BREAKS

It's not chasing women and having sex that tires out young footballers. It's staying up all night looking for it. ~ CLEMENS WESTERHOF

The only thing I have in common with George Best is that we came from the same place, play for the same club and were discovered by the same man. ~ NORMAN WHITESIDE

We keep kicking ourselves in the foot.
~ RAY WILKINS

The gelling period has just started to knit. ~ RAY WILKINS

That was an inch-perfect pass to no one. ~ RAY WILKINS

It's strange for me to respect a manager who every previous time we have met has stuck his studs in my jockstrap. ~ RAY WILKINS ON GRAEME SOUNESS

Having Wasps here gives us that little buzz around the place. ~ RAY WILKINS AT QPR

I am a firm believer that if you score one goal, the other team have to score two to win. ~ HOWARD WILKINSON

I think if they hadn't scored, we might have got a better result. ~ HOWARD WILKINSON

We did not deserve to lose today; we weren't beaten, we lost. ~ HOWARD WILKINSON

We need the players, because without the players, we wouldn't have a team.
~ HOWARD WILKINSON

We have to roll up our sleeves and get our knees dirty.   ~ HOWARD WILKINSON

Once Tony Daley opens his legs, you've got a problem.   ~ HOWARD WILKINSON

As one door closes, another one shuts.
~ HOWARD WILKINSON

Going behind that early made it like trying to run uphill in treacle.
~ HOWARD WILKINSON

There's only two types of manager. Those who've been sacked and those who will be sacked in the future.   ~ HOWARD WILKINSON

Eric Cantona gave interviews on art, philosophy and politics. A natural room-mate for David Batty, I thought immediately…   ~ HOWARD WILKINSON

I feel like Corky the Cat, who has been run over by a steamroller, got up and had someone punch him in the stomach.
~ HOWARD WILKINSON AFTER LEEDS LOSE TO ARSENAL IN THE FA CUP

So that's what you look like. I've played you three times and all I've seen is your arse.   ~ GRAHAM WILLIAMS, WELSH FULL-BACK, AFTER BEING
GIVEN THE RUNAROUND BY GEORGE BEST

The linesman flagged initially because he thought I was an Oldham player. Fair enough, I did have a replica shirt on – but I also have a big furry head.
~ KEVIN WILLIAMS, AKA OLDHAM MASCOT CHADDY THE OWL, GIVEN OFFSIDE IN A GAME

A player with a heart the size of a diamond ear-stud.
~ RICHARD WILLIAMS ON HARRY KEWELL

If that's not a sending-off offence, what is? What do we need, a leg with blood dripping off the stump? ~ PETER WILLIS

There have been a lot of rumours about players sleeping with each other's wives. But it's not true. We're all pulling together. ~ FABIEN WILNIS

You would put David Beckham's achievements for our national team in the same rank as you'd place his wife as a singer. Bargain basement. ~ A.N. WILSON

Gascoigne has pissed a fartness test. ~ BOB WILSON

Diego Maradona – a flawed genius who has now become a genius who is flawed. ~ BOB WILSON

There's one match that hasn't been cancelled because of the Arctic conditions – it's been cancelled because of a frozen pitch. ~ BOB WILSON

There was nothing between the teams apart from seven goals.
~ BARNSLEY BOSS DANNY WILSON FOLLOWING A HAMMERING AT OLD TRAFFORD

It's the end-of-season curtain raiser. ~ PETER WITHE

Both sides have scored a couple of goals and both sides have conceded a couple of goals. ~ PETER WITHE

I don't think my girlfriend would be too happy to hear I've been chasing Totti round Rome.
~ LEEDS DEFENDER JONATHAN WOODGATE PREPARING TO FACE ROMA'S FRANCESCO TOTTI

There is a refreshing honesty about football. At least they stab you in the chest.
~ CLIVE WOODWARD, MAKING THE SWITCH FROM RUGBY

The rules of soccer are very simple. Basically it is this: if it moves, kick it. If it doesn't move, kick it until it does.　　　　　　　　~ PHIL WOOSNAM

When people ask me what was my biggest thrill in football, I can't help but think of Raquel Welch and the day she walked down the touchline at Stamford Bridge in a pair of skin-tight blue leather trousers. Much nicer than 'Chopper' Harris.　　　　　　　　~ FRANK WORTHINGTON

If you can get through the first round you have a good chance of getting into the next one.　　　　　　　　~ NIGEL WORTHINGTON

It came in so quickly, he tried to get a head on it and it came off the wrong corner of his head.　~ NIGEL WORTHINGTON

To be defeated by the United States at football was like the MCC being beaten by Germany at cricket.　　　　　　　　~ BILLY WRIGHT

The referee was booking everyone. I thought he was filling in his lottery numbers.　　　　　　　　~ IAN WRIGHT

Without being too harsh on David [Beckham], he cost us the match.　~ IAN WRIGHT

It took a lot of bottle for Tony [Adams] to own up to being an alcoholic.　　　　　　　　~ IAN WRIGHT

I've got the passion but no idea of tactics – I'd be like a black Kevin Keegan.　　　　　　　　~ IAN WRIGHT, PONDERING A CAREER IN MANAGEMENT

I don't really believe in targets, because my next target is to beat Stoke City.　　　　　　　　~ RON WYLIE

Will the owner of a horse attached to a rag and bone cart in the visitors' car park return to his vehicle immediately.

~ ALI YASSIN, CARDIFF CITY PA ANNOUNCER, JOKINGLY WELCOMES WEST HAM TO NINIAN PARK

It will be quite a contest. We've got a manager who thinks he's the best-looking in the League and so have they.

~ TERRY YORATH, HUDDERSFIELD ASSISTANT MANAGER, AFTER THE FA CUP DRAW
PITTED MANAGERS PETER JACKSON AND JOSE MOURINHO AGAINST EACH OTHER

He's tall, he's quick, his name's a porno flick, Emmanuel, Emmanuel.

~ YORK CITY FANS SING THE PRAISES OF STRIKER EMMANUEL PANTHER

Man offers marriage proposal to any woman with ticket for Leeds v Sheffield United game. Must send photograph (of ticket). ~ *YORKSHIRE EVENING POST* ADVERT

Which team do I fear? No one. I fear nobody in the world, except my wife.

~ BURKHARD ZIESE

FOOTBALL (OTHER)

American Football

Football is a game for trained apes. That, in fact, is what most of the players are – retarded gorillas wearing helmets and uniforms. The only thing more debased is the surrounding mob of drunken monkeys howling the gorillas on.

~ EDWARD ABBEY

Losing the Super Bowl is worse than death. With death you don't have to get up next morning.

~ GEORGE ALLEN

Lou [Holtz] is a great talker. If he were God, Moses would have to send out for more tablets.

~ BARRY ALVAREZ

If me and King Kong went into an alley, only one of us would come out. And it wouldn't be the monkey.

~ LYLE ALZADO

American football is rugby after a visit from a Health and Safety inspector.

~ ANON

My wife calls me 'Much-Maligned'. She thinks that's my first name. Every time she reads a story about me, that's always in front of my name.

~ CHRIS BAHR

It's a good thing William 'The Refrigerator' Perry didn't need acupuncture. They'd have had to use a harpoon.

~ BUDDY BARON

A 'good hit' is a tackle that causes at least one major internal organ to actually fly out of a player's body.

~ DAVE BARRY

You have to play this game like somebody just hit your mother with a two-by-four.

~ DAN BIRDWELL

Officials are the only guys who can rob you and then get a police escort out of the stadium.

~ RON BOLTON

Thanksgiving dinners take 18 hours to prepare. They are consumed in 12 minutes. Half-times take 12 minutes. This is not coincidence.   ~ ERMA BOMBECK

The Rose Bowl is the only bowl I've ever seen that I didn't have to clean.

~ ERMA BOMBECK

If a man watches three football games in a row, he should be declared legally dead.

~ ERMA BOMBECK

I may be dumb, but I'm not stupid.   ~ TERRY BRADSHAW

After three failed marriages, I know what it's like to be replaced.~ TERRY BRADSHAW

You tend to learn more by mistakes and by failure than you do by positives. With the mistakes I've made, I'll probably be Einstein pretty soon.   ~ DAVE BROWN

I wouldn't ever set out to hurt anyone deliberately unless it was, you know, important – like a League game or something.   ~ DICK BUTKUS

My gluteus maximus is hurteus enormous.

~ TONY CAMPBELL AFTER LANDING AWKWARDLY

It's like being a ballet dancer – tight pants, a little contact and a whole lot of kicking. ~ JASON CHAFFETZ ON THE POSITION OF PLACEKICKER

It's a humbling thing being humble.   ~ MAURICE CLARETT

If this keeps up, our team picture this year will be an X-ray.

~ JOHN COOPER ON ARIZONA STATE'S INJURY LIST

We're not attempting to circumcise rules.   ~ BILL COWHER

Hopefully that will get done in time, and if not, shortly thereafter.   ~ BILL COWHER

He's about the size of a lot of guys that size.

~ GARY CROWTON

Football is not a contact sport; it is a collision sport. Dancing is a contact sport.

~ DUFFY DAUGHERTY

My only feeling about superstition is that it's unlucky to be behind at the end of the game.

~ DUFFY DAUGHERTY

Not only is he ambidextrous, but he can throw with either hand. ~ DUFFY DAUGHERTY

I could have been a Rhodes scholar, except for my grades.

~ DUFFY DAUGHERTY

A tie is like kissing your sister.

~ DUFFY DAUGHERTY

Elvin [Bethea] is so old he had to use a jump cable to get started last year.

~ DOUG DIEKEN

The reason women don't play football is because 11 of them would never wear the same outfit in public.

~ PHYLLIS DILLER

John Madden's one man who didn't let success go to his clothes.

~ MIKE DITKA

They can't fire me because my family buys too many tickets.

~ LaVELL EDWARDS, FOOTBALL COACH AND ONE OF 14 CHILDREN

Physically, he's a world-beater. Mentally, he's an eggbeater.

~ MATT ELLIOTT ON ALONZO SPELLMAN

Some defensive-minded, some offensive-minded and some no-minded.

~ BOOMER ESIASON ASSESSING THE MERITS OF THE SIX COACHES
IN HIS SIX SEASONS WITH THE ARIZONA CARDINALS

Does Tom Landry ever smile? I don't know. I only played there nine years.

~ WALT GARRISON

Pro football is like nuclear warfare. There are no winners, only survivors.

~ FRANK GIFFORD

They boo for a living in Cleveland and Cincinnati. We played on Christmas Eve and they even booed Santa Claus.   ~ JERRY GLANVILLE

If you're a pro coach, NFL stands for 'Not For Long'.   ~ JERRY GLANVILLE

If there's a pile-up, they'll have to give some of the players artificial insemination.   ~ CURT GOWDY

A good coach needs a patient wife, a loyal dog and a great quarterback, but not necessarily in that order.   ~ BUD GRANT

He didn't know anything about drugs. He thought uppers were dentures.

~ ARCHIE GRIFFIN ON COACH WOODY HAYES

Old place-kickers never die, they just go on missing the point.   ~ LOU GROZA

It's a retirement community. If it wasn't for mouth-to-mouth resuscitation, there'd be no romance at all in that town.

~ ARGUS HAMILTON ON PHOENIX AS A SUPER BOWL VENUE

I'd catch a punt naked in the snow in Buffalo for a chance to play in the NFL.

~ STEVE HENDRICKSON

The man who complains about the way the ball bounces is likely the one who dropped it.   ~ LOU HOLTZ

On this team, we were all united in a common goal: to keep my job. ~ LOU HOLTZ

I knew Rocket Ismail was fast, but I never knew how fast until I saw him playing tennis by himself.   ~ LOU HOLTZ

He put together a very difficult jigsaw puzzle in 18 months. Now, we've got to be impressed, because on the box it says three to five years.
                                        ~ LOU HOLTZ ON WIDE RECEIVER DERRICK MAYES

College football is a sport that bears the same relation to education that bullfighting does to agriculture.   ~ ELBERT HUBBARD

Playing middle linebacker is like walking through a lion's cage dressed in a three-piece pork-chop suit.   ~ CECIL JOHNSON

You've got a better chance of completing a pass to the Venus de Milo.
                                                              ~ VANCE JOHNSON

Coach Lombardi is very fair. He treats us all like dogs.   ~ HENRY JORDAN

I've never seen such skinny legs on a football player before. I wonder if they ever caught the rustler who stole his calves.   ~ STEVE JORDAN ON ANTHONY CARTER

I never graduated from college, but I was only there for two terms – Truman's and Eisenhower's.   ~ ALEX KARRAS

Most of my clichés aren't original.
                                                                ~ CHUCK KNOX

Football is an incredible game. Sometimes it's so incredible, it's unbelievable.
                                                                ~ TOM LANDRY

American football makes rugby look like a Tupperware party.   ~ SUE LAWLEY

I wanted to have a career in sports when I was young, but I had to give it up. I'm only six feet tall, so I couldn't play basketball. I'm only 190 pounds, so I couldn't play football. And I have 20-20 vision, so I couldn't be a referee.   ~ JAY LENO

According to a *Sports Illustrated* poll, 30 per cent of male readers said they would rather watch a big play-off game than have sex. The other 70 said, 'Hey, that's why they have half-time.'

~ JAY LENO

Dom Capers is so stingy he has a burglar alarm on his garbage can.   ~ MARV LEVY

Pain is only temporary, no matter how long it lasts.   ~ RAY LEWIS

One of my uncles was a classic paranoid who couldn't sit through a football game. He thought the guys in the huddle were talking about him.
~ FRANZ LIDZ

I just wrap my arms around the whole backfield and peel 'em one by one until I get to the ball carrier. Him I keep.   ~ BIG DADDY LIPSCOMB

We didn't lose the game; we just ran out of time.   ~ VINCE LOMBARDI

Winning is not the most important thing: it's the only thing.   ~ VINCE LOMBARDI

If winning isn't everything, why do they keep score?   ~ VINCE LOMBARDI

If you aren't fired with enthusiasm, you will be fired with enthusiasm.

~ VINCE LOMBARDI

I don't care what the tape says, I didn't say it.   ~ RAY MALAVASI

The mooning allegation? I'd just like to put it behind me.   ~ PEYTON MANNING

My boy, get in there and play like you did in the last game. I've got five dollars bet on the other team.   ~ GROUCHO MARX, *HORSE FEATHERS*

When he didn't remember our anniversary, I knew he was OK.

~ LISA McCAFFREY AFTER HUSBAND ED SUFFERED CONCUSSION DURING A DENVER BRONCOS GAME

If a contest had 97 prizes, the 98th would be a trip to Green Bay.   ~ JOHN McKAY

—Reporter: Another loss. What about your team's execution?
—John McKay: I'm all for it.

Defensively, I think it's important for us to tackle.   ~ KARL MECKLENBURG

Big deal, so he scored. The last time I saw someone dance like that I had to pay her $20 and have my pants dry-cleaned the next day.   ~ DENNIS MILLER

I've seen women pee standing up with better aim.   ~ DENNIS MILLER

The quarterback's spending so much time behind the centre that he may jeopardise his right to lead a Boy Scout troop.   ~ DENNIS MILLER

It's a once-in-a-lifetime thing that only happens every so often.   ~ RANDY MOSS

Nothing is ever so bad it can't be made worse by firing the coach.   ~ JIM MURRAY

Do I prefer Astroturf to grass? I don't know. I've never smoked Astroturf.   ~ JOE NAMATH

One of the great disappointments of a football game is that the cheerleaders never seem to get injured.   ~ *NEW YORK TRIBUNE*

That kid grew up so far out in the country, he had to go toward town to hunt.   ~ BILL PARCELLS ON DEMARCUS WARE

There are a lot of guys available, although some of them are in rest homes.   ~ BILL PARCELLS SEEKING EXPERIENCED REPLACEMENTS FOR INJURED PLAYERS

I looked in the mirror one day and I said to my wife, 'How many great coaches do you think there are?' She said, 'One less than you think.' ~ JOE PATERNO

Gary Anderson's a great player. He ceases to amaze me every day. ~ RAY PERKINS

I've been big ever since I was little. ~ WILLIAM 'THE REFRIGERATOR' PERRY

You guys line up alphabetically by height. ~ BILL PETERSON

I'm the football coach around here and don't you remember it! ~ BILL PETERSON

We're not giving away any football players who could hurt us later. I don't mind people thinking I'm stupid, but I don't want to give them any proof. ~ BUM PHILLIPS

Why do I take my wife on all the road trips? Because she is too damn ugly to kiss goodbye. ~ BUM PHILLIPS

When I coached, players carried a six-pack. Now they have a briefcase on one hand and a lawyer on the other. ~ BUM PHILLIPS

If I drop dead tomorrow, at least I'll know I died in good health. ~ BUM PHILLIPS, AFTER PASSING A MEDICAL

Marv's more likely to quote Homer, and I'm more likely to quote Homer Simpson. ~ BUFFALO BILLS COACH WADE PHILLIPS ON HIS PREDECESSOR, MARV LEVY

Most football teams are temperamental. That's 90 per cent temper and ten per cent mental.
~ DOUG PLANK

He treats us like men. He lets us wear earrings. ~ TORRIN POLK ON HIS COACH JOHN JENKINS

I have contempt for a game in which players have to wear so much equipment. Men play basketball in their underwear, which seems just right to me.

~ ANNA QUINDLEN

The football season is like pain. You forget how terrible it is until it seizes you again.

~ SALLY QUINN

When I went to Catholic High School in Philadelphia, we just had one coach for football and basketball. He took all of us who turned out and had us run through a forest. The ones who ran into the trees were on the football team.

~ GEORGE RAVELING

If Dick Butkus was a cab driver and he had Ray Charles in the back seat, he'd rev up the engine for 50 minutes and charge him full fare. ~ BENNY RICARDO

I feel like I'm the best, but you're not going to get me to say that. ~ JERRY RICE

I've found that prayers work best when you have big players. ~ KNUTE ROCKNE

I want to rush for 1,000 or 1,500 yards, whichever comes first. ~ GEORGE ROGERS

Midwestern farmers are now using equipment that turns manure into energy. You know, the reverse of the [Chicago] Bears. ~ STEVE ROSENBLOOM

One player was lost because he broke his nose. How do you go about getting a nose in condition for football? ~ DARRELL ROYAL

We would like to find 53 guys on our team who do not need a sheepdog to find their way home at night. ~ NICK SABAN

Watching football is like watching pornography. There's plenty of action, and I can't take my eyes off it, but when it's over, I wonder why the hell I spent an afternoon doing it. ~ LUKE SALISBURY

It was like taking Miss America home after a date and discovering that she had just won a garlic-eating contest.

~ BLACKIE SHERROD, AFTER THE AUTHORITIES TOOK AWAY FLORIDA STATE'S FIRST-EVER TITLE

Sure, luck means a lot in football. Not having a good quarterback is bad luck.

~ DON SHULA

I'm fairly confident that if I died tomorrow, Don would find a way to preserve me until the season was over and he had time for a nice funeral. ~ DOROTHY SHULA

If we didn't have a huddle, Jim [Burt] would have no social life.   ~ PHIL SIMMS

If God wanted women to understand men, football would never have been created.   ~ ROGER SIMON

If women were meant to play football, God would have put their tits somewhere else.   ~ GORDON SINCLAIR

We've got [Mike] Keeney on the lettuce diet. Unfortunately, he eats 40 pounds of lettuce a day.   ~ STEVE SLOAN

The sun doesn't shine on the same dog's butt every day but we sure didn't expect a total eclipse.   ~ STEVE SLOAN

I like to believe that my best hits border on felonious assault.   ~ JACK TATUM

The word 'genius' isn't applicable in football. A genius is a guy like Norman Einstein.   ~ JOE THEISMAN

If the Super Bowl is the ultimate game, why are they playing it again next year?   ~ DUANE THOMAS

IQ? Sure, I've got one. It's a perfect 20-20.   ~ DUANE THOMAS

I think the first thing my dad ever bought me was a football. And I was very young. He didn't know a lot about it. He came from the old country. I mean, we tried to pass it and throw it and kick it, and we couldn't do it. And it was very discouraging for him and for me. We almost quit. And finally we had a nice enough neighbour who came over and put some air in it, and what a difference!

~ BOB UECKER

Football has affected my entire family's lifestyle. My little boy can't go to bed unless we give him a two-minute warning.

~ DICK VERMEIL

I have two weapons – my legs, my arms and my brains.

~ MICHAEL VICK

As you all know, there is no 'I' in 'championship'.

~ BARRY WAGNER

The University of Maryland football team members all made straight As. But their Bs are a little crooked.

~ JOHNNY WALKER

We're still shooting ourselves in the mouth.

~ MARCEL WEST

Football combines two of the worst things in American life. It is violence punctuated by committee meetings.

~ GEORGE WILL

There are no opportune times for a penalty, and this is not one of those times.

~ JACK YOUNGBLOOD

Australian Rules Football

Shaun [McManus] goes to collect the ball, a free kick, and several teeth.

~ DENNIS COMETTI

The Magpies ought to be kicking themselves right now, but with their luck, they'd probably miss.

~ DENNIS COMETTI

Gaspar, the unfriendly post.

~ DENNIS COMETTI, AFTER DARREN GASPAR HIT A POST FROM 40 METRES OUT

Ashley McIntosh, like a good hairspray, capable of a subtle hold. ~ DENNIS COMETTI

Barlow to Bateman, the Hawks are attacking alphabetically. ~ DENNIS COMETTI

[Jeff] Farmer may have an injury to his calf… Hmm, a farmer with a calf problem. ~ DENNIS COMETTI

If you are not in bed by twelve o'clock, go home. ~ COACH JACK DYER TO HIS PLAYERS

Australian Rules football might best be described as a game devised for padded cells, played in the open air. ~ JIM MURRAY

Gaelic Football

That referee wouldn't see a foul in a henhouse. ~ ANON

He'll regret this to his dying day, if he lives that long. ~ ANON

Now listen, lads, I'm not happy with our tackling. We're hurting them but they keep getting up. ~ JOHN B. KEANE

How would you know a Cork footballer? He's the one who thinks that oral sex is just talking about it. ~ JOHN B. KEANE

A fan is someone who, if you have made an idiot of yourself on the pitch, doesn't think you've done a permanent job. ~ JACK LYNCH

Colin Corkery on the 45 lets go with the right boot. It's over the bar. This man shouldn't be playing football. He's made an almost Lazarus-like recovery from a heart condition. Lazarus was a great man, but he couldn't kick points like Colin Corkery. ~ MICHAEL O'MUIRCHEARTAIGH

You get more contact in an old-time waltz at the old folks' home than in a National League final.   ~ PAT SPILLANE

The first half was even, the second half was even worse.   ~ PAT SPILLANE

ICE AND SNOW

Bobsled

Always remember, your bones will not break in a bobsled. No, no, no. They shatter.

~ *COOL RUNNINGS*

Bobsledding is a sport in which demented people sit on a sled that goes 2,000mph down an ice ditch. The same sport is often practised without ice – when four drunks leave a fraternity party in a BMW.

~ DAN JENKINS

One word: intersections.

~ DENNIS MILLER'S SUGGESTION FOR LIVENING UP THE BOBSLED EVENT

She's got what I call bobsled looks: going downhill fast.

~ CRAIG NOVA

The Winter Olympics is nothing more than 40 kinds of sliding.

~ DARA O'BRIAIN

Curling

Curling is sweeping the nation.

~ ANON

You can tell your lady that she is wide without fear of getting whacked upside the head with a cast iron pan. Or proclaim out loud that she is too heavy, knowing that your comment has been heard by countless bystanders. In curling, you are the king of the house.

~ ANON

I'm a curling addict. I need a hit, and I want to get stoned.

~ ANON

If curling were easy, they'd call it hockey.

~ ANON

Curling is not a sport. I called my grandmother and told her she could win a gold medal because they have dusting in the Olympics now.

~ CHARLES BARKLEY

Curling is just housework on ice.

~ LINDA SMITH

Ice Hockey

Ice hockey players can walk on water. ~ ANON

Four out of five dentists recommend playing hockey. ~ ANON

Hockey is figure skating in a war zone. ~ ANON

Hockey players wear numbers because you can't always identify the body with dental records. ~ ANON

You're playing worse every day and right now you're playing like the middle of next week. ~ HERB BROOKS TO THE 1980 US OLYMPIC TEAM

A puck is a hard rubber disc that hockey players strike when they can't hit one another. ~ JIMMY CANNON

After a year of no NHL, I got so much to say I can hardly wait to hear myself. ~ DON CHERRY

We take the shortest route to the puck and arrive in ill humour. ~ BOBBY CLARKE

It's something we're doing for team bondage. ~ CURTIS COOPER

The only difference between this and Custer's last stand was Custer didn't have to look at the tape afterwards. ~ TERRY CRISP AFTER TAMPA BAY LIGHTNING SUFFERED A 10-0 DEFEAT

I went to a fight the other night and a hockey game broke out. ~ RODNEY DANGERFIELD

They had to take a piece of bone out of my head in order to rebuild my nose. It was kind of a pain in the ass. ~ ROB DiMAIO

If hockey fights were fake, you would see me in more of them. ~ ROD GILBERT

The thing I'm going to miss most is showering with 23 guys.

~ RON GRESCHNER ON HIS RETIREMENT

I love playing and living in New York. There's such a high energy here. Everybody's fighting for that same cab.   ~ WAYNE GRETZKY

That's so when I forget how to spell my name, I can still find my clothes.

~ STU GRIMSON ON WHY HE KEPT A COLOUR PHOTO OF HIMSELF ABOVE HIS LOCKER

On a windy day, I don't know which side of my face my nose is going to be on.

~ KYLE HAVILAND, WHOSE NOSE HAD BEEN BROKEN EIGHT TIMES IN HOCKEY BRAWLS

All hockey players are bilingual: they speak English and profanity. ~ GORDIE HOWE

I was a multi-millionaire from playing hockey. Then I got divorced, and now I am a millionaire.   ~ BOBBY HULL

One was on the ice and we put that one back in. Another was up my nose and they had to pull it down.   ~ SAMI KAPANEN AFTER A COLLISION SMASHED HIS FRONT TEETH

Ice hockey is a form of disorderly conduct in which the score is kept.

~ DOUG LARSON

Half the game is mental; the other half is being mental. ~ JIM McKENNY

I've been fired more times than Custer's pistol.   ~ TOM McVIE

Is my improved play due to maturity? Not so much maturity as growing up.

~ JAY MILLER

Hockey is murder on ice.   ~ JIM MURRAY

Hockey is the only game that can be played equally well with the lights out.

~ JIM MURRAY

Playing 'Send In The Clowns' when the referee and the officials went on to the ice was inappropriate, and was compounded when he played 'Three Blind Mice' when they left.

~ NOTTINGHAM PANTHERS OFFICIAL ANNOUNCING THE SACKING OF THE STADIUM ORGANIST

We get nose jobs all the time in the NHL, and we don't even have to go to the hospital.

~ BRAD PARK

This type of injury is very painful. Especially when it hurts.

~ JEAN PERRON

Goaltending is a normal job. Sure! How would you like a job where, every time you make a mistake, a big red light goes on and 18,000 people boo?

~ JACQUES PLANTE

The difference between John Hart and an arsonist is that an arsonist doesn't throw away his last two matches.

~ BRENT POPE

Where's the rest of your goalkeeper?

~ LARRY ROBINSON, SEEING CHICAGO BLACKHAWKS' 5FT 5IN GOALMINDER DARREN PANG

Black people dominate sports in the United States. Basketball, baseball, football, golf, tennis, and as soon as they make a heated hockey rink we'll take that too.

~ CHRIS ROCK

Yeah, I'm cocky and I am arrogant, but that doesn't mean I'm not a nice person.

~ JEREMY ROENICK

By the age of 18, the average American has witnessed 200,000 acts of violence on television, most of them occurring during the NHL play-off series.

~ STEVE RUSHIN

Hockey belongs to the Cartoon Network, where a person can be pancaked by an ACME anvil, then expanded – accordion-style – back to full stature, without any lasting side effect.   ~ STEVE RUSHIN

That's an OK sacrifice for the gold. You can always get new teeth.
~ FINLAND'S TEEMU SELANNE WHO LOST THREE TEETH DURING A QUARTER-FINAL
MATCH AGAINST THE UNITED STATES AT THE 2006 WINTER OLYMPICS

Once someone hits that puck it's going to keep going until it stops.
~ PAUL STEIGERWALD

Red ice sells hockey tickets.   ~ BOB STEWART

Better teams win more often than the teams that are not so good.
~ CANADIAN COACH TOM WATT

It felt like a golf swing and my head was on the tee.
~ TYLER WRIGHT ON BEING CLUBBED

Luge

Sliding along an ice chute at 90mph on what is essentially a tea tray.   ~ ANON

That's what I call the ultimate laxative.
~ OTTO JELINEK, CANADIAN SPORTS MINISTER, AFTER HIS FIRST LUGE RUN

President Clinton is now telling close friends and associates that he and Monica Lewinsky were practising for the two-man luge.   ~ DAVID LETTERMAN

Imagine being on a rollercoaster, except with your chin just above the frame.
~ SHELLEY RUDMAN ON SKELETON

You think the luge is a sport. It's not a sport. It's a bet.   ~ JON STEWART

Skating

This is a sport where you can talk about sequins, earrings and plunging necklines – and you are talking about the men. ~ CHRISTINE BRENNAN

Remember: when they make the ice, they make it slippery side up.

~ DEWY BROWNING

Ice skating – with its meticulously preordinated choreography, fanciful dress and movements that consist of wandering around in apparently pointless, ever-decreasing circles – is closer to Trooping the Colour than to a sport.

~ JULIE BURCHILL

I've seen the entire world and I've met some amazing friends. But it's honestly a pretty ridiculous thing. I mean, I skate around in tights!

~ JOEY CHEEK AFTER WINNING AN OLYMPIC SPEED-SKATING GOLD MEDAL AT THE 2006 GAMES

Torvill and Dean, oh, they're very good on ice. But you get them out on the street ... all over the place!

~ HARRY HILL

Tonya Harding: history's first disfigure skater. ~ LEIGH HILL

Just what does a person have to do in figure skating to be banned for life? Wear bib overalls to the long programme? Or maybe slip some Slim Whitman into a competitor's music? ~ STEVE HUMMER

[Jan] Hoffman knocked off triples with the awesome precision of a fighter pilot swatting flies. He made the same artistic impression as a fringe theatre company producing a minor play by Brecht in the back room of a pub. ~ CLIVE JAMES

Olympic figure skating – a sport where competitors are dressed as dinner mints.

~ JERE LONGMAN

Olympic skating champion Oksana Baiul was charged with drink-driving in Connecticut. They took her blood alcohol level, and she received .18, .16, .17, .16, .16 and .17.

~ DON McMILLAN

Russian women are not very good for figure skating. They are good for building rail tracks in Siberia, for example.

~ ALEXEI MISHIN

You have to kiss a few toads before you find the right prince.

~ CALLA URBANSKI, AFTER DUMPING HER SIXTH PAIRS PARTNER

Skiing

Skiing: the art of catching cold and going broke while rapidly heading nowhere at great personal risk.

~ ANON

All things are possible, except for skiing through a revolving door.

~ ANON

Stretch pants: the garment that made skiing a spectator sport.

~ ANON

There are 206 bones in the human body, but don't worry: the two in the middle ear have never been broken while skiing.

~ ANON

Skiing combines outdoor fun with knocking down trees with your face.

~ DAVE BARRY

Alain Baxter faces an uphill struggle in the slalom tomorrow.

~ BBC PRESENTER

Skiing is the only sport where you spend an arm and a leg to break an arm and a leg.

~ HENRY BEARD, *SKIING*

Skis are a pair of long, thin flexible runners that permit a skier to slide across the snow and into debt.   ~ HENRY BEARD, *SKIING*

A ski jacket is the larval stage of a blimp.   ~ HENRY BEARD, *SKIING*

I do not participate in any sport with ambulances at the bottom of the hill.
                                                              ~ ERMA BOMBECK

In St Moritz everyone who is anything goes around in plaster.   ~ NOËL COWARD

I remember when I did my first jump, I looked from the top and was so frightened that my bum shrivelled up like a prune.   ~ EDDIE 'THE EAGLE' EDWARDS

Skiing? Why break my leg at 40 degrees below zero when I can fall downstairs at home?   ~ COREY FORD

There are really only three things to learn in skiing: how to put on your skis, how to slide downhill, and how to walk along the hospital corridor.
                                                              ~ LORD MANCROFT

[Eddie] The Eagle doesn't jump – he drops like a stone.   ~ ROB McCORMACK

I got to party and socialise at Olympic level.
        ~ BODE MILLER, THE AMERICAN HOPEFUL WHO FLOPPED AT THE 2006 WINTER OLYMPICS

The sport of skiing consists of wearing $3,000 worth of clothes and equipment and driving for 200 miles in the snow in order to stand around at a bar and get drunk.   ~ P.J. O'ROURKE

I went skiing and I knew I was going too fast when I suddenly realised that I was actually getting younger.
                                                              ~ JOHN ROSS

I really lack the words to compliment myself today.   ~ ALBERTO TOMBA

Most skiers are really motorcyclists in cute clothes.   ~ BOB WILKERSON

Cross-country skiing is great if you live in a small country.   ~ STEVEN WRIGHT

Snowboarding

Snowboarding is an activity that is very popular with people who do not feel that regular skiing is lethal enough. I now realise that the small hills you see on ski slopes are formed around the bodies of 47-year-olds who tried to learn snowboarding.   ~ DAVE BARRY

IN THE POOL

Diving

Synchronised diving: two svelte young men with hairless chests jump off a board and land in a swimming pool at the same time head first. It's not clever, it's not artistic. It's gravity.
~ *THE GUARDIAN*

It's the safest thing in the world, but it could kill you.
~ JOHN MAXSON ON DIVING FROM AN 80FT BOARD

Swimming

I wanted to be an Olympic swimmer, but I had some problems with buoyancy.
~ WOODY ALLEN

It's a good idea to begin at the bottom in everything, except in learning to swim.
~ ANON

And she is on the shoulder of the Hungarian swimmer who is two lanes away.
~ BOB BALLARD

And the race is all about first, second and third.
~ HAMILTON BLAND

I enjoy most sports with a passion, but I think I'd struggle to get excited by synchronised swimming.
~ IAN BOTHAM

If our swimmers want to win any more medals, they'll have to put their skates on.
~ DAVID BRENNER

Swimming isn't a sport. It's just a way to keep from drowning.
~ GEORGE CARLIN

I won Wales' bachelor of the year – I jumped from number 41 to number one. Catherine Zeta Jones, Charlotte Church – I'm interested, definitely. ~ DAVID DAVIES

The swimmers are swimming out of their socks.   ~ SHARRON DAVIES

It's really quite bizarre but apparently when I swim the 1,500 at this level, I can conceive babies for people. I suppose they're lucky I'm not a sprinter because that's all over in a minute.   ~ GRANT HACKETT ON E-MAILS HE RECEIVED FROM WOMEN
WHO GOT PREGNANT DURING HIS MARATHON OLYMPIC TRIUMPHS

I swim a lot. It's either that or buy a new golf ball.   ~ BOB HOPE

On the correctly formed pubescent girl, a Speedo looked wonderful. When it was wet, it was an incitement to riot.   ~ CLIVE JAMES

It's obvious these Russian swimmers are determined to do well on American soil.   ~ ANITA LONSBOROUGH

Michelle Ford is Australia's first Olympic medal for four years.   ~ NORMAN MAY

We are hoping that our swimmers are going to do something big in the pool.   ~ DIANE MODAHL

This boy swims like a greyhound.   ~ ATHOLE STILL

I don't see myself competing again. I don't think it will happen. I won't rule it out, I never rule anything out, but it won't happen.   ~ IAN THORPE

When I saw the French coast in the distance I thought, 'We're out of the World Cup so Britain needs a cross-dressing comedian to restore its pride.'   ~ DAVID WALLIAMS

Marie Scott, from Fleetwood, the 17-year-old who has really plummeted to the top.   ~ ALAN WEEKS

If one synchronised swimmer drowns, do the rest have to drown too?

~ STEVEN WRIGHT

If swimming is so good for your figure, how do you explain whales?

~ STEVEN WRIGHT

If it had been the backstroke, I obviously would have stopped.

~ MATT ZELEN, WHOSE SWIMMING TRUNKS SLIPPED OFF DURING THE BUTTERFLY

Water Polo

Water polo is terribly dangerous. I had two horses drown under me.

~ TONY CURTIS

That's what I get for kicking Sans in his face.

~ MIKE EVANS OF THE US, EJECTED AFTER KICKING SPAIN'S JORDI SANS IN THE FACE

MIND GAMES

Bridge

Having sex is like playing bridge. If you don't have a good partner, you'd better have a good hand. ~ WOODY ALLEN

Bridge is the only game that bruises more shins than hockey. ~ ANON

Bridge is a great comfort in your old age. It also helps you get there faster. ~ ANON

Bridge is a game that separates the men from the boys. It also separates husbands and wives. ~ GEORGE BURNS

Let's banish bridge. Let's find some pleasant way of being miserable together. ~ DON HEROLD

When my bridge partner excused himself to go to the bathroom, it was the only time all night I knew what he had in his hand. ~ GEORGE S. KAUFMAN

My friend Imran Khan, who is a famous cricketer and a very popular man with the ladies, has bodyguards outside his room, warding women off. I have guys warding them in.

~ ZIA MAHMOOD, PAKISTAN BRIDGE PLAYER

Since the average person's small supply of politeness must last him all his life, he can't afford to waste it on bridge partners. ~ ALFRED SHEINWOLD

Chess

I failed to make the chess team because of my height.   ~ WOODY ALLEN

Life is too short for chess.   ~ LORD BYRON

Chess is the most elaborate waste of human intelligence that you can find outside of an advertising agency.   ~ RAYMOND CHANDLER

No chess grandmaster is normal; they only differ in the extent of their madness.   ~ VIKTOR KORCHNOI

There just isn't enough televised chess.   ~ DAVID LETTERMAN

A computer once beat me at chess, but it was no match for me at kick boxing.   ~ EMO PHILIPS

Chess is ruthless: you've got to be prepared to kill people.   ~ NIGEL SHORT

I had lunch with a chess champion the other day. I knew he was a chess champion because it took him 20 minutes to pass the salt.   ~ ERIC SYKES

It's always better to sacrifice your opponent's men.   ~ SAVIELLY TARTAKOVER

A chess game is divided into three stages: the first, when you hope you have the advantage, the second, when you believe you have the advantage, and the third, when you know you're going to lose.   ~ SAVIELLY TARTAKOVER

Victory goes to the player who makes the next-to-last mistake.   ~ SAVIELLY TARTAKOVER

ON THE COURT

Basketball

Bill Walton is incredible. If you drop a toothpick on his foot, he'll have a stress fracture.

~ STAN ALBECK

Manute Bol is so skinny, they save money on road trips – they just fax him from city to city.

~ WOODY ALLEN

We have 44 defences for him, but he has 45 ways to score.

~ AL ATTLES ON NATE ARCHIBALD

If I weren't earning $3 million a year to dunk a basketball, most people on the street would run in the other direction if they saw me coming. ~ CHARLES BARKLEY

We don't need referees in basketball, but it gives the white guys something to do.

~ CHARLES BARKLEY

I don't hate anyone, at least not for more than 48 minutes, barring overtime.

~ CHARLES BARKLEY

I miss America. I miss crime and murder. I miss Philadelphia. There hasn't been a brutal stabbing or anything here the last 24 hours.

~ CHARLES BARKLEY AT THE 1992 BARCELONA OLYMPICS

They're getting dumber. They run like deer, they jump like deer, and they think like deer. ~ CHARLES BARKLEY ON THE LATEST CROP OF NBA PLAYERS

I don't create controversies. They're there long before I open my mouth. I just bring them to your attention. ~ CHARLES BARKLEY

You got to believe in yourself. Hell, I believe I'm the best-looking guy in the world, and I might be right. ~ CHARLES BARKLEY

I was misquoted. ~ CHARLES BARKLEY ON HIS AUTOBIOGRAPHY

I haven't been able to slam-dunk the basketball for the past five years. Or, for the 38 years before that, either. ~ DAVE BARRY

I've never had major knee surgery on any other part of my body. ~ WINSTON BENNETT

I'm going to graduate on time, no matter how long it takes. ~ ROD BROOKIN

After you go to the bathroom, you don't just stand there and look at what you dropped in there for all night long. At some point you gotta flush it, man. ~ KOBE BRYANT, EXPLAINING HOW THE LA LAKERS HAD TO MOVE ON AFTER LOSING TO THE PHOENIX SUNS IN GAME 6 OF THEIR 2006 PLAY-OFF SERIES

The trouble with referees is that they just don't care which side wins. ~ TOM CANTERBURY

They say that nobody is perfect. Then they tell you practice makes perfect. I wish they'd make up their minds. ~ WILT CHAMBERLAIN

The kid is slower than erosion. ~ GORDON CHIESA ON TIM CAIN

Any time Detroit scores more than 100 points and holds the other team below 100 points, they almost always win. ~ DOUG COLLINS

He has so many fish hooks in his nose, he looks like a piece of bait.
~ BOB COSTAS ON DENNIS RODMAN'S NOSE PIERCINGS

When I die, I want to come back as me. ~ MARK CUBAN

Manute Bol is so tall that if he fell down, he'd be halfway home. ~ DARRYL DAWKINS

I'm six foot eleven. My birthday covers three days. ~ DARRYL DAWKINS

I don't want to shoot my mouth in my foot, but those are games we can win.

~ SHERMAN DOUGLAS

The first time I saw Dick Vitale, his hair was blowing in the breeze. And he was too proud to chase it.

~ CLIFF ELLIS

We're the only team in history that could lose nine games in a row and then go into a slump.

~ BILL FITCH ON THE CLEVELAND CAVALIERS

Last year wasn't all that bad. We led the league in flu shots.

~ BILL FITCH ON THE MISERABLE RUN OF THE CLEVELAND CAVALIERS

I don't have an ulcer. I'm a carrier. I give them to other people.

~ BILL FITCH

I love Charles [Barkley] because he's so honest. You can see a thought form in his head and then come right out his mouth without stopping in between.

~ CHRIS FORD

To get into college they asked me to spell Mississippi. I said, 'Which one? The state or the river?'

~ PETE GILLEN

I've had to overcome a lot of diversity.

~ DREW GOODEN

I'm often mentioned in the same sentence as Michael Jordan. You know, 'That Scott Hastings, he's no Michael Jordan.'

~ SCOTT HASTINGS

The way defences are operating these days, the other team starts picking you up when you walk out of the hotel lobby.

~ DOC HAYES

Am I a basketball player? No, I clean giraffe ears.

~ 6FT 11IN ELVIN HAYES

Girls shouldn't play with men's balls. Their hands are too small.

~ WALLY HORN

Not only is there more to life than basketball, there's a lot more to basketball than basketball.
~ PHIL JACKSON

Shooting is just like toenails. They may fall off occasionally, but you know they'll always come back.
~ CHARLES JOHNSON

It's almost like we have ESPN.
~ MAGIC JOHNSON ON HOW WELL HE AND JAMES WORTHY WORK TOGETHER

We are going to turn this around 360 degrees.
~ JASON KIDD

That was the nail that broke the coffin's back.
~ JACK KRAFT

Cleveland Cavaliers star Shawn Kemp, who's fathered seven children by six women, may be a great basketball player but he obviously knows nothing about safe sex. What does he think HIV means? High five?
~ BOB LACEY

I told him, 'Son, what is it with you? Is it ignorance or apathy?' He said, 'Coach, I don't know and I don't care.'
~ FRANK LAYDEN

Finish last in your league and they call you 'Idiot'. Finish last in medical school and they call you 'Doctor'.
~ ABE LEMONS

You did great, son. You scored one more point than a dead man.
~ ABE LEMONS AFTER HIS MAJOR PLAYER SCORED JUST ONE POINT IN A GAME

We are just about to start March Madness. That's the college basketball tournament where we start with 64 teams and whittle them down to just one. You know, kind of like our allies.
~ US CHAT SHOW HOST JAY LENO

I can't believe how physical the NBA is getting lately. Shaquille O'Neal – what is he, 320 pounds – comes down the court and crashes into Dennis Rodman. Luckily, Dennis was wearing a padded bra, so he's OK.
~ JAY LENO

The new Dennis Rodman doll is $19.95, assault and battery not included.

~ DAVID LETTERMAN

He's been out of the league so long they must have lost his scouting report. When he was playing, they probably pounded out the scouting reports on stone tablets.   ~ GRANT LONG ON THE COMEBACK OF HIS 40-YEAR-OLD COUSIN JOHN LONG

I never thought I'd lead the NBA in rebounding, but I got a lot of help from my team-mates – they did a lot of missing.   ~ MOSES MALONE

Clark Kent went into the phone booth and came out as Lois Lane.

~ JACK McCALLUM ON KURT RAMBIS'S SUDDEN LOSS OF FORM

I come from New York, where if you fall down someone will pick you up by your wallet.   ~ AL McGUIRE

Damn, that's the same nose I broke a couple of years ago!   ~ JOE MERIWEATHER

War is the only game in which it doesn't pay to have the home-court advantage.

~ DICK MOTTA

When he sits down, his ears pop.   ~ DON NELSON ON 7FT 6IN SHAWN BRADLEY

My sister's expecting a baby, and I don't know if I'm going to be an uncle or an aunt.   ~ CHUCK NEVITT

We were the quintessence of athletic atrocity.   ~ MIKE NEWLIN

—Reporter: How do you pronounce your name?
—Tom Nissalke: Tom.

If he was on fire, he couldn't act as if he were burning.

~ SHAQUILLE O'NEAL ON DENNIS RODMAN'S ACTING SKILLS

I'm tired of hearing about money, money, money, money, money. I just want to play the game, drink Pepsi, wear Reebok.   ~ SHAQUILLE O'NEAL

Did we go to the Parthenon on our visit to Greece? I can't really remember the names of the clubs that we went to.   ~ SHAQUILLE O'NEAL

I've won at every level, except college and pro.   ~ SHAQUILLE O'NEAL

Drug tests? I'm in favour of them, as long as they're multiple choice.
               ~ KURT RAMBIS

Fans never fall asleep at our games, because they're afraid they might get hit by a pass.   ~ GEORGE RAVELING

I know the Virginia players are smart because you need a 1,500 SAT score to get in. I have to drop breadcrumbs to get our players to and from classes.
               ~ GEORGE RAVELING

They've had so many injuries, they get to park their team bus in the handicapped zone.   ~ GEORGE RAVELING

What does the Orlando Magic PA announcer say at half-time to get the crowd going? 'Please drive carefully.'   ~ ALAN RAY, AFTER A 19-GAME LOSING RUN

Billy Tubbs is what's known as a contact coach – all con and no tact.
               ~ BOB REINHARDT

If God had an agent, the world wouldn't be built yet. It'd only be about Thursday.   ~ JERRY REYNOLDS

It's always fun to be around a white park knowing you're going to get picked to play basketball. It's like you're the Loch Ness Monster. 'We've heard you existed, but we never thought we'd see you.'   ~ CHRIS ROCK

I've got to stop this. My entourages are getting entourages.   ~ JALEN ROSE

I love exercise. I could watch it all day.   ~ BILL RUSSELL

If cocaine were helium, the NBA would float away.   ~ ART RUST

Left hand, right hand, it doesn't matter. I'm amphibious.   ~ CHARLES SHACKLEFORD

In my prime I could have handled Michael Jordan. Of course, he would be only 12 years old.   ~ JERRY SLOAN

Quit fouling like a wimp. If you're gonna foul, knock the crap outta him.   ~ NORM STEWART

We're shooting 100 per cent – 60 per cent from the field and 40 per cent from the free-throw line!   ~ NORM STEWART

Ball handling and dribbling are my strongest weaknesses.   ~ DAVID THOMPSON

I'm an optometrist – I always believe in good stuff.   ~ MYCHAL THOMPSON

I asked a referee if he would give me a technical foul for thinking bad things about him. He said, 'Of course not.' I said, 'Well, I think you stink.' And he gave me a technical. You can't trust 'em.   ~ JIM VALVANO

This is the second most exciting indoor sport, and the other one shouldn't have spectators.   ~ DICK VERTLEIB

George McGinnis has got the body of a Greek god and the running ability of a Greek goddess.   ~ DICK VITALE

It's a muscle pull, pull in the oblique. That's a muscle on your side. Or, for you reporters, about where your third spare tyre would be.   ~ JAYSON WILLIAMS

We can't win at home and we can't win on the road. My problem as general manager is I can't think of another place to play. ~ PAT WILLIAMS

We were so bad last year, the cheerleaders stayed home and phoned in their cheers. ~ PAT WILLIAMS

Shaquille O'Neal's house is in such a great neighbourhood, the bird feeders have salad bars and the Salvation Army band has a string section. ~ PAT WILLIAMS

Crime is down in Miami. They ran out of victims. ~ PAT WILLIAMS

NBA commissioner David Stern bought another yacht. The other one got wet. ~ PAT WILLIAMS

Charles Barkley was so fat, he fell down and rocked himself to sleep trying to get up. ~ PAT WILLIAMS

We got Stanley Roberts eating the seven basic food groups, and now there are only three left. ~ PAT WILLIAMS

You know the old saying 'no man is an island'? Well, Stanley [Roberts] comes close.
~ PAT WILLIAMS

What do you have when you've got an agent buried up to his neck in sand? Not enough sand. ~ PAT WILLIAMS

When I left, I said I'd like to give Harold [Katz] something to commemorate our five years together. But I never could figure out how to get an ulcer framed. ~ PAT WILLIAMS

Manute Bol is so skinny, his pyjamas have only one pinstripe. ~ PAT WILLIAMS

When the list of great coaches is finally read out, I believe Frank Layden will be there … listening.
~ PAT WILLIAMS

I have a God-given talent. I got it from my dad.
~ JULIAN WINFIELD

Are you any relation to your brother Marv? ~ LEON WOOD TO ANNOUNCER STEVE ALBERT

Volleyball

The only thing missing from their 'uniforms' were the garter belts stuffed with dollar bills.
~ MIKE BIANCHI ON THE WOMEN'S OLYMPIC BEACH VOLLEYBALL OUTFITS

It would increase our attendance with just the Secret Service alone.
~ COACH DON SHAW ON NEWS THAT CHELSEA CLINTON MIGHT JOIN THE STANFORD WOMEN'S TEAM

Twenty-two people on the beach who quit playing when the hamburgers are ready.
~ STEVE TIMMONS

PLAYING
THE GREEN

Bowls

I'm not an athlete, more a gymnast and golfer, soldered together.   ~ DAVID BRYANT

Bowls are built with a bias, and so for that matter are many of the players.

~ HERBERT COLLINGS

He's got no weaknesses. That's one of the strengths of Greg [Harlowe].

~ DAVID GOURLAY

Greg Harlowe has covered himself at the rear in case Jenkins gets too excited.

~ DAVID GOURLAY

If I'm going to lie on my back for an hour, I expect to be enjoying myself.

~ MARGARET JOHNSTON PROTESTS AT THE INTRODUCTION OF RELAXATION THERAPY IN BOWLS

—David Vine: What's he going to do with this, do you think?
—David Rhys-Jones: Well, he's got to be thinking that he's got to do something with this.

Strut must be happy to see that ball struggle on and die as short as a carrot.

~ HARRY RIGBY

Croquet

The clunk of the ball against mallet is a lovely sound, just like ice cubes in a gin and tonic. ~ *SUNDAY TIMES*

My doctor forbids me to play, unless I win. ~ ALEXANDER WOOLLCOTT

Golf

It took me 17 years to get 3,000 hits in baseball. I did it in one afternoon on the golf course.

~ HANK AARON

I had a wonderful experience on the golf course today. I had a hole in nothing. Missed the ball and sank the divot.

~ DON ADAMS

Most people play a fair game of golf – if you watch them.

~ JOEY ADAMS

If you break 100, watch your golf. If you break 80, watch your business.

~ JOEY ADAMS

Sorry, I don't know much about you. I don't follow tennis.

~ SINGER CHRISTINA AGUILERA TO TIGER WOODS

I'm the best. I just haven't played yet.

~ MUHAMMAD ALI, ASKED ABOUT HIS GOLF GAME

The fun you get from golf is in direct ratio to the effort you don't put in.

~ BOB ALLEN

He had the most incredible misdemeanour.

~ FULTON ALLEN PRAISING THE COMPOSURE OF 19-YEAR-OLD
AMATEUR MATT KUCHAR AT THE 1998 US MASTERS

Playing golf is like going to a strip joint. After 18 holes you're tired and most of your balls are missing.

~ TIM ALLEN

I can't see, unless the weather changes, the conditions changing dramatically.

~ PETER ALLISS

As the cock crows, it's only about 200 yards.

~ PETER ALLISS

And now to hole eight, which is in fact the eighth hole.

~ PETER ALLISS

Although it's a narrow green, it's a wide green. ~ PETER ALLISS

He's got to go in for a hernia operation, but when he gets over that he'll be back in harness again. ~ PETER ALLISS

You couldn't really find two more completely different personalities than these two men, Tom Watson and Brian Barnes; one the complete golf professional and the other the complete professional golfer. ~ PETER ALLISS

Wentworth Golf Course is in remarkable condition, after the wettest drought in history.

~ PETER ALLISS, MOCKING THE HOSE BAN IMPOSED ON
SOUTH-EAST ENGLAND DURING THE SUMMER OF 2006

One good thing about rain in Scotland – most of it ends up as scotch. ~ PETER ALLISS

In technical terms, he's making a real pig's ear of this hole. ~ PETER ALLISS

He hasn't got any good points to his swing that a bit of tuition couldn't ruin. ~ PETER ALLISS ON AMATEUR RICKY BARNES

What a lot of fuss about a little thing like that! ~ PETER ALLISS, AS A STREAKER RUNS ACROSS THE GREEN

The game of golf is an enigma wrapped in a mystery impaled on a conundrum. ~ PETER ALLISS

It's like turning up to hear Pavarotti sing and finding out he has laryngitis. ~ PETER ALLISS AFTER TIGER WOODS SHOOTS AN 81 AT THE 2002 OPEN

It's a funny old game. One day you're a statue, the next you're a pigeon. ~ PETER ALLISS AFTER TIGER WOODS LOSES IN THE FIRST ROUND OF THE 2006 WORLD MATCH PLAY

—Peter Alliss: What do you think of the climax of this tournament?
—Peter Thomson: I'm speechless.
—Peter Alliss: That says it all.

Playing with your spouse on the golf course runs almost as great a marital risk as getting caught playing with someone else's anywhere else. ~ PETER ANDREWS

An interesting thing about golf is that no matter how badly you play, it is always possible to get worse. ~ ANON

Only Hitler has spent more time in a bunker. ~ ANON

A caddie is someone who accompanies a golfer and didn't see the ball either. ~ ANON

When I die, bury me on the golf course so my husband will visit. ~ ANON

Golf is a game invented by the same people who think music comes out of a bagpipe. ~ ANON

Golfers always carry a spare sock in case they get a hole in one. ~ ANON

When golf starts getting in the way of work and family, give up work and family. ~ ANON

If it goes right, it's a slice; if it goes left, it's a hook; if it goes straight, it's a miracle. ~ ANON

Is my friend in the bunker or is the bastard on the green? ~ ANON

In primitive society, when native tribes beat the ground and yelled, it was called witchcraft; today, in civilised society, it is called golf. ~ ANON

Golf is a lot of walking, broken up by disappointment and bad arithmetic.

~ ANON

Golfer's diet: live on greens as much as possible.

~ ANON

Advice to golfers: hit the ball hard and straight and not too often.

~ ANON

Arnie Palmer, usually a great putter, seems to be having trouble with his long putts. However, he has no trouble dropping his shorts.

~ ANON

My knee's only a few months old, my back is only 17, and I recently got a new hip. I might be too young now.

~ GEORGE ARCHER, WORRIED THAT HIS REPLACED BODY
PARTS MIGHT MAKE HIM INELIGIBLE FOR THE SENIOR TOUR

Golf is an awkward set of bodily contortions designed to produce a graceful result.

~ TOMMY ARMOUR

Love and putting are mysteries for the philosopher to solve. Both subjects are beyond golfers.

~ TOMMY ARMOUR

I don't enjoy playing video golf because there is nothing to throw. ~ PAUL AZINGER

He [Tiger Woods] could be the first player to win the Masters who doesn't shave.

~ PAUL AZINGER, 1997

There was never much said on the course when I played with Nick [Faldo]. I probably knew him 20 years before I heard him complete a sentence.

~ PAUL AZINGER

A professional will tell you the amount of flex you need in the shaft of your club. The more the flex, the more strength you will need to break the thing over your knees.

~ STEPHEN BAKER

If you don't succeed at first, don't despair. Remember, it takes time to learn to play golf; most players spend their entire lifetime finding out about the game before they give up.
~ STEPHEN BAKER

John Daly's driving is unbelievable. I don't go that far on my holidays.
~ IAN BAKER-FINCH

I wish my name was Tom Kite.
~ IAN BAKER-FINCH SIGNING DOZENS OF AUTOGRAPHS

Everything was fine until I walked on to the first tee.
~ SEVE BALLESTEROS

I'd like to see the fairways more narrow. Then everybody would have to play from the rough, not just me.
~ SEVE BALLESTEROS

Vijay Singh apologised for saying he hopes Annika Sorenstam misses the cut at the 2003 Colonial. He even said he would love one day to personally help her into the traditional green apron.
~ JIM BARACH

I need two sherpas – one to carry my clubs, the other to carry me.
~ BRIAN BARNES BEFORE THE 1991 GERMAN OPEN ON THE HILLY DUSSELDORF COURSE

Few pleasures on earth match the feeling that comes from making a loud bodily function noise just as a guy is about to putt.
~ DAVE BARRY

Although golf was originally restricted to wealthy, overweight Protestants, today it's open to anybody who owns hideous clothing.
~ DAVE BARRY

'Play it as it lies' is one of the fundamental dictates of golf. The other is 'Wear it if it clashes.'
~ HENRY BEARD

A ball will always come to rest halfway down a hill, unless there is sand or water at the bottom.
~ HENRY BEARD

It is as easy to lower your handicap as it is to reduce your hat size.

~ HENRY BEARD, *MULLIGAN'S LAW*

Never try to keep more than 300 separate thoughts in your mind during your swing.

~ HENRY BEARD, *MULLIGAN'S LAW*

Fairway: a narrow strip of mown grass that separates two groups of golfers looking for lost balls in the rough.

~ HENRY BEARD AND ROY MCKIE, *GOLFING: A DUFFER'S DICTIONARY*

Follow-through: the part of the swing that takes place after the ball has been hit, but before the club has been thrown.

~ HENRY BEARD AND ROY MCKIE, *GOLFING: A DUFFER'S DICTIONARY*

Practice tee: the place where golfers go to convert a nasty hook into a wicked slice.

~ HENRY BEARD AND ROY MCKIE, *GOLFING: A DUFFER'S DICTIONARY*

If you pick up a golfer and hold it close to your ear, like a conch shell, and listen… You will hear an alibi.

~ FRED BECK

Man blames fate for other accidents, but feels personally responsible when he makes a hole in one.

~ MARTHA BECKMAN

If the following foursome is pressing you, wave them through and then speed up.

~ DEANE BEMAN

Give me my golf clubs, fresh air and a beautiful partner, and you can keep my golf clubs and the fresh air.

~ JACK BENNY

You got a new driver for your wife? Great trade!

~ PATTY BERG

Ninety per cent of putts that are short don't go in.

~ YOGI BERRA

I have a golf handicap of 27 but have often been mistaken for a 28.

~ BOB 'THE CAT' BEVAN

You're not going to believe this, but a golf ball just landed on my laptop. David Duval must be on the practice range again.

~ MIKE BIANCHI

Golf is played by 20 million mature American men whose wives think they are out having fun.

~ JIM BISHOP

Gimme: an agreement between two losers who can't putt.

~ JIM BISHOP

The way I putted today, I must have been reading the greens in Spanish and putting them in English.

~ HOMERO BLANCAS

—Reporter: Did you have any uphill putts?
—Homero Blancas: Yeah, after each of my downhill putts.

Have you ever noticed what golf spells backwards?

~ AL BOLISKA

Always throw your clubs ahead of you. That way you don't have to waste energy going back to pick them up.

~ TOMMY BOLT

Never break your putter and your driver in the same round, or you're dead.

~ TOMMY BOLT

Golf is a game where guts and blind devotion will always net you absolutely nothing but an ulcer.

~ TOMMY BOLT

Putting allows the touchy golfer two to four opportunities to blow a gasket in the short space of two to 40 feet.

~ TOMMY BOLT

Retire to what? I'm a golfer and a fisherman. I've got no place to retire to.

~ JULIUS BOROS

I don't like watching golf on TV. I can't stand whispering.   ~ DAVID BRENNER

I was three over — one over a house, one over a patio and one over a swimming pool.

~ GEORGE BRETT

Thomas Bjorn gets more wrist action than anyone in Europe.   ~ KEN BROWN

Some weeks Nick likes to use Fanny; other weeks he prefers to do it by himself.

~ KEN BROWN ON THE WORKING RELATIONSHIP BETWEEN
NICK FALDO AND HIS CADDIE, FANNY SUNNESON

And Vijay Singh lampoons another one down the fairway.   ~ KEN BROWN

You know you're on the Senior Tour when your back goes out more than you do.   ~ BOB BRUCE

What's nice about the Senior Tour is you can't remember your bad shots.

~ BOB BRUCE

My back swing off the first tee had put him in mind of an elderly woman of dubious morals trying to struggle out of a dress too tight around the shoulders.

~ PATRICK CAMPBELL

Golf is the only game in the world in which a precise knowledge of the rules can win a reputation for bad sportsmanship.   ~ PATRICK CAMPBELL

Everyone is studying golf technique like mad. Every young lad now aspires to be another Palmer or Nicklaus. We may go centuries before we produce another playwright.   ~ JOE CARR

Like a lot of fellows on the Senior Tour, I have a furniture problem. My chest has fallen into my drawers.
~ BILLY CASPER

Who watches golf on TV? Who calls eight friends over and gets a keg of beer? Landscapers, I guess. They sit around the TV, yelling: 'Will you look at that golf path? Pure pea gravel.'
~ JEFF CESARIO

Being left-handed is a big advantage. No one knows enough about your swing to mess you up with advice.
~ BOB CHARLES

I regard golf as an expensive way of playing marbles.
~ G.K. CHESTERTON

Golf is a game whose aim is to hit a very small ball into an even smaller hole, with weapons singularly ill designed for the purpose.
~ WINSTON CHURCHILL

Playing golf is like chasing a quinine pill around a cow pasture.
~ WINSTON CHURCHILL

Difficult couple of holes here: 15, 16, and 17.
~ HOWARD CLARK

Guinness ability – that's why they picked me for the team. There was no other reason whatsoever.
~ DARREN CLARKE CELEBRATING EUROPE'S 2006 RYDER CUP WIN

On one hole I'm like Arnold Palmer, and on the next I'm like Lilli Palmer.
~ SEAN CONNERY

When male golfers wriggle their feet to get their stance right, they look exactly like cats preparing to pee.
~ JILLY COOPER

I used to play golf with a man who cheated so badly that he once had a hole in one and wrote down zero on his scorecard.
~ RONNIE CORBETT

If God had wanted man to play golf, He would have given him an elbowless left arm, short asymmetrical legs with side-hinged knees, and a trapezoid rib cage from which diagonally jutted a two-foot neck topped by a three-eyed head.

~ ALAN COREN

I didn't hit the ball like I was 46. But I putted like I was 66.   ~ FRED COUPLES

Have I ever played in Asia? I've played in Japan. Is that anywhere near Asia?

~ FRED COUPLES

My golf game's gone off so much that when I went fishing a couple of weeks ago my first cast missed the lake.   ~ BEN CRENSHAW

I'm about five inches from being an outstanding golfer. That's the distance my left ear is from my right.   ~ BEN CRENSHAW

You don't need a roadmap for this one, you need a passport.

~ JAY CRONLEY ON A 614-YARD HOLE AT SOUTHERN HILLS, TULSA

Was I intimidated by Tiger Woods? A little bit. He's got this aroma about him.

~ BEN CURTIS

Golf is like a love affair: if you don't take it seriously, it's no fun; if you do take it seriously, it breaks your heart.   ~ ARNOLD DALY

They don't let you smoke or drink in gyms so you know I'm not going to have any fun doing that.

~ JOHN DALY, DENYING A NEW FITNESS PUSH

Woosie and I are talking about marriage. He says it's the longest relationship he's ever had.   ~ JOHN DALY, AFTER PLAYING ALL FOUR ROUNDS OF THE MASTERS WITH IAN WOOSNAM

I think I'd rather go to the dentist than play a practice round.   ~ LAURA DAVIES

The trouble is I hit my putts as long as my drives.

~ LAURA DAVIES ON HER REPUTATION AS A BIG DRIVER

Golf is based on honesty. Where else would you admit to a seven on a par three?

~ JIMMY DEMARET

Golf and sex are the only things you can enjoy without being good at it.

~ JIMMY DEMARET

You know what they say about big hitters ... the woods are full of them.

~ JIMMY DEMARET

Bob Hope has a beautiful short game. Unfortunately it's off the tee.

~ JIMMY DEMARET

The only emotion Ben [Hogan] shows in defeat is surprise.   ~ JIMMY DEMARET

Some players would complain if they had to play on Dolly Parton's bedspread.

~ JIMMY DEMARET

I can airmail the golf ball but sometimes I don't put the right address on it.

~ BIG-HITTER JIM DENT

The difference in golf and government is that in golf you can't improve your lie.

~ GEORGE DEUKMEJIAN

The reason the pro tells you to keep your head down is so you can't see him laughing.   ~ PHYLLIS DILLER

Water creates a neurosis in golfers. The very thought of this harmless fluid robs them of their normal powers of rational thought, turns their legs to jelly, and produces a palsy of the upper limbs.   ~ PETER DOBEREINER

Half of golf is fun; the other half is putting. ~ PETER DOBEREINER

These days I'm a columnist, a technical term meaning a writer who hides in the mountains during the heat of battle and then comes down to bayonet the wounded. ~ PETER DOBEREINER

Golf is like an 18-year-old girl with big boobs. You know it's wrong but you can't keep away from her. ~ VAL DOONICAN

The ardent golfer would play Mount Everest if somebody would put a flagstick on top. ~ PETE DYE

How has retirement affected my golf game? A lot more people beat me now. ~ DWIGHT D. EISENHOWER

From 1 to 10 in difficulty, it's an 11. ~ ERNIE ELS ON THE SHINNECOCK COURSE IN THE US

I'm into golf now. I'm getting pretty good. I can almost hit the ball as far as I can throw the clubs. ~ BOB ETTINGER

He may be a great golfer, but socially he's a 24-handicapper. ~ GILL FALDO ON EX-HUSBAND NICK

When the wind blows at St Andrews, even the seagulls walk. ~ NICK FALDO

If you can imagine a hole halfway down the bonnet of a Volkswagen Beetle – and then you have to putt it from the roof. ~ NICK FALDO AT ROYAL MELBOURNE

Fred Couples is so hot he must be wearing asbestos shorts. ~ NICK FALDO

John Daly certainly gives it a good hit, doesn't he? My Sunday best is Wednesday afternoon compared to him. ~ NICK FALDO

I would like to thank the Press from the heart of my bottom. ~ NICK FALDO

Can I just give this team a bit of deodorant, a quick clean, a fresh shirt and take them over to America with me now?

~ NICK FALDO, EUROPE'S INCOMING RYDER CUP CAPTAIN, SPEAKING AFTER THE 2006 TRIUMPH ABOUT HIS PLANS FOR 2008

Justin Leonard's the most organised individual in the world. He probably vacuums in straight lines. ~ BRAD FAXON

Colin Montgomerie has a face like a warthog that has been stung by a wasp.

~ DAVID FEHERTY

Colin Montgomerie is a few French fries short of a Happy Meal. ~ DAVID FEHERTY

John Daly has the worst haircut I've ever seen in my life. It looks like he has a divot over each ear. ~ DAVID FEHERTY

The only time Nick Faldo opens his mouth is to change feet. ~ DAVID FEHERTY

I don't know him but I've seen him smile, and that's quite enough to put me off wanting to know anything about him. ~ DAVID FEHERTY ON PHIL MICKELSON

Jim Furyk has a swing like a man trying to kill a snake in a phone booth.

~ DAVID FEHERTY

I was swinging like a toilet door on a prawn trawler. ~ DAVID FEHERTY

I play the game because my sole ambition is to do well enough to give it up.

~ DAVID FEHERTY

I really don't enjoy playing this game at all any more. You would have to be a pervert to enjoy the sort of feelings that I went through out there.

~ DAVID FEHERTY

I keep thinking that I might go out and play like Jack Nicklaus, but instead it's more like Jacques Tati. ~ DAVID FEHERTY

John Daly's divots go further than my drives. ~ DAVID FEHERTY

The Crooked Stick course is so long that figuring distances on some holes, you have to reckon in the curvature of the earth. ~ DAVID FEHERTY

Playing Augusta is like playing a Salvador Dali landscape. I expected a clock to fall out of the trees and hit me in the face. ~ DAVID FEHERTY

It's not like something from Ireland or Scotland; it's like something from Mars.

~ DAVID FEHERTY ON THE KIAWAH ISLAND COURSE

I considered beating the living daylights out of it but it's probably got a wife and snakelets to look after.

~ DAVID FEHERTY AFTER BEING BITTEN BY AN ADDER DURING A TOURNAMENT

It's hard to tell who's going to win this week, but it probably won't be a big, fat guy.

~ DAVID FEHERTY ON THE HEAT AND HUMIDITY AT THE 2001 US PGA CHAMPIONSHIP

You know why I like talking to corporate America? It looks good on a parole application. ~ DAVID FEHERTY

If I were allowed to rewrite the Rules of Golf, I would insert a new rule: 'You are allowed to tackle your opponent.' ~ DAVID FEHERTY

They are the same people who knock the Pyramids because they don't have elevators. ~ JIM FERREE ON GOLFERS WHO MOAN ABOUT ST ANDREWS

They call it golf because all the other four-letter words were taken.
~ RAYMOND FLOYD

I went to bed and I was old and washed up. I woke up a rookie. What could be better? ~ RAYMOND FLOYD, ON TURNING 50 AND QUALIFYING FOR THE SENIOR TOUR

I know I'm getting better at golf because I'm hitting fewer spectators.
~ GERALD FORD

I would like to deny all allegations by Bob Hope that during my last game of golf, I hit an eagle, a birdie, an elk and a moose. ~ GERALD FORD

A woman I know is engaged to a real golf nut. They are supposed to get married next Saturday ... but only if it rains. ·· BRUCE FORSYTH

My luck is so bad that if I bought a cemetery, people would stop dying.
~ ED FURGOL

I won't try to describe his game, beyond saying the way he played, it would have taken three years of solid practice to work up to where he could be called a duffer. ~ PAUL GALLICO

It would have been a great week if we could have turned the scoreboard upside-down. ~ SERGIO GARCIA AFTER FINISHING SECOND FROM BOTTOM IN THE 2006 MASTERS

Augusta is the closest thing to heaven for a golfer – and it's just about as hard to get into. ~ JOE GESHWILER

Obviously a deer on the fairway has seen you tee off before and knows that the safest place to be when you play is right down the middle. ~ JACKIE GLEASON

I played crap, he played crap. He just out-crapped me.
~ WAYNE GRADY AFTER LOSING TO GREG NORMAN IN THE WORLD MATCHPLAY CHAMPIONSHIP

The only time my prayers are never answered is on the golf course. ~ BILLY GRAHAM

I owe everything to golf. Where else could a guy with an IQ like mine make this much money? ~ HUBERT GREEN

—Interviewer: What was the difference between your first-round 81 and your second-round 67?
—Hubert Green: Fourteen strokes.

A coarse golfer is one who has to shout 'fore' when he putts.
~ MICHAEL GREEN, THE ART OF COARSE GOLF

The number of shots taken by an opponent who is out of sight is equal to the square root of the sum of the number of curses heard plus the number of swishes. ~ MICHAEL GREEN, THE ART OF COARSE GOLF

The interesting thing about a coarse golfer's language is that to listen to him one would think that his bad shots came as a surprise.
~ MICHAEL GREEN, THE ART OF COARSE GOLF

The secret of missing a tree is to aim straight at it. ~ MICHAEL GREEN, THE ART OF COARSE GOLF

Golf balls are attracted to water as unerringly as the eye of a middle-aged man to a female bosom. ~ MICHAEL GREEN, THE ART OF COARSE GOLF

Golfers are dull robots carrying sticks. They don't even spit or scratch their privates like other athletes. ~ LEWIS GRIZZARD

By the time a man can afford to lose a golf ball, he can't hit it that far.
~ LEWIS GRIZZARD

I've had a good day when I don't fall out of the cart. ~ BUDDY HACKETT

Golf is more fun than walking naked in a strange place, but not much.

~ BUDDY HACKETT

I had a hangover for two days – and I only drank about half of what Darren Clarke and Lee Westwood knocked back.

~ PADRAIG HARRINGTON AFTER EUROPE'S 2004 RYDER CUP VICTORY

When you start driving your ball down the middle, you meet a different class of people. ~ PHIL HARRIS

Golf is a game in which you yell 'fore', shoot six, and write down five.

~ PAUL HARVEY

I played golf. I did not get a hole in one, but I did hit a guy. That's way more satisfying. ~ MITCH HEDBERG

Wee Woosie [Ian Woosnam] is a chatterbox. He makes Lee Trevino look like Marcel Marceau. ~ STEVE HERSHEY

The golf swing is like sex. You can't be thinking about the mechanics of the act while you are performing. ~ DAVE HILL

My game is so bad I gotta have three caddies – one to walk the left rough, one for the right rough, and one down the middle. And the one in the middle doesn't have to do much. ~ DAVE HILL

Some guys get so nervous playing for their own money, the greens don't need fertilising for a year. ~ DAVE HILL

Golf is the hardest game in the world to play, and the easiest to cheat at.

~ DAVE HILL

If God had intended a round of golf to take more than three hours, He would not have invented Sunday lunch.　　　　　　　　　　~ JIMMY HILL

I've got a good mind to jump in and make it four!

~ SIMON HOBDAY, AFTER HITTING TWO BALLS INTO THE WATER

The last year's Masters champion serves as the host. He chooses the menu and picks up the tab. When I discovered that the cost of the dinner was more than the prize money, I finished second four times.　　　　~ BEN HOGAN

If you watch a game, it's fun. If you play it, it's recreation. If you work at it, it's golf.　　　　　　　　　　　　　　　　　　~ BOB HOPE

I play golf every chance I get. The world needs more laughter.　~ BOB HOPE

I like to play in the low 70s. If it gets any hotter than that, I'll stay in the bar.

~ BOB HOPE

At one stage I gave up golf and took up ten-pin bowling. At least I didn't lose so many balls.　　　　　　　　　　　　　　　　　~ BOB HOPE

Some of these legends have been around golf a long time. When they mention a good grip, they're talking about their dentures.　　　　~ BOB HOPE

Arnold Palmer is the biggest crowd-pleaser since the invention of the portable sanitary facility.　　　　　　　　　　　　　　　　~ BOB HOPE

Sammy Davis Jr hits the ball 130 yards and his jewellery goes 150.　~ BOB HOPE

Gerald Ford is the most dangerous driver since Ben Hur.　　　~ BOB HOPE

There are over 150 golf courses in the Palm Springs area and Gerry Ford is never sure which one he's going to play until his second shot.　　~ BOB HOPE

Whenever I play golf with Gerry Ford, I usually try to make it a foursome –
Ford, me, a paramedic, and a faith healer.   ~ BOB HOPE

At least Gerry Ford can't cheat on his score, because all you have to do is look
back down the fairway and count the wounded.   ~ BOB HOPE

Alan Shepard walking on the moon found a golf ball with Gerald Ford's initials
on it.   ~ BOB HOPE

It's fun to run down the fairway and have the trees run with you.
                    ~ BOB HOPE ON PLAYING WITH PRESIDENT FORD AND HIS SECURITY GUARDS

I never kick my ball in the rough or improve my lie in a sand trap. For that I
have a caddie.   ~ BOB HOPE

If I'm on the course and lightning starts, I get inside fast. If God wants to play
through, let him.   ~ BOB HOPE

If golf is relaxing, you're not playing it right.   ~ BOB HOPE

Take nine strokes off your score. Skip the last hole.   ~ BOB HOPE

I'd give up golf if I didn't have so many sweaters.   ~ BOB HOPE

It was a great honour to be inducted into the Golf Hall of Fame. I didn't know
they had a caddie division.   ~ BOB HOPE

I'll shoot my age if I have to live to be 105.   ~ BOB HOPE

That putt was so good, I could feel the baby applaud.
                                     ~ A SEVEN MONTHS PREGNANT DONNA HORTON-WHITE

Real golfers don't cry when they line up their fourth putt. ~ KAREN HURWITZ

Golf is a game to be played between cricket and death. ~ COLIN INGLEBY-MACKENZIE

When a pro hits it left to right, it's called a fade. When an amateur hits it left to right, it's called a slice. ~ PETER JACOBSEN

My most common mistake at St Andrews is turning up. ~ MARK JAMES

I couldn't live anywhere other than Britain, but I'd quite like it parked off the coast of Australia. ~ MARK JAMES

I'll take a two-shot penalty, but I'll be damned if I'm going to play the ball where it lies. ~ ELAINE JOHNSON AFTER HER SHOT REBOUNDED FROM A TREE AND INTO HER BRA

I was like a lobotomised baboon. In fact, a blind lobotomised baboon. ~ TONY JOHNSTONE ON A POOR PERFORMANCE

Dividing a golf swing into its parts is like dissecting a cat. You'll have blood and guts and bones all over the place. But you won't have a cat. ~ ERNEST JONES

My best score is 103, but I've only been playing for 15 years. ~ ALEX KARRAS

A playing partner called one of my drives a Rock Hudson ('looks straight but turns out to be anything but'). ~ DES KELLY, *DAILY MAIL*

A drive that scuttles along the ground off the tee is a Sally Gunnell – 'ugly but a good runner'. ~ DES KELLY

A tricky short putt is a Dennis Wise – 'a nasty five-footer'. ~ DES KELLY

A lucky bounce is an O.J. Simpson – 'got away with it somehow'. ~ DES KELLY

I made that putt. It just didn't go in. ~ TOM KITE

Find a man with both feet firmly on the ground and you've found a man about to make a difficult putt.

~ FLETCHER KNEBEL

He certainly didn't appear as cool as he looked.

~ RENTON LAIDLAW

This is the 12th, the green is like a plateau with the top shaved off.

~ RENTON LAIDLAW

Azinger is wearing an all black outfit: black jumper, blue trousers, white shoes and a pink 'tea cosy' hat.

~ RENTON LAIDLAW

Talking to a golf ball won't do you any good. Unless you do it while your opponent is teeing off.

~ BRUCE LANSKY

I'll always remember the day I broke 90. I had a few beers in the clubhouse and was so excited I forgot to play the back nine.

~ BRUCE LANSKY

My psychiatrist prescribed a game of golf as an antidote to the feelings of euphoria I experience from time to time.

~ BRUCE LANSKY

I don't think I'll live long enough to shoot my age. I'm lucky to shoot my weight!

~ BRUCE LANSKY

Never putt until the cup stops moving.

~ BRUCE LANSKY

On a recent survey, 80 per cent of golfers admitted cheating. The other 20 per cent lied.

~ BRUCE LANSKY

The main problem with keeping your eye on the ball is you have to take your eye off your opponent.

~ BRUCE LANSKY

Alaska would be an ideal place for a golf course – mighty few trees and damn few ladies' foursomes.

~ REX LARDNER

Golf may be played on Sunday, not being a game within view of the law, but being a form of moral effort.   ~ STEPHEN LEACOCK

I'm third in earnings, and first in spending.   ~ TONY LEMA

If you think it's difficult to meet new people, try picking up the wrong golf ball.   ~ JACK LEMMON

Learning to play golf is like learning to play the violin. It's not only difficult to do, it's very painful to everyone around you.   ~ HAL LINDEN

All I've got against golf is that it takes you so far from the clubhouse.
                                                               ~ ERIC LINKLATER

You drive for show, but putt for dough.   ~ BOBBY LOCKE

They say practice makes perfect. Of course it doesn't. For the vast majority of golfers it merely consolidates imperfection.   ~ HENRY LONGHURST

It's like learning to play golf. Just when you think you've cracked it, they move the goalposts.   ~ ADRIAN LOVE

What's the penalty for killing a photographer – one stroke or two? ~ DAVIS LOVE III

What do I think of Tiger Woods? I don't know. I've never played there.
                                                             ~ SANDY LYLE, 1992

What do I have to shoot to win this tournament? The rest of the field.
                                                             ~ ROGER MALTBIE

That son of a bitch was able to hole a putt over 60 feet of peanut brittle.
                                                ~ LLOYD MANGRUM ON BOBBY LOCKE

Fifty years ago, 40 white men chasing a black man was the Ku Klux Klan. Now it's the US Open golf championship. ~ BERNARD MANNING

The only sure rule in golf is, he who has the fastest cart never has to play the bad lie. ~ MICKEY MANTLE

Never bet with anyone you meet on the first tee, who has a deep suntan, a one-iron in his bag and squinty eyes. ~ DAVE MARR

Doug Sanders' outfit has been described as looking like the aftermath of a direct hit on a pizza factory. ~ DAVE MARR

Golf's three ugliest words: still your shot. ~ DAVE MARR

If you drink, don't drive. Don't even putt. ~ DEAN MARTIN

No game designed to be played with the aid of personal servants by right-handed men who can't even bring along their dogs can be entirely good for the soul. ~ BRUCE McCALL

These greens are so fast they must bikini wax them. ~ GARY McCORD ON AUGUSTA

My playing career started slowly and then tapered off. ~ GARY McCORD

People have been asking me what the Irish – in one word – will bring to the Ryder Cup. Alcohol. ~ PAUL McGINLEY

Now, here's Jack Lemmon, about to play an all-important eighth shot. ~ JIM McKAY

His future is ahead of him.
~ STEVE MELNYK ON PHIL MICKELSON

If I had my way, any man guilty of golf would be ineligible for any office of trust in the United States. ~ H.L. MENCKEN

I have come to understand and appreciate writers much more recently since I started working on a book last fall. Before that, I thought golf writers got up every morning, played a round of golf, had lunch, showed up for our last three holes and then went to dinner.

~ PHIL MICKELSON

I played so bad I got a get-well card from the IRS.

~ JOHNNY MILLER

When [Jack] Nicklaus plays well he wins, when he plays badly he comes second. When he's playing terribly, he's third.

~ JOHNNY MILLER

You start your soft-boiled eggs by the time he's ready.

~ JOHNNY MILLER ON NICK FALDO'S SLOW PUTTING

This is a fun guy. He's like a David Feherty who can play.

~ JOHNNY MILLER ON KENNETH FERRIE

Golf is so popular simply because it is the best game in the world at which to be bad.

~ A.A. MILNE

It's like eating an elephant. I can do it, but you have to do it bite by bite.

~ COLIN MONTGOMERIE ON SLOWLY CLIMBING THE WORLD RANKINGS

Corey Pavin is a little on the slight side. When he goes through a turnstile, nothing happens.

~ JIM MORIARTY

If your caddie coaches you on the tee, 'Hit it down the left side with a little draw,' ignore him. All you do on the tee is try not to hit the caddie.

~ JIM MURRAY

Show me a man who is a good loser and I'll show you a man who is playing golf with his boss.

~ JIM MURRAY

Pebble Beach Golf Club is a 300-acre unplayable lie.

~ JIM MURRAY

Walter Hagen once said that every golfer can expect to have four bad shots in a round and when you do, just put them out of your mind. This, of course, is hard to do when you're not even off the first tee when you've had them.

~ JIM MURRAY

The only time I ever took out a one-iron was to kill a tarantula – and I took seven to do that.

~ JIM MURRAY

Arnold Palmer attacked the game of golf like a cop busting a crap game.

~ JIM MURRAY

Anyone who would pass up an opportunity to see Sam Snead swing a golf club at a golf ball would pull down the shades when driving past the Taj Mahal.

~ JIM MURRAY

Hubert Green swings like a drunk trying to find a keyhole in the dark.

~ JIM MURRAY

John Daly hit a tee shot – and two tracking stations picked it up as a satellite!

~ JIM MURRAY

Corey Pavin plays the game as if he has a plane to catch; as if he were double parked and left the meter running. Guys move slower leaving hotel fires.

~ JIM MURRAY

Golf is the cruellest of sports. Like life, it's unfair. It's a harlot. A trollop. It leads you on. It never lives up to its promises. It's a boulevard of broken dreams. It plays with men. And runs off with the butcher.

~ JIM MURRAY

Nothing dissects a man in public quite like golf.

~ BRENT MUSBERGER

When [Bernhard] Langer practises on his own, he can hold up a fourball.

~ DAVE MUSGROVE

If you want to take long walks, take long walks. If you want to hit things with a stick, hit things with a stick. But there's no excuse for combining the two and putting the results on TV. Golf is not so much a sport as an insult to lawns.

~ *NATIONAL LAMPOON*

It's nice to look down the fairway and see your mother on the left and your father on the right. You know that no matter whether you hook it or slice it, somebody is going to be there to kick it back in the fairway.   ~ LARRY NELSON

Lost: golfing husband and dog – last seen at Ratliff Ranch Golf Links. Reward for dog.   ~ NEWSPAPER ADVERT

Nothing goes down slower than a golf handicap.   ~ BOBBY NICHOLS

I tee the ball high because through years of experience I have found that the air offers less resistance than dirt.   ~ JACK NICKLAUS

The older you get the stronger the wind gets – and it's always in your face.

~ JACK NICKLAUS

—Reporter: You really know your way around a course. What's your secret?
—Jack Nicklaus: The holes are numbered.

The game is an absolutely closed book to me and I would not even know which end to swing a caddie.   ~ DENIS NORDEN

I owe a lot to my parents, especially my mother and father.   ~ GREG NORMAN

We should be allowed to wear shorts. LPGA women are allowed to wear them and we've got better legs than them!   ~ GREG NORMAN

When I putt, my emotions collide like tectonic plates. It's left my memory circuits full of scars that won't heal.   ~ MAC O'GRADY

That round of golf was like a first date. She didn't care for me and I didn't like her. I tried to kiss her, but she slapped me. I was afraid to come back for a second date.

~ MAC O'GRADY, WITHDRAWING FROM A TOURNAMENT FOLLOWING A FIRST-ROUND 79

Golf is essentially an exercise in masochism conducted out of doors. ~ PAUL O'NEIL

Golf combines two favourite American pastimes: taking long walks and hitting things with a stick. ~ P.J. O'ROURKE

Golf is a lot like sex. You have to get it up and in. And that gets tougher and tougher to do every year. ~ BILLY ORVILLE

A player at my club is so slow he moves through a nine-hole course the way a meal moves through a python. ~ DAVID OWEN

I have a tip that can take five strokes off anyone's golf game. It's called an eraser. ~ ARNOLD PALMER

Can you imagine Jack [Nicklaus] getting beat by a guy smoking a pipe? ~ ARNOLD PALMER ON BRIAN BARNES AT THE 1975 RYDER CUP

You know you're getting older when all the names in your black book have M.D. after them. ~ ARNOLD PALMER

I'd rather watch a cabbage grow than a man worrying his guts over a two-foot putt. ~ MICHAEL PARKINSON

There are more golf books than sex manuals, surely the clearest indication that we have our priorities in the wrong order. ~ MICHAEL PARKINSON

It's really expensive. I don't know why. It tastes just like regular dirt. ~ JESPER PARNEVIK, EATING VOLCANIC DUST TO CLEANSE HIS SYSTEM

Make your backswing as though you are being paid by the hour. ~ HARVEY PENICK

Golf tips are like aspirin. One may do you good, but if you swallow the whole bottle you will be lucky to survive. ~ HARVEY PENICK

The worst club in my bag is my brain.

~ CHRIS PERRY

Headline writers, we hear, are flooding psychiatry hotlines after experiencing the same recurring nightmare, in which Mark Calcavecchia announces he is engaged to fellow golfer Virada Nirapathpongporn. And the sequels only get worse: they've decided to hyphenate. ~ DWIGHT PERRY

The way I play, I'd set the game back 100 yards.
~ AMERICAN FOOTBALL COACH BILL PETERSON, DECLINING AN OFFER TO PLAY GOLF

Real golfers, no matter what the provocation, never strike a caddie with a driver. The sand wedge is far more effective. ~ HUXTABLE PIPPEY

Golf is a marriage. If I had to choose between my wife and my putter, well, I'd miss her. ~ GARY PLAYER

It takes a lot of guts to play this game, and by looking at Billy Casper you can tell he certainly has a lot of guts. ~ GARY PLAYER ON THE CORPULENT CASPER

If he [Lee Trevino] didn't have an Adam's apple, he'd have no shape at all.
~ GARY PLAYER

If there's a golf course in heaven, I hope it's like Augusta National. I just don't want an early tee time. ~ GARY PLAYER

I retired from competition at 28, the same age as Bobby Jones. The difference was that Jones retired because he beat everybody; I retired because I couldn't beat anybody. ~ CHARLES PRICE

David Toms' putt is slightly straight. ~ RONAN RAFFERTY

Golf is a fascinating game. It has taken me nearly 40 years to discover that I can't play it. ~ TED RAY

The man who once ruled it as smoothly as Bob Charles is presently putting more like Ray Charles. ~ MARK REASON ON JOSE-MARIA OLAZABAL

The man has ruined more pictures than Sylvester Stallone.

~ RICK REILLY, AFTER TIGER WOODS' CADDIE, STEVE WILLIAMS,
GRABBED PHOTOGRAPHERS' CAMERAS AT THE US OPEN

Eighteen holes of match or medal play will teach you more about your foe than will 18 years of dealing with him across a desk. ~ GRANTLAND RICE

Ballesteros felt much better today after a 69. ~ STEVE RIDER

The par here at Sunningdale is 70 and anything under that will be a score in the 60s. ~ STEVE RIDER

This Walker Cup team is very laid back. In fact, we're so laid back, I doubt that any of us could lean forward. ~ DEAN ROBERTSON

My favourite shots are the practice swing and the conceded putt. The rest can never be mastered. ~ LORD ROBERTSON

You know it's gone to hell when the best rapper out there is a white guy and the best golfer is a black guy. ~ CHRIS ROCK

I think I'll go to Hertz and see if I can rent a game. ~ A STRUGGLING PHIL RODGERS

I don't fear death, but I sure do hate those three-footers for par.

~ CHI CHI RODRIGUEZ

For most amateurs, the best wood in the bag is the pencil.   ~ CHI CHI RODRIGUEZ

The first time I played the Masters, I was so nervous I drank a bottle of rum before I teed off. I shot the happiest 83 of my life.   ~ CHI CHI RODRIGUEZ

Golf is the most fun you can have without taking your clothes off.
~ CHI CHI RODRIGUEZ

A golf ball is like a clock. Always hit it at six o'clock and make it go toward twelve o'clock. But make sure you're in the same time zone.   ~ CHI CHI RODRIGUEZ

I'm playing like Tarzan, but scoring like Jane.   ~ CHI CHI RODRIGUEZ

The winds were blowing 50mph and gusting to 70. I hit a par three with my hat.
~ CHI CHI RODRIGUEZ

Putting isn't golf. Greens should be treated almost the same as water hazards: you land on them, then add two strokes to your score.   ~ CHI CHI RODRIGUEZ

The only useful putting advice I ever got from my caddie was to keep the ball low.

~ CHI CHI RODRIGUEZ

I never pray to God to make a putt. I pray to God to help me react good if I miss a putt!   ~ CHI CHI RODRIGUEZ

After all these years, it's still embarrassing for me to play on the American golf tour. Like the time I asked my caddie for a sand wedge and he came back ten minutes later with a ham on rye.   ~ CHI CHI RODRIGUEZ

When you retire, your wife gets twice as much husband and half as much money. I have to keep playing.   ~ CHI CHI RODRIGUEZ

The good thing is, I don't have to play Tiger Woods until I'm 90.

~ CHI CHI RODRIGUEZ ON THE SENIORS TOUR

I was distracted by Jesper Parnevik's outfit. I simply couldn't believe the colour of his trousers.

~ MARK ROE, DISQUALIFIED FOR SIGNING THE WRONG SCORECARD

Income Tax has made more liars out of the American people than golf.

~ WILL ROGERS

Golf is a wonderful exercise. You can stand on your feet for hours, watching somebody else putt.

~ WILL ROGERS

Golf is good for the soul. You get so mad at yourself you forget to hate your enemies.

~ WILL ROGERS

I have never been depressed enough to take up the game.

~ WILL ROGERS

Anyone who likes golf on television would enjoy watching the grass grow on the greens.

~ ANDY ROONEY

There are so many doglegs here, Lassie must have designed the course.

~ BOB ROSBURG ON HAZELTINE NATIONAL GOLF CLUB, MINNESOTA

Golf is a game where the ball always lies poorly and the player always lies well.

~ ART ROSENBAUM

And on the eve of the Bob Hope Classic is an interview with the man himself, Gerry Ford.

~ JIM ROSENTHAL

Golf is a passion, an obsession, a romance, a nice acquaintanceship with trees, sand, and water.

~ BOB RYAN

In my house in Houston I still have that putter with which I missed that two and a half foot putt to win the Open. It's in two pieces. ~ DOUG SANDERS

I'm working as hard as I can to get my life and my cash to run out at the same time. If I can just die after lunch Tuesday, everything will be perfect.

~ DOUG SANDERS

All men are created equal. I am just one stroke better than the rest.

~ GENE SARAZEN AFTER WINNING THE 1922 US OPEN

I told the Masters chairman I was getting too old to play, but he kept saying, 'Gene, they don't want to see you play; they just want to see if you're still alive.'

~ GENE SARAZEN, AGED 90, AS AN HONORARY PLAYER AT THE US MASTERS

Far be it from me to pile it on about Hal Sutton, but do you really want a guy who's been married four times trying to match up people?

~ BILL SCHEFT ON THE 2004 US RYDER CUP CAPTAIN

Watching Sam Snead practise hitting a golf ball is like watching a fish practise swimming. ~ JOHN SCHLEE

I like the thought of playing for money instead of silverware. I never did like to polish. ~ PATTY SHEEHAN, ON TURNING PROFESSIONAL

Be funny on a golf course? Do I kid my best friend's mother about her heart condition? ~ PHIL SILVERS

I just about shot my age about a week after my 80th birthday, but I three-putted the hole with the windmill. ~ LON SIMMONS

The reason most people play golf is to wear clothes they would not be caught dead in otherwise. ~ ROGER SIMON

Golf is to Fiji what cricket is to America.

~ VIJAY SINGH, FIJIAN WINNER OF THE 2000 US MASTERS

I get my exercise on the golf course. When I see my friends collapse, I run for the paramedics.

~ RED SKELTON

My putting's so bad, I could putt off a tabletop and still leave the ball halfway down the leg.

~ J.C. SNEAD

You've just one problem: you stand too close to the ball – after you've hit it.

~ SAM SNEAD

Those greens are so fast I have to hold my putter over the ball and hit it with the shadow.

~ SAM SNEAD

The greens there are harder than a whore's heart.

~ SAM SNEAD

If some players took a fork to their mouths the way they take the club back, they'd starve to death.

~ SAM SNEAD

There is an old saying: If a man comes home with sand in his cuffs and cockleburs in his pants, don't ask him what he shot.

~ SAM SNEAD

Lay off for three weeks, then quit for good.

~ SAM SNEAD'S ADVICE TO A PUPIL

Why am I using a new putter? Because the last one didn't float too well.

~ CRAIG STADLER

I think it's funny that almost all the sports writers who are always asking why Craig doesn't lose weight are heavier than he is.

~ SUE STADLER, CRAIG'S WIFE

Even the men's room has a double dogleg.

~ DAVE STOCKTON, ON THE POPPY HILLS COURSE AT PEBBLE BEACH, CALIFORNIA

I don't think television work has screwed up my golf. I've pretty much taken care of that on my own.

~ CURTIS STRANGE

What a terrible round of golf! I only hit two good balls all day and that was when I stood on a rake.

~ JIMMY TARBUCK

I was playing so bad, I said, 'I think I'm going to drown myself in the lake.' My caddie said, 'Do you think you can keep your head down that long?'

~ JIMMY TARBUCK

Ronnie Corbett is so small, he might get lost in an unreplaced divot.

~ JIMMY TARBUCK

We had to fill in the ovaries recently, because people kept getting stuck in them.

~ FLORIAN TEVES, DIRECTOR OF LA SALLE, A FRENCH COURSE
DESIGNED AROUND THE FEMALE ANATOMY

I'm hitting the woods just great, but I'm having a terrible time getting out of them.

~ HARRY TOFCANO

There are two things you can do with your head down – play golf and pray.

~ LEE TREVINO

My swing is so bad, I look like a caveman killing his lunch.

~ LEE TREVINO

I'm not saying my golf game went bad, but if I grew tomatoes they'd come up sliced.

~ LEE TREVINO

Someone once said that nobody murders Troon. The way I played the Open they couldn't even arrest me for second-degree manslaughter.

~ LEE TREVINO

I still swing the way I used to, but when I look up the ball is going in a different direction.

~ LEE TREVINO

You can talk to a fade, but a hook won't listen. ~ LEE TREVINO

Nobody but you and your caddie care what you do out there, and if your caddie is betting against you, he doesn't care either. ~ LEE TREVINO

There are two things which don't last – dogs who chase cars and professional golfers who putt for pars. ~ LEE TREVINO

A rough should have high grass. When you go bowling, they don't give you anything for landing in the gutter, do they? ~ LEE TREVINO

My three playing partners drove into the woods. I asked them what was over there, a nudist colony? ~ LEE TREVINO

If there's a thunderstorm on a golf course, walk down the middle of the fairway, holding a one-iron over your head. Even God can't hit a one-iron. ~ LEE TREVINO

I always know which side a putt will break. It always slopes toward the side of the green Herman's standing.

~ LEE TREVINO ON HIS HEAVYWEIGHT CADDIE HERMAN MITCHELL

He'll be tougher than a 50-cent steak.

~ LEE TREVINO, ON RAYMOND FLOYD JOINING THE SENIOR TOUR

At one time I had 15 clubs. When we left the fifth green, Nicklaus couldn't find his putter. He had put it in my bag. I told him I'd take the two-shot penalty if he didn't use the putter for the rest of the round. ~ LEE TREVINO

At 15 we put down my bag to hunt for a ball, found the ball, lost the bag.

~ LEE TREVINO, ON THE ROUGH AT ROYAL BIRKDALE

Columbus went around the world in 1492. That isn't a lot of strokes when you consider the course. ~ LEE TREVINO

Arnie [Palmer] would go for the flag from the middle of an alligator's back.

~ LEE TREVINO

I've never had a coach in my life. When I find one who can beat me, then I'll listen.

~ LEE TREVINO

Real pressure in golf is playing for $10 when you've only got $5 in your pocket.

~ LEE TREVINO

If it wasn't for golf, I don't know what I'd be doing. If my IQ had been two points lower, I'd have been a plant.

~ LEE TREVINO

I was 20 before I realised that Manual Labour wasn't a Mexican.

~ LEE TREVINO

One of the nice things about the Senior Tour is that we can take a cart and cooler. If your game is not going well, you can always have a picnic. ~ LEE TREVINO

You can make a lot of money out of golf. Just ask my ex-wives!

~ LEE TREVINO

His nerve, his memory, and I can't remember the third thing.

~ LEE TREVINO ON THE THREE THINGS AN AGEING GOLFER LOSES

I didn't even bother to go look for the first ball. I would have gotten scratches all over my back and I would have had to explain that to my wife.

~ LEE TREVINO, AFTER HITTING A BALL INTO THE WOODS

—Reporter: When did you start wearing a corset for your bad back?
—Lee Trevino: Ever since my wife found it in the glove compartment.

One of the reasons Arnie Palmer is playing so well is that, before each tee shot, his wife takes out his balls and kisses them.

~ TV COMMENTATOR

Mmmm. That's a little on the heavy side. A little less than perfect. A bit like Kate Winslet really.   ~ TV COMMENTATOR

Golf is a good walk spoiled.   ~ MARK TWAIN

It's good sportsmanship to not pick up lost balls while they are still rolling.
                                                                       ~ MARK TWAIN

Golf appeals to the idiot in us and the child. Just how childlike golf players become is proven by their frequent inability to count past five.   ~ JOHN UPDIKE

The golf swing is like a suitcase into which we are trying to pack one too many things.   ~ JOHN UPDIKE

If we accept that women can enter our tournaments, then it applies that men can play with women. I am definitely going to approach them to get an application and if they let me play in the qualifying event, then I will. I'll even wear a kilt and shave my legs.   ~ JEAN VAN DE VELDE

If your opponent is playing several shots in vain attempts to extricate himself from a bunker, do not stand near him and audibly count his strokes. It would be justifiable homicide if he wound up his pitiable exhibition by applying his niblick to your head.   ~ HARRY VARDON

Moderation is essential in all things, madam, but never in my life have I failed to beat a teetotaller.   ~ HARRY VARDON

—Harry Vardon: What should I take here?
—Vardon's caddie: Well, sir, I'd recommend the 4.05 train.

Art Rosenbaum said he wanted to get more distance. I told him to hit it and run backwards.   ~ KEN VENTURI

Watching a golf tournament is different from attending other sports arenas. For one thing, the drunks are spread out in a larger area. ~ DON WADE

I've seen turtles move faster than Bernhard Langer. ~ LANNY WADKINS

I never heard of them before. I thought it was some kind of sunglasses.
~ LANNY WADKINS ON BETA BLOCKERS

Keep your eye on the club. Nothing is more embarrassing than to throw a club and then have to ask a playing partner where it went. ~ GLEN WAGGONER

I tell myself that Jack Nicklaus probably has a lousy curveball.
~ BASEBALL PITCHER BOB WALK, STRUGGLING TO MASTER GOLF

My golf swing is a bit like ironing a shirt. You get one side smoothed out, turn it over and there is a big wrinkle on the other side. Then you iron that one out, turn it over and there is yet another wrinkle. ~ TOM WATSON

Muirfield without a wind is like a lady undressed. No challenge. ~ TOM WATSON

First, hitting the ball. Second, finding out where it went.
~ TOM WATSON, ASKED WHAT WOULD HELP PRESIDENT GERALD FORD'S GOLF GAME

My kids used to come up to me and say, 'Daddy, did you win?' Now they say, 'Daddy, did you make the cut?'
~ TOM WATSON

The uglier a man's legs are, the better he plays golf. It's almost a law. ~ H.G. WELLS

The intensity of Tiger Woods's life is just ridiculous. He says the reason he loves scuba diving so much is because the fish don't recognise him. ~ LEE WESTWOOD

Sergio Garcia can switch from a kid apparently playing for the heck of it to someone with the predatory instincts of an alligator. The kid is all smiles, but watch out for his teeth.   ~ LEE WESTWOOD

I'll be voting for Zara Phillips. Can you imagine what Darren [Clarke] would be like if he won? ~ LEE WESTWOOD, CONSIDERING THE 2006 BBC SPORTS PERSONALITY OF THE YEAR

Golf is a game where white men can dress up as black pimps and get away with it.   ~ ROBIN WILLIAMS

Golf … is the infallible test. The man who can go into a patch of rough alone, with the knowledge that only God is watching him, and play his ball where it lies, is the man who will serve you faithfully and well.   ~ P.G. WODEHOUSE

Golf, like measles, should be caught young.   ~ P.G. WODEHOUSE

Sudden success in golf is like the sudden acquisition of wealth. It is apt to unsettle and deteriorate the character.   ~ P.G. WODEHOUSE

The least thing upset him on the links. He missed short putts because of the uproar of butterflies in the adjoining meadows.   ~ P.G. WODEHOUSE

There was the man who seemed to be attempting to deceive his ball and lull it into a false sense of security by looking away from it and then making a lightning slash in the apparent hope of catching it off its guard.   ~ P.G. WODEHOUSE

He enjoys that perfect peace, that peace beyond all understanding, which comes at its maximum only to the man who has given up golf.   ~ P.G. WODEHOUSE

When Tiger got out of the high chair, he had a golf swing.   ~ EARL WOODS

Everyone wants to give me advice. I go into the grocery store and someone tells me what I did wrong with the four-iron I hit on the 15th.   ~ TIGER WOODS

Do I ever wake up at night and find myself amazed at what I have accomplished in golf? Usually when I wake up in the middle of the night, it's to do something else.   ~ TIGER WOODS

The other day I broke 70. That's a lot of clubs.   ~ HENNY YOUNGMAN

If conversation was fertiliser, [Lee] Trevino would be up to his neck in grass all the time.   ~ LARRY ZIEGLER

I have never led the tour in money winnings, but I have many times in alcohol consumption.   ~ FUZZY ZOELLER

Seve Ballesteros drives into territory Daniel Boone couldn't find. ~ FUZZY ZOELLER

What changes would I like to see in golf? I'd like to see the holes made bigger.
                                                             ~ FUZZY ZOELLER

RACQUETS

Badminton

They are always trying to get me into something I couldn't get one boob in, let alone my arse. ~ GAIL EMMS, OLYMPIC SILVER MEDALLIST, ON SPONSORS' DEMANDS

Squash

Squash is boxing with racquets. ~ JONAH BARRINGTON

Squash – that's not exercise, it's flagellation. ~ NOËL COWARD

Crystallising my feelings about the game, I find that squash is less frustrating than golf, less fickle than tennis. It is easier than badminton, cheaper than polo. It is better exercise than bowls, quicker than cricket, less boring than jogging, drier than swimming, safer than hang gliding. ~ JOHN HOPKINS

Tennis

Years ago we discovered the exact point, the dead centre of middle age. It occurs when you are too young to take up golf and too old to rush up to the net.

~ FRANKLIN P. ADAMS

Nobody should be ranked number one who looks like he just swung from a tree.

~ ANDRE AGASSI ON PETE SAMPRAS

My feelings are Yevgeny Kafelnikov should take his prize money when he is done here and go and buy some perspective. ~ ANDRE AGASSI

I feel old when I see mousse in my opponent's hair. ~ ANDRE AGASSI

The skirts look like they're a little difficult to run in. I think they need to be shorter. ~ ANDRE AGASSI ON THE MODEL BALL GIRLS AT THE MADRID MASTERS

He told me how much he enjoyed playing me, and that he hoped it happens a lot more in the future. And that makes one of us.

~ ANDRE AGASSI AFTER LOSING TO ROGER FEDERER AT THE 2005 AUSTRALIAN OPEN

Federer was too good. I would suggest to his next opponent that he doesn't look to me for advice. ~ ANDRE AGASSI

The loudest sound in the world is 23,000 quiet New Yorkers.

~ ANDRE AGASSI AFTER A FOUR-SET VICTORY OVER ANDREI PAVEL IN HIS LAST US OPEN

She always wins. The problem is I can't always keep my eyes on the ball.

~ ANDRE AGASSI ON PLAYING HIS WIFE, STEFFI GRAF

Roger [Federer] can produce tennis shots that should be declared illegal!

~ TRACY AUSTIN

A wading pool has more depth than women's tennis. Women's tennis is in trouble. Lindsay Davenport beat the world's 13th-ranked player, Vera Zvonareva, in less time than it takes Andre Agassi to comb his hair. Earlier in the tournament Australian Sam Stosur lost to Hungarian Aniko Kapros, who serves slower than a bad restaurant. ~ THE AUSTRALIAN

We don't always get from slow motion the pace at which they play. ~ JOHN BARRETT

As Boris Becker sits there, his eyes staring out in front of him, I wonder what he's thinking. I think he's thinking, 'I am Boris Becker.' At least, I hope that's what he's thinking. ~ JOHN BARRETT

The only thing I had on my mind was tennis, and sometimes girls. ~ BORIS BECKER

The most expensive five seconds of my life.

~ BORIS BECKER ON THE BROOM-CUPBOARD FLING THAT COST HIM MILLIONS

Arantxa Sanchez-Vicario bustled this way and that, as if mounted on castors and hurtling across a highly polished floor. ~ REX BELLAMY

Charlie Pasarell moves so slowly between points that at times he seems to be flirting with reverse gear. ~ REX BELLAMY

When I was 40 my doctor advised me that a man in his forties shouldn't play tennis. I heeded his advice carefully and could hardly wait until I reached 50 to start again. ~ HUGO L. BLACK

Martina Navratilova is the 'Tootsie' of tennis. ~ MR BLACKWELL

I have finally mastered what to do with the second tennis ball. Having small hands, I was becoming terribly self-conscious about keeping it in a can in the car while I served the first one. I noted some women tucked the second ball just inside the elastic leg of their tennis panties. I tried, but found the space already occupied by a leg. Now, I simply drop the second ball down my cleavage, giving me a chest that often stuns my opponent throughout an entire set. ~ ERMA BOMBECK

You don't play people, you play a ball. You don't ever hit a guy in the butt and knock him over the net – unless you're really upset. ~ VIC BRADEN

Soderling wanted that first set – it was part of his game plan. ~ CHRIS BRADNAM

Martina [Navratilova] was so far in the closet she was in danger of being a garment bag. ~ RITA MAE BROWN

What have I learned from my crushing defeats by Martina Navratilova? How to shake hands. ~ BETTINA BUNGE

Serena [Williams] played some great shots, but so did I, and that was the only difference. ~ JENNIFER CAPRIATI

Andrea Jaeger plays tennis like she's double-parked.   ~ MARY CARILLO

It's quite clear that Virginia Wade is thriving on the pressure now that the pressure on her to do well is off.   ~ HARRY CARPENTER

We haven't had any more rain since it stopped raining.   ~ HARRY CARPENTER

If someone says tennis is not feminine, I say screw it.   ~ ROSIE CASALS

What would I do to improve Wimbledon? How about moving it to the summer?

~ PAT CASH

Lleyton Hewitt's two greatest strengths are his legs, his speed, his agility and his competitiveness.   ~ PAT CASH

Roger Federer's only weakness is heavy metal music.   ~ ANDREW CASTLE

Pete Sampras does have a weakness. He cannot cook for a start.   ~ MICHAEL CHANG

The primary conception of tennis is to get the ball over the net and at the same time to keep it within bounds of the court; failing this, within the borders of the neighbourhood.   ~ ELLIOT CHAZE

In tennis the addict moves about a hard rectangle and seeks to ambush a fuzzy ball with a modified snow-shoe.   ~ ELLIOT CHAZE

When Ilie Nastase's winning, he's objectionable. When he's losing, he's highly objectionable.   ~ ADRIAN CLARK

The pace of this match is really accelerating, by which I mean it's getting faster all the time.   ~ DAVID COLEMAN

While Ivan Lendl suffers for being too little a man and too much a machine, Martina Navratilova suffers for being too much of both.   ~ BUD COLLINS

New Yorkers love it when you spill your guts out there. Spill your guts at Wimbledon and they make you stop and clean it up.   ~ JIMMY CONNORS

I don't know that my behaviour has improved that much with age. They just found someone worse.   ~ JIMMY CONNORS ON JOHN McENROE

The serve was invented so that the net could play.
~ BILL COSBY

Even after dropping his drawers, he still had on more clothes than Serena Williams.   ~ GREG COTE, AFTER MARAT SAFIN MOONED THE CROWD AT THE FRENCH OPEN

You'd have to think that if he'd been around today, Rod Laver would have been Rod Laver.   ~ JIM COURIER

Unbelievable, yet what else could it be?   ~ JIM COURIER

It was like an alien abduction out there. Someone invaded his body and turned him into the greatest volleyer in the universe.   ~ JIM COURIER AFTER LOSING TO TIM HENMAN

That shot he's got to obliterate from his mind a little bit.   ~ MARK COX

Chip Hooper is such a big man that it is sometimes difficult to see where he is on the court.   ~ MARK COX

Even when he has to move back, he moves back so that he's moving forwards.   ~ MARK COX

He certainly looks older than he did last year.   ~ MARK COX

Lindsay Davenport has the turning circle of a station wagon.   ~ MIKE DICKSON

Wimbledon weather is always the same. Either it's rainy with sunny intervals or sunny with rainy intervals.   ~ PAT DuPRE

I remember when Jimmy [Connors] and I went into confession and he came out a half-hour later and I said, 'How'd it go?' He said, 'I wasn't finished. The priest said come back next Sunday.'   ~ CHRIS EVERT

If you put two monkeys on to play, you'd still pack the Centre Court.   ~ NEIL FRASER

Everyone thinks my name is Jerry Laitis and they call me Mr Laitis. What can you do when you have a name that sounds like a disease?   ~ VITAS GERULAITIS

And let that be a lesson to you all. Nobody beats Vitas Gerulaitis 17 times in a row.   ~ VITAS GERULAITIS, FINALLY BEATING BJORN BORG IN AN EXHIBITION MATCH

Hardy Amies once told me that the sexiest thing he had seen was nuns playing tennis.   ~ PRUDENCE GLYNN

The one foolproof way of putting the ticket touts out of business – a Wimbledon final between Pete Sampras and Jim Courier.   ~ THE GUARDIAN

Winning or losing, she [Lindsay Davenport] has the demeanour of a bored teenager who's been dragged off Tomb Raider to kiss a mad auntie with whiskers.   ~ THE GUARDIAN

Svetlana Kuznetsova has legs of which Mark Hughes would be proud.
~ THE GUARDIAN

If Tim Henman was any more wholesome you could take him for constipation.
~ THE GUARDIAN

Compared with British tennis, Mars appears brimming with life. ~ *THE GUARDIAN*

Arantxa Sanchez-Vicario is the only sports person whose name is worth 175 in Scrabble. ~ NICK HANCOCK

The depressing thing about tennis is that no matter how good I get, I'll never be as good as a wall. They're so relentless. ~ MITCH HEDBERG

If you don't do something special against Chris Evert, you find yourself losing concentration after 35 shots. ~ JULIE HELDMAN

You can almost watch a couple play mixed doubles and know whether they should stay together. ~ DR HERBERT HENDIN

I played a great first point.
~ TIM HENMAN AFTER LOSING 6-0, 6-3 TO PETE SAMPRAS

Tim Henman is going to be a father again. So that means at least one British seed got through. ~ LENNY HENRY

I just couldn't lose to a bloke wearing a shirt like that.
~ LLEYTON HEWITT FOLLOWING HIS US OPEN VICTORY OVER DOMINIK HRBATY, WHO WORE A PINK AND BLACK SHIRT WITH TWO OVAL HOLES CUT OUT OF THE BACK

I'm sure it's not pleasant for players who have been on the tour for five or six years when a little brat wins against them.
~ MARTINA HINGIS, TURNING PROFESSIONAL AT 14

I've always said I'm a good horse but still an underdog. ~ MARTINA HINGIS

Look, Nastase, we used to have a famous cricket match in this country called Gentlemen versus Players. The Gentlemen were put down on the scorecard as 'Mister' because they were gentlemen. By no stretch of the imagination can anybody call you a gentleman.
~ TRADER HORN, WIMBLEDON UMPIRE, AFTER BEING TOLD TO ADDRESS ILIE NASTASE AS 'MISTER'

Zivojinovic seems to be able to pull the big bullet out of the top drawer.

~ MIKE INGHAM

Tim Henman, I guess, is sitting in the locker room, pacing up and down.

~ JOHN INVERDALE

She [Dokic] left the court with a face as long as thunder.   ~ JOHN INVERDALE

I like to play fast. Too many players bounce the ball, they look at me, they look at the ground. They bounce it ten times. They look at the sky. They bounce it again and I fall asleep.   ~ GORAN IVANISEVIC

Actually, I tossed it nicely, landed nicely, like airplane. No warning, beautiful. That's the art of throwing rackets.   ~ GORAN IVANISEVIC

I was pretty nice to the racket all last week. I was surprised how easy it broke. Maybe there is something wrong with it, or I'm too strong.   ~ GORAN IVANISEVIC

I pay more fines than some guys' career prize money on the tour.

~ GORAN IVANISEVIC

After so much time I decided they can start to travel together. So they are travelling together and they are being good friends. When they are good friends, I play good tennis.   ~ GORAN IVANISEVIC ON 'GOOD' AND 'BAD' GORAN

Ivan Lendl's never going to be a great player on grass. The only time he comes to the net is to shake your hand.   ~ GORAN IVANISEVIC

She's from another planet. She's 48, 50, I don't know, and she won 6-0, 6-1. At 47, I'm probably going to be in a wheelchair.   ~ GORAN IVANISEVIC ON MARTINA NAVRATILOVA

I can go on the women's tour with this second serve.

~ GORAN IVANISEVIC ON HIS SHOULDER PROBLEMS

Yes, I said that I would marry if I won Wimbledon, but this is a new century, new rules are valid now.

~ GORAN IVANISEVIC

I am going to miss everything about Wimbledon, the guys, serving aces on 15-40, talking to the umpire, watching the Teletubbies.

~ GORAN IVANISEVIC

John McEnroe looks as if he is serving round the edge of an imaginary building.

~ CLIVE JAMES

McEnroe is as charming as a dead mouse in a loaf of bread.

~ CLIVE JAMES

McEnroe has hair like badly turned broccoli.

~ CLIVE JAMES

Bjorn Borg looks like a hunchbacked, jut-bottomed version of Lizabeth Scott impersonating a bearded Apache princess.

~ CLIVE JAMES

Like a Volvo, Bjorn Borg is rugged, has good after-sales service, and is very dull.

~ CLIVE JAMES

Nastase rarely grins and bears it. More commonly he grins, groans, shrugs, slumps, spins around, shakes his head, puffs out his cheeks, rolls on the ground and bears it. Even more common, he does all that and doesn't bear it.

~ CLIVE JAMES

Jimmy Connors likes the ball to come at him in a straight line, so that he can hit it back in another straight line. When it comes to him in a curve, he uses up half of his energy straightening it up again.

~ CLIVE JAMES

Jimmy Connors has unleashed his new tactic, the Early Grunt. Now he has taken to grunting loudly at the instant of hitting the ball instead of just afterwards. Since the grunt travels at the speed of sound, it arrives in the opponent's court marginally before the ball does. Opponents try to hit the grunt.   ~ CLIVE JAMES

A traditional fixture at Wimbledon is the way the BBC TV commentary box fills up with British players eliminated in the early rounds.   ~ CLIVE JAMES

He's now letting Chang play his own game – and he does that better than anyone.   ~ CHRISTINE JANES

It's like trying to return a serve that comes from the Eiffel Tower.
~ THOMAS JOHANSSON ON TOWERING CROAT IVO KARLOVIC

Diane … keeping her head beautifully on her shoulders.   ~ ANN JONES

She puts her head down and bangs it straight across the line.   ~ ANN JONES

And when Chrissie is playing well, I always feel that she is playing well.
~ ANN JONES

He's got his hands on his knees and holds his head in despair.   ~ PETER JONES

Today something didn't feel right. I guess it's the puberty's fault.
~ SESIL KARATANTCHEVA AFTER LOSING 6-0, 6-1 TO MARIA SHARAPOVA

McEnroe claims John Lloyd is more popular than him because Lloyd married Chris Evert. McEnroe wouldn't be popular if he was married to Marie Osmond.
~ TERRY KELLEHER

If you're up against a girl with big boobs, bring her to the net and make her hit backhand volleys.   ~ BILLIE JEAN KING

You usually feel like you're playing uphill against them.

~ MARK KNOWLES ON DOUBLES EXPERTS MARK WOODFORDE AND TODD WOODBRIDGE

Ivan Lendl is a robot, a solitary, mechanical man who lives with his dogs behind towering walls at his estate in Connecticut. A man who so badly wants to have a more human image that he's having surgery to remove the bolts from his neck.

~ TONY KORNHEISER

I may have exaggerated a bit when I said that 80 per cent of the top women tennis players are fat pigs. It's only 75 per cent. ~ RICHARD KRAJICEK

An otherwise happily married couple may turn a mixed doubles game into a scene from *Who's Afraid of Virginia Woolf?* ~ ROD LAVER

I often surprise myself. You can't plan some shots that go in, not unless you're on marijuana, and the only grass I'm partial to is Wimbledon's. ~ ROD LAVER

I'm very jealous: one of Rafael Nadal's biceps is bigger than my chest!

~ JOHN LLOYD

Noah always beats Curren. He has a sort of Houdini against him. ~ JOHN LLOYD

Why did I lose? No reason, though you might like to know that I got tired, my ears started popping, the rubber came off my shoes, I got cramp, and I lost one of my contact lenses. Other than that I was in great shape. ~ BOB LUTZ

She sounds like a live pig being slaughtered.
~ FREW MacMILLAN ON MARIA SHARAPOVA'S GRUNTING

That shot knocked the stuffing out of his sails. ~ FREW MacMILLAN

Ten of the world's greatest rarities. Number 4: A British tennis player with a can of silver polish. ~ *MAIL ON SUNDAY*

It's difficult to play against a man … I mean against Martina [Navratilova]. She scares you with her muscles. ~ HANA MANDLIKOVA

The Gullikson twins here. An interesting pair, both from Wisconsin.
~ DAN MASKELL

And here's Zivojinovic, six foot six inches tall and 14 pounds ten ounces.
~ DAN MASKELL

Lendl has remained throughout as calm as the proverbial iceberg. ~ DAN MASKELL

He slips, but manages to regroup himself. ~ DAN MASKELL

Nobody has worked harder than Gottfried to get to the top of the tennis tree, and certainly nobody more so than Borg. ~ DAN MASKELL

When Martina Navratilova is tense it helps her to relax. ~ DAN MASKELL

You can almost hear the silence as they battle it out. ~ DAN MASKELL

Billie Jean has always been conscious of wind on the centre court. ~ DAN MASKELL

The British boys are adopting the attacking position: Cox up at the net.
~ DAN MASKELL

I'd rather be number two in Chile and number one in the world. ~ NICOLAS MASSU

—Interviewer: How different was it holding up that plate today than in Australia?
—Amelie Mauresmo: It's a different trophy. It's round, it's smaller.

That's one of the best sets I've seen him [Tomas Zib] play, although I should preface that by saying I haven't seen him play before. ~ JOHN McENROE

This [defeat] has taught me a lesson, but I'm not sure what it is.   ~ JOHN McENROE

Let's hope his nerves will run through his veins.   ~ JOHN McENROE

Do you have any other problems, other than that you're unemployed and a moron and a dork?

~ JOHN McENROE TO A SPECTATOR

If you believe that, I've never questioned a call in my life.

~ JOHN McENROE ON ANNA KOURNIKOVA'S SUPPOSED VIRGINAL STATUS

He seems like he's moving farther and farther back in the court. You need binoculars to see him sometimes.

~ JOHN McENROE ON ANDY RODDICK'S CLAY-COURT TACTICS

I play four or five times a week. I'd still rather win than lose. I'm more competitive than the average bear.   ~ JOHN McENROE PLAYING THE SENIORS TOUR

I want to get into the top ten – then maybe I can get a date with Maria Sharapova!   ~ ANDY MURRAY

I'm supposed to be seeing Coldplay tonight, so I want to be out of Wimbledon.

~ ANDY MURRAY, LOSING IN THE 2005 MIXED DOUBLES

I can't believe how hard Agassi hits the ball. Ion Tiriac didn't drive that fast.

~ ILIE NASTASE

I can make him into the player who swears most on the court.

~ ILIE NASTASE, COACHING SWEDISH HOPEFUL HENRIK SUNDSTROM

Why haven't I reported the theft of my credit card? Because whoever stole it is spending less money than my wife!   ~ ILIE NASTASE

I'm not just involved in tennis but committed. Do you know the difference between involvement and commitment? Think of ham and eggs. The chicken is involved. The pig is committed.

~ MARTINA NAVRATILOVA

Whoever said, 'It's not whether you win or lose that counts,' probably lost.

~ MARTINA NAVRATILOVA

I had a feeling today that Venus Williams would either win or lose.

~ MARTINA NAVRATILOVA

Sure I know where the Press room is. I just look for where they throw the dog meat.

~ MARTINA NAVRATILOVA

—Male reporter: Are you still a lesbian?
—Martina Navratilova: Are you still the alternative?

Serena Williams' breasts alone must weigh more than Justine Henin-Hardenne.

~ MATTHEW NORMAN

Federer is an immeasurably more charming human being than McEnroe (then again, so was Pol Pot).

~ MATTHEW NORMAN

She was beside herself, which, come to think of it, would make a great doubles team.

~ SCOTT OSTLER, WITNESSING A MARTINA NAVRATILOVA TANTRUM

Tim Henman's injured shoulder has raised its ugly head again.

~ JONATHAN OVEREND

Just what is the nationality of a child with a Russian mother and German father conceived in a Japanese restaurant in England?

~ DWIGHT PERRY, AFTER BORIS BECKER ADMITTED BEING THE
FATHER OF A BABY GIRL BORN TO A RUSSIAN MODEL

Strangely enough, Kathy Jordan is getting to the net first, which she always does.

~ FRED PERRY

McEnroe has got to sit down and work out where he stands.   ~ FRED PERRY

It's good to get out on court and get that monkey that turned into a gorilla off my shoulders.   ~ MARK PHILIPPOUSSIS

If ice cream is a steroid, I'm definitely positive for that.   ~ MARK PHILIPPOUSSIS

They said, 'Well job, good done.'   ~ TSVETANA PIRONKOVA, ASKED ABOUT THE PLAYERS'
REACTION TO HER VICTORY OVER VENUS WILLIAMS AT THE 2006 AUSTRALIAN OPEN

Sure, on a given day I could beat him. But it would have to be a day he had food poisoning.   ~ MEL PURCELL AFTER LOSING TO IVAN LENDL IN UNDER AN HOUR

He was a great tennis player, rather like a chess player, always trying to thread the ball through the eye of a needle.   ~ RADIO COMMENTATOR

She comes from a tennis-playing family. Her father's a dentist.

~ RADIO COMMENTATOR

Strawberries, cream and champers flowed like hot cakes.   ~ RADIO 2 AT WIMBLEDON

Michael Chang has all the fire and passion of a public service announcement.

~ ALEX RAMSEY

The only thing faster in women's tennis than Venus Williams' serve is Anna Kournikova's exit.   ~ ALAN RAY

I don't know if he's in a class by himself, but it sure don't take long to call the roll.   ~ GIL REYES ON ANDRE AGASSI

Don't marry a tennis player – love means nothing to them.　　　~ JOAN RIVERS

Billie Jean King, with the look on her face that says she can't believe it, because she never believes it, and yet, somehow, I think she does.　　　~ MAX ROBERTSON

If she gets the jitters now, then she isn't the great champion that she is.

~ MAX ROBERTSON

This is a sheer game of chess between these two players. But Borg has an ace in the pack.　　　~ MAX ROBERTSON

These ball boys are marvellous. You don't even notice them. There's a left-handed one over there. I noticed him earlier.　　　~ MAX ROBERTSON

I threw the kitchen sink at him. He went into the bathroom and threw back the tub.　　　~ ANDY RODDICK AFTER LOSING TO ROGER FEDERER AT WIMBLEDON

You run out of options because he's become such a complete player. Maybe I'll just punch him or something.　　　~ ANDY RODDICK ON ROGER FEDERER

I'm gonna have to start winning some of the matches to call it a rivalry!

~ ANDY RODDICK, ASKED WHETHER HE AND ROGER FEDERER
HAD A RIVALRY THAT WOULD LAST FOR YEARS

What are my chances of winning the US Open? As good as anybody not named Roger.　　　~ ANDY RODDICK

By the time I wake up he is about five cups of coffee deep! I can't get a word in edgeways.　　　~ ANDY RODDICK ON COACH BRAD GILBERT

Whatever I said last year, just copy it. I'm sure it still fits.

~ ANDY RODDICK TO THE MEDIA AFTER LOSING IN THE FIRST ROUND AT THE 2006 FRENCH OPEN

Umpiring, the only job in the world where you can screw up on a daily basis and still have one! ~ ANDY RODDICK

One of the reasons I like to do well here is because I know I will talk to you afterwards. I have a bit of a crush on you. ~ ANDY RODDICK TO SUE BARKER AT WIMBLEDON

—Anne Robinson: What letter in the English language sounds like a female sheep?
—Andy Roddick: Baah? ~ *THE WEAKEST LINK*

If I had won half the games I should have, I would have a different ranking. ~ MARAT SAFIN

It's one-on-one out there. There ain't no hiding. I can't pass the ball. ~ PETE SAMPRAS

Professional tennis: I don't understand all the shushing. Why are they always shushing? Don't the players know that we're there? Should we duck down behind the seats so they don't see us watching them? ~ JERRY SEINFELD

Tennis is basically just ping-pong and the players are standing on the table. ~ JERRY SEINFELD

I'm done growing. I only grow when I put my high heels on now. ~ MARIA SHARAPOVA

I'm not the next Kournikova – I want to win matches. ~ MARIA SHARAPOVA

Every time Venus tossed up to serve, I was thinking, 'Oh no, they won't fall out, will they?'
~ PAM SHRIVER ON THE LOW-CUT OUTFIT WORN BY VENUS WILLIAMS AT THE AUSTRALIAN OPEN

Henman is trying his very best to get tough. He's grunting and growling and returning serves with the kind of filthy looks he hasn't had cause to throw since his wild teenage years when he threw a strop over not being allowed to watch *Pogle's Wood* and he had to be sent to bed without any tea.   ~ AIDAN SMITH

Tim Henman is the human equivalent of beige.   ~ LINDA SMITH

Andre Agassi was recently born again. Now, if he can only grow up.

~ *SPORTS ILLUSTRATED*

The unstoppable juggernaut of women's tennis has just been run over by a Lori.

~ *THE SUN* ON STEFFI GRAF'S FIRST-ROUND LOSS TO LORI MCNEIL AT WIMBLEDON IN 1994

I feel like dog trainer who teach dog manners and graces and just when you think dog knows how should act with nice qualities, dog make big puddle and all is wasted.   ~ ION TIRIAC ON COACHING ILIE NASTASE

Nastase does not have a brain; he has a bird fluttering around in his head.

~ ION TIRIAC

Why should a player be denied the sheer pleasure and release of smashing his own expensive racket into pieces occasionally?   ~ PETER USTINOV

I excused myself by expressing myself flattered by the offer, but begged them to renew it when my eyesight had deteriorated sufficiently for me to be able to make wrong decisions with absolute conviction.

~ PETER USTINOV, ON BEING ASKED TO BE A LINESMAN AT WIMBLEDON

The one drawback, of course, is that it looks a lot better than it performs.

~ MICHAEL VENTRE ON THE NEW 'ANNA BRA', NAMED AFTER ANNA KOURNIKOVA

We have no differences because we have nothing in common.   ~ GUILLERMO VILAS

Ann's got to take her nerve by the horns. ~ VIRGINIA WADE

Chris Lloyd came out of the dressing room like a pistol. ~ VIRGINIA WADE

Martina, she's got several layers of steel out there like a cat with nine lives.
~ VIRGINIA WADE

Tim's got a big job to do, so he's got to get out there and do the business.
~ VIRGINIA WADE

She [Monica Seles] has so much control of the racket with those double-handed wrists. ~ VIRGINIA WADE

Taut and tight-lipped mistress of the baseline, Chris Evert is the all-American golden girl become the champion of monotony. ~ PAUL WEST

Miss Stove seems to be going off the boil. ~ PETER WEST

This is the third week the fish seem to be getting away from British tennis players. ~ GERALD WILLIAMS

First thing is, it's inevitable. The second thing is, it's going to happen anyway.
~ GERALD WILLIAMS ON THE DANGERS OF BUILDING UP ANDY MURRAY

When the Williams sisters play tennis, it gets pretty hot. When they start grunting, I'm in. ~ ROBIN WILLIAMS

I was looking in the mirror today and my waist is still 28 inches. I think it is all because I have a large bosom and a large ass. I have a large ass and it always just looks like I'm bigger than the rest of the girls. I could lose 20 pounds and I'm still going to have this ass and that's just the way it is. ~ SERENA WILLIAMS

It must be a comedy if a British player is winning at Wimbledon!

~ SERENA WILLIAMS LOOKS FORWARD TO *WIMBLEDON*, THE MOVIE IN WHICH
A PLUCKY BRIT COMES FROM NOWHERE TO WIN THE TOURNAMENT

Serena just called me and said, 'Could I have your autograph?'

~ VENUS WILLIAMS AFTER BEATING DEFENDING CHAMPION MARIA SHARAPOVA AT WIMBLEDON

If you see a tennis player who looks as if he is working very hard, then that means he isn't very good.

~ HELEN WILLS MOODY

The crowds at Flushing Meadow are about as impartial as a Nuremberg Rally.

~ IAN WOOLDRIDGE

Though your game is hardly the best, you can fray your opponent's nerves by methodically bouncing the ball at least ten times before your serves.

~ ARNOLD J. ZARETT

RUGBY

Rugby League

Not many of my players will be able to satisfy their wives tonight after they were hurt by the Huddersfield players in sensitive places.

~ HALIFAX COACH TONY ANDERSON ALLEGING UNDERHAND TACTICS

Rugby League is war without the frills.

~ ANON

Give Blood. Play Rugby League.

~ ANON

To play Rugby League, you need three things: a good pass, a good tackle and a good excuse.

~ ANON

Not many people in Batley speak Latin, so the first thing we did was change the motto.

~ CLUB CHAIRMAN STEPHEN BALL

Worry is like a rocking chair. It gives you something to do but gets you nowhere.

~ WAYNE BENNETT

Eddie Waring has done as much for Rugby League as Cyril Smith would do for hang-gliding.

~ REG BOWDEN

The main difference between playing League and Union is that now I get my hangovers on Monday instead of Sunday.

~ TOM DAVID

I think you enjoy the game more if you don't know the rules. Anyway, you're on the same wavelength as the referees.

~ JONATHAN DAVIES

The refereeing over here is atrocious. It's like Manuel out of *Fawlty Towers.*

~ BRAD DAVIS IN FRANCE

Wigan doesn't offer much in the way of waves.

~ AUSTRALIAN CLUB EXECUTIVE PETER DOUST FENDING OFF
A BID FROM WIGAN WARRIORS FOR CENTRE MARK GASNIER

And he's got the icepack on his groin there, so possibly not the old shoulder injury.
~ RAY FRENCH

And there we see the sad sight of Martin Offiah limping off with a broken finger.
~ RAY FRENCH

These kicking tees get stranger by the minute. I was up in Humberside the other day, and there was a lad using one which looked like a traffic cone off the M62!
~ RAY FRENCH

It's Great Britain in the all-white strip, with the red and blue V, the dark shorts and dark socks.
~ RAY FRENCH

League is much, much more physical than Union, and that's before anyone starts breaking the rules.
~ ADRIAN HADLEY

A game for ape-like creatures watched by gloomy men in cloth caps.
~ MICHAEL HERD

Trying to explain this performance is like trying to row upstream in a barbed wire canoe.
~ SHAUN McNALLY

This will put the pressure back on Great Britain, which they can ill afford to do without.
~ ALEX MURPHY

Every time he gets the ball he moves around like a banana-shaped umbrella to cut the park off.
~ ALEX MURPHY

We were prepared to fight George Foreman … and we got George Formby.
~ BRIAN NOBLE AFTER HIS BRADFORD BULLS CRUSH A WEAKENED ST HELENS

I had a commitment to his mum that his face would not get changed, so that was the only disappointing element for me.

~ GREAT BRITAIN COACH BRIAN NOBLE ON THE NOSE INJURY SUFFERED
BY SCRUM-HALF PAUL DEACON IN A VICTORY OVER NEW ZEALAND

I believe it is the best sport in the world. It's got everything – speed and tough, ugly men.

~ TERRY O'CONNOR

I've broken my nose this year and I put my teeth all the way through my lip. This is not good for my modelling career.

~ ROBBIE PAUL

I can't see into the future but I predict he is destined for great things.

~ ROBBIE PAUL

Anyone who doesn't watch Rugby League is not a real person. He's a cow's hoof or comes from Melbourne.

~ JOHN SINGLETON

And let's see where that move started. And it started from its origins…

~ EDDIE WARING

There's one minute 60 seconds to go.

~ EDDIE WARING

I don't know whether that's the ball or his head. We'll know if it stands up.

~ EDDIE WARING

In south-west Lancashire, babes don't toddle, they side-step. Queueing women talk of 'nipping round the blindside'. Rugby League provides our cultural adrenalin.

~ COLIN WELLAND

Even Princess Di would think twice about getting too close to that lot.

~ COLIN WELLAND ON THE WIGAN PLAYERS

Rugby Union

There's no such thing as lack of confidence. You either have it or you don't.

~ ROB ANDREW

A game for hooligans played by gentlemen.

~ ANON

Since when did a Welsh three-quarter wear a fake tan, spiked hair and silver boots?

~ ANON ON GAVIN HENSON

The Shed at Gloucester is full of unpleasant yobs, akin to the sort of mob that cheered public executions.

~ ANON

The best way of stopping Carlos Spencer is to lock him in the dressing room.

~ BRIAN ASHTON

Scotland are staring down the barrel of a wooden spoon.

~ MARTIN BAYFIELD

Playing in the second row doesn't require a lot of intelligence really. You have to be bloody crazy to play there for a start.

~ BILL BEAUMONT

Look what these bastards have done to Wales. They've taken our coal, our water, our steel. They buy our houses and they only live in them for a fortnight every 12 months. What have they given us? Absolutely nothing. We've been exploited, raped, controlled and punished by the English. And that's who you are playing this afternoon!

~ PHIL BENNETT

If you can't take a punch, you should play table tennis.

~ PIERRE BERBIZIER

I'd rather crawl across broken glass naked than speak to Will Carling. ~ DICK BEST

The French pulled up the Scots' kilts and discovered they had no balls.

~ NEW ZEALAND'S ZINZAN BROOKE AFTER SCOTLAND CRASH 51-9 TO FRANCE

He was better than some of our players. At least he showed some aggression.
~ SIMON BULLARD, CHAIRMAN OF OLD DUNSTABLIANS,
AFTER BERT, AN ESCAPED VULTURE, LANDED ON THEIR PITCH

His intensity of commitment was such that he was to dismiss dislocation of his left kneecap, after just five minutes, as little more than a minor inconvenience.
~ MICHAEL CALVIN ON JAPAN'S TOSHIYUKI HAYASHI

Will Carling runs like a castrated calf.
~ DAVID CAMPESE

I'm still an amateur, of course, but I became rugby's first millionaire five years ago.
~ DAVID CAMPESE

I'm short. I don't drink. I don't know the words to any dirty songs. I'm pretty useless really.
~ WILL CARLING

Martin Corry reminds me of an old Morris Minor trying to get up a hill.
~ WILL CARLING

—Eddie Jones: If you take the scrum out of the equation, we played well.
—Mike Carlton: If you take the assassination out of the equation, the President and Mrs Kennedy quite enjoyed the drive from Dallas to the airport.

We [Saracens] have all the ingredients for a good mayonnaise; all we need is the stove at the right temperature.
~ THOMAS CASTAIGNEDE

At least this time I haven't been the subject of a poll comparing me with Saddam Hussein and Osama bin Laden.
~ COLIN CHARVIS, CAPTAIN OF WALES, ON HIS POPULARITY IN THE PRINCIPALITY

I thought I would have a quiet pint … and about 17 noisy ones.
~ GARETH CHILCOTT ON PLAYING HIS LAST GAME FOR BATH

The idea of the tackle is to smash your opponent into next week. ~ GEORGE CHUTER

And Dusty Hare kicked 19 of the 17 points. ~ DAVID COLEMAN

How do I know Zak Fea'unati has a fractured eye socket? When he blows his nose, his eye bulges. And that's usually a pretty sure sign. ~ JOHN CONNOLLY

Playing rugby at school I once fell on a loose ball and, through ignorance and fear, held on despite a fierce pummelling. After that it took me months to convince my team-mates I was a coward. ~ PETER COOK

They were lucky to get nought.

~ GEOFF COOKE ON HIS ENGLAND SIDE'S 11-0 VICTORY OVER FRANCE, 1989

I don't know about us not having a Plan B when things went wrong; we looked like we didn't have a Plan A.

~ GEOFF COOKE, AFTER ENGLAND WERE BEATEN BY NEW ZEALAND IN THE 1995 WORLD CUP

The Pacific Islands' Elvis Seveali'i has three icons in his name, so he has a lot to live up to. ~ ANDREW COTTER

I really must work on my try-scoring face. One of my friends said, 'You've got a silly face when you score a try, Cus.'

~ CHRIS CUSITER AFTER SCORING FOR SCOTLAND AGAINST ROMANIA IN 2006

If I haven't taken too many bangs on the head by the end of my career, I might just start thinking about using my brain again. ~ LAWRENCE DALLAGLIO

We've lost seven of our last eight matches. The only team that we've beaten was Western Samoa. Good job we didn't play the whole of Samoa. ~ GARETH DAVIES

Of course they don't play to any sort of pattern and if you're not careful you will start playing to that pattern. ~ MIKE DAVIES

I described Kyran Bracken last year as a tube of toothpaste we keep squeezing.
I think we have opened up a Stanley knife and scraped out the last dregs.

~ STEVE DIAMOND

And which lamp-post did you bump into?

~ DUKE OF EDINBURGH BEING PRESENTED TO SCOTLAND'S BRUCE HAY

And if they can get some pressure going, they'll put them under pressure.

~ GARETH EDWARDS

Bloody typical, isn't it? The car's a write-off. The tanker's a write-off. But JPR [Williams] comes out of it all in one piece!

~ GARETH EDWARDS

Every time I went to tackle him, Horrocks went one way, Taylor went the other, and all I got was the bloody hyphen.

~ MICK ENGLISH ON TRYING TO STOP PHIL HORROCKS-TAYLOR

If you were looking for indications in recent years of performance enhancement then I would not have thought that Welsh Rugby was the obvious starting point!

~ DENIS EVANS, SECRETARY OF THE WELSH RUGBY UNION,
ON ALLEGATIONS OF PERFORMANCE-ENHANCING DRUG ABUSE, 1991

Sometimes even Campo's brain doesn't know where his feet are taking him.

~ NICK FARR-JONES ON DAVID CAMPESE

Forwards are the gnarled and scarred creatures who have a propensity for running into and bleeding all over each other.

~ PETER FITZSIMMONS

We were too dumb. We're training well, but when we go on the field it's as if we take off the head and replace it with a pumpkin.

~ SARACENS' ALAN GAFFNEY

His shyness is derivative of not having a high intellect.

~ SCOTT GIBBS ON GAVIN HENSON

Tony Ward is the most important rugby player in Ireland. His legs are far more important to his country than even those of Marlene Dietrich were to the film industry. A little hairier, maybe, but a pair of absolute winners.   ~ MIKE GIBSON

I may not have been very tall or athletic, but the one thing I did have was the most effective backside in world rugby.   ~ JIM GLENNON

You've got to get your first tackle in early, even if it's late.   ~ RAY GRAVELL

A game played by fewer than 15 a side, at least half of whom should be totally unfit.   ~ MICHAEL GREEN

I can no longer perform to the levels I wish, and my body is falling apart; six operations, broken bones, a near-death experience, torn ligaments, dislocated shoulders and hamstrings tighter than guitar strings.
~ WILL GREENWOOD, ANNOUNCING HIS RETIREMENT

I've had a text from Granny – she's going to throw a party for you.
~ PRINCE HARRY TO MIKE TINDALL AFTER ENGLAND'S 2003 WORLD CUP SUCCESS

And there's Gregor Townsend's knee, looking very disappointed.   ~ GAVIN HASTINGS

There's no doubt about it, he's a big bastard.   ~ GAVIN HASTINGS ON JONAH LOMU

You'd think I'd rounded up every kangaroo in the land and drowned them in front of a class of orphans.   ~ AUSTIN HEALEY, BRIDLING AT AUSTRALIAN CRITICISM

While the state of British sport may be mostly serious but never hopeless, the state of Irish sport, although usually hopeless, is never serious.
~ NOEL HENDERSON, PRESIDENT OF THE IRISH RUGBY FOOTBALL UNION

I really like her family – they are all pretty cool. Let's be fair, it's not bad that they own a pub either.   ~ GAVIN HENSON ON LIFE WITH CHARLOTTE CHURCH

Being hit by Victor Costello is like being hit by a cement mixer travelling at 40mph.
~ GEORGE HOOK

A major rugby tour by the British Isles to New Zealand is a cross between a medieval crusade and a prep school outing.
~ JOHN HOPKINS

Condom Is Back In French Pack
~ *INDEPENDENT* HEADLINE ON THE RECALL OF FRANCE'S LOCK FORWARD JEAN CONDOM

Get your retaliation in first.
~ CARWYN JAMES

Good ball is when you have it and bad ball is when the opposition have it.
~ DICKIE JEEPS

The sooner that little so-and-so goes to Rugby League, the better it will be for us.
~ DICKIE JEEPS ON GARETH EDWARDS

The one-handed palmer can always reach higher, they say. They may be right, but the result is that nearly every line-out is like a tropical island – all waving palms.
~ VIVIAN JENKINS

I wasn't misquoted. I just got it slightly wrong. I actually said, 'It's a poxy little island in the Pacific.' In fact, it's two islands.
~ SCOTT JOHNSON ON NEW ZEALAND

To my mind we are not far from being a good side. If I could use a cricket analogy, it is the difference at the moment of being caught at first slip and edging just wide of first slip. I will enjoy seeing how that can be translated into French!
~ EDDIE JONES TO THE PRESS AFTER AUSTRALIA LOSE TO FRANCE

They had to use brassieres to thaw it out.
~ KEN JONES, ON A FROZEN PITCH

Bob Hillier had the hair of a city slicker and the hoofing toecap of a Tunisian mule.
~ FRANK KEATING

When they [England] ran onto the field, it was like watching a tribe of white orcs on steroids.
~ MICHAEL LAWS

For an 18-month suspension, I feel I probably should have torn it off. Then at least I could say, 'Look, I've returned to South Africa with the guy's ear.'
~ JOHAN LE ROUX

Dean Richards is nicknamed 'Warren', as in warren ugly bastard. ~ JASON LEONARD

I went to the bank the other day and got a standing ovation.
~ JASON LEONARD AFTER ENGLAND'S WORLD CUP TRIUMPH

The knee doesn't trouble me when I'm walking. But it's painful when I kneel, like before the bank manager.
~ DAVID LESLIE

I once dated a famous Aussie rugby player who treated me just like a football; made a pass, played footsie, then dropped me as soon as he'd scored.
~ KATHY LETTE

The time for reminiscing is after rugby. Then you can sit down and get fat.
~ JOSH LEWSEY

Wade Dooley, with a handle like that, sounds more like a western sheriff than the Lancashire bobby that he is.
~ NORMAN MAIR

O'Reilly, your best attacking move today will be to shake your jowls at your opposite number.
~ WILLIE JOHN McBRIDE

Like a woman, different scrimmaging machines can take some getting used to.
~ IAN McGEECHAN

He's all right, but he'll not be able to go through any airport security scanners for a while.

~ IAN McGEECHAN AFTER DEREK WHITE HAS EIGHT METAL STAPLES INSERTED IN A HEAD WOUND

Rafter, again doing much of the unseen work which the crowd relishes so much.

~ BILL McLAREN

It was just sheer luck that nobody got drowned.

~ IAN McLAUCHLAN AFTER SCOTLAND LOST ON A WATERLOGGED PITCH IN NEW ZEALAND

We have 41 caps between us.

~ FELIM McLOUGHLIN ON THE IRISH INTERNATIONAL APPEARANCES OF HE AND HIS BROTHER RAY. FELIM HAD ONE CAP, RAY THE OTHER 40.

I've seen better centres in a box of Black Magic.   ~ JOE McPARTLIN

This looks a good England team on paper; let's see how it looks on grass.

~ NIGEL MELVILLE

You don't like to see hookers going down on players like that.   ~ MURRAY MEXTED

He's looking for some meaningful penetration into the backline.   ~ MURRAY MEXTED

It's groping in a sense – it's like a blind man in a brothel.

~ MURRAY MEXTED ON THE SCRAMBLE FOR A LOOSE BALL

Everybody knows that I have been pumping Martin Leslie for a couple of seasons now.   ~ MURRAY MEXTED

This is like celebrating getting life instead of the death penalty.

~ BRIAN MOORE, AFTER AN UNCONVINCING ENGLAND VICTORY OVER SOUTH AFRICA IN NOVEMBER 2006 PROVIDES A BRIEF STAY OF EXECUTION FOR BELEAGUERED HEAD COACH ANDY ROBINSON

My advice: one, don't run into Dean Richards; two, don't get in the way of Dean Richards.

~ DEWI MORRIS

Spread out in a bunch.

~ NOEL MURPHY

The Empire Strikes Back

~ NIKE ADVERT AFTER ENGLAND BEAT AUSTRALIA TO LIFT THE RUGBY WORLD CUP

Don't ask me about emotions in the Welsh dressing room. I'm someone who cries when he watches *Little House on the Prairie*.

~ ROBERT NORSTER

It is true. Despite the rumours, we have signed Jonah Lomu, not Joanna Lumley!

~ ROBERT NORSTER AT CARDIFF BLUES

When I toured with the Irish rugby team I found social contact with other members of the squad very difficult. They were always using big words like 'galvanise' and 'marmalade'.

~ PHIL O'CALLAGHAN

Was I speared? I think so. Slam-dunked is probably the expression which sums it up best.

~ BRIAN O'DRISCOLL

Colin Meads is the kind of player you expect to see emerging from a ruck with the remains of a jockstrap between his teeth.

~ TONY O'REILLY

Twice around Barry McGann and you qualify as a bona fide traveller.

~ TONY O'REILLY

I was in direct communication with the Vatican.

~ TONY O'REILLY, EXPLAINING WHY HE WAS LOOKING THE OTHER WAY AS JACK VAN DER SCHYFF MISSED THE KICK THAT WOULD HAVE GIVEN SOUTH AFRICA VICTORY OVER THE BRITISH LIONS IN 1955

Australia are a different bag of hammers but still very dangerous.

~ EDDIE O'SULLIVAN, IRELAND COACH

Jonah Lomu is a figure who inspires hero worship among even those who think a fly-half is a glass of beer consumed when 'er indoors is looking the other way.

~ ROBERT PHILIP

[The ball] is specially shaped like a lozenge so it cannot roll, bounce properly or do any of the things for which a ball was designed.   ~ STEPHEN PILE

Australian Customs have a lot to answer for, letting this bloke into the country. If there has ever been a case of a person having foot and mouth disease, it's this bloke.   ~ SIMON POIDEVIN ON AUSTIN HEALEY

We shot ourselves in both feet, both hands, everywhere, with a pump-action shotgun.   ~ BUDGE POUNTNEY

When you are attacked in a very sensitive, personal area you can't guarantee to control other parts of your body.   ~ JEFF PROBYN

One of the things a forward always finds difficult is to run and think at the same time.
~ DEREK QUINNELL

And Matt Dawson, who has been dropped by England, is this morning in hospital suffering from concussion.   ~ RADIO 4

The three loose forwards are working in tandem.   ~ RADIO COMMENTATOR

I think Brian Moore's gnashers are the kind you get from a DIY shop and hammer in yourself. He is the only player we have who looks like a French forward.   ~ ENGLAND'S PAUL RANDALL

If rugby between New Zealand and Wales was a boxing contest, they would have stopped it many rounds ago and revoked the Welsh licence. Let's face it, Wales are rubbish. They are the village idiots of world rugby.

~ CHRIS RATTUE, *NEW ZEALAND HERALD*, 2006

Jack Rowell has the acerbic wit of Dorothy Parker and, according to most New Zealanders, a similar knowledge of rugby. ~ MARK REASON

The job of Welsh coach is like a minor part in a Quentin Tarantino film: you stagger on, you hallucinate, nobody seems to understand a word you say, you throw up, you get shot. ~ MARK REASON

Winger Simon Geoghegan resembles Mother Brown, running with a high knee-lift and sometimes not progressing far from the spot where he started.

~ MARK REASON

Grandmother or tails, sir? ~ REFEREE TO PRINCESS ANNE'S SON, PETER PHILLIPS, AT THE COIN TOSS BEFORE A GORDONSTOUN SCHOOL GAME

In the opening 20 minutes at Murrayfield, Portugal bought more dummies than a nurse on a maternity ward. ~ ALASDAIR REID

That's the first time I've seen a try scored live and in slow motion at the same time. ~ JIM RENWICK TO BRUCE HAY

A player of ours has been proven guilty of biting. That's a scar that will never heal. ~ ANDY ROBINSON

Rugby's a game of two halves – it's all about the last third. ~ ANDY ROBINSON

The advantage law is the best law in rugby, because it lets you ignore all the others. ~ DEREK ROBINSON

In my time, I've had my knee out, broken my collarbone, had my nose smashed, a rib broken, lost a few teeth, and ricked my back; but as soon as I get a bit of bad luck I'm going to quit the game. ~ J.W. ROBINSON

For Jonny Wilkinson to win the BBC Sports Personality of the Year, England have to win the World Cup, he has to kick the most points – and marry Kylie Minogue.
~ GRAHAM SHARPE

Footballer Stan Collymore got beat up by rugby players. They say he was bragging about the last time he met a rugby player. They thought Stan said he had a fight with him outside a pub and gave him a really good hiding, but he hadn't said that at all. What he actually said was that the last time he was in a car park he splattered an Austin Healey.
~ FRANK SKINNER

As Phil De Glanville said, each game is unique, and this one is no different to any other.
~ JOHN SLEIGHTHOLME

Colin may not have looked too good but I'm told he smelled lovely.
~ STEVE SMITH AFTER PROP-FORWARD COLIN SMART APPARENTLY DRANK AFTERSHAVE AT A POST-MATCH ENGLAND BANQUET

Hey, skipper, there's a bird just run on the pitch and she's wearing your bum on her chest!
~ STEVE SMITH TO BILL BEAUMONT AFTER ERICA ROE'S STREAK AT TWICKENHAM

The French selectors never do anything by halves; for the first international of the season against Ireland they dropped half the three-quarter line.
~ NIGEL STARMER-SMITH

If you didn't know him, you wouldn't know who he was.
~ NIGEL STARMER-SMITH

I enjoy the violence in rugby, except when they start biting each other's ears off.
~ ELIZABETH TAYLOR

Like a sweet-natured version of the Nuremberg rally.
~ *THE TIMES* DESCRIBING THE PARADE IN HONOUR OF ENGLAND'S WORLD CUP-WINNING TEAM

I used to milk 100 cows six days a week, and then go to a place like Newbridge in Wales on a wet Wednesday night and have my head kicked in. It was a tough apprenticeship, but you know what? I miss those days.

~ PHIL VICKERY ON BEING APPOINTED ENGLAND CAPTAIN

I've got a steel plate across my cheek, three along the jaw area and eight staples in my head. I went to a practice session in London last night and it was raining so heavily I had to pack it in after half an hour because I was starting to rust.

~ DEREK WHITE

Rugby is a good occasion for keeping 30 bullies far from the city centre.

~ OSCAR WILDE

The strain on my groin from years of bashing balls around needs to be changed.

~ JONNY WILKINSON

No leadership, no ideas. Not even enough imagination to thump someone in the line-out when the ref wasn't looking.

~ JPR WILLIAMS AFTER WALES ARE CRUSHED BY AUSTRALIA

Each side is allowed to put in a certain amount of assault and battery and do things to its fellow man which, if done elsewhere, would result in 14 days without the option, coupled with some strong remarks from the Bench.

~ P.G. WODEHOUSE, *VERY GOOD, JEEVES*

The relationship between the Welsh and the English is based on trust and understanding. They don't trust us and we don't understand them.

~ DUDLEY WOOD

The heart is willing, the head is willing, but the body's had enough.

~ KEITH WOOD, DECIDING TO HANG UP HIS BOOTS

I could hear a few people outside shouting 'boring, boring'. I was in bed with my wife at the time.
~ CLIVE WOODWARD, AFTER AUSTRALIAN FANS
BARRACKED THE ENGLAND PARTY OUTSIDE THE TEAM HOTEL

STICKS

Hockey

Street hockey is great for kids. It's energetic, competitive and skilful. And best of all it keeps them off the street.

~ ANON

The worst thing about playing for Great Britain is the sleeveless shirts. It means you have to shave your armpits before every game.

~ KAREN BROWN

It was worth getting your knickers wet for.

~ JENNY CARDWELL, AFTER GREAT BRITAIN DEFEATED SPAIN IN THE RAIN

Where oh where were the Germans? And frankly, who cares?

~ BARRY DAVIES, AFTER GREAT BRITAIN'S SECOND GOAL IN THE 1988 OLYMPIC FINAL AGAINST GERMANY

An umpire in Australia undoubtedly needs to be deaf – in both ears.

~ PATRICK ROWLEY

Hurling

I'm always suspicious of games where you're the only ones that play it.

~ JACK CHARLTON

Hurling is a combination of hockey, football, golf, baseball, battle, and sudden death.

~ *DAILY MAIL*

There is something pigheaded about Wexford this season, something pigheaded and perverse and oddly beautiful. In certain lights they are starting to look heroic.

~ TOM HUMPHRIES

There is a level of politics in hurling. I don't think Henry Kissinger would have lasted a week on the Munster council.

~ GER LOUGHNANE

Teddy McCarthy to John McCarthy, no relation. John McCarthy back to Teddy McCarthy, still no relation.

~ MICHAEL O'MUIRCHEARTAIGH

Teddy looks at the ball, the ball looks at Teddy. ~ MICHAEL O'MUIRCHEARTAIGH

Sean Og O'Hailpin ... his father's from Fermanagh, his mother's from Fiji, neither a hurling stronghold. ~ MICHAEL O'MUIRCHEARTAIGH

Pat Fox out to the 40 and grabs the sliothar. I bought a dog from his father last week. Fox turns and sprints for goal, the dog ran a great race last Tuesday in Limerick. Fox to the 21 fires a shot, it goes to the left and wide ... and the dog lost as well. ~ MICHAEL O'MUIRCHEARTAIGH

Pat Fox has it on his hurley and is motoring well now. But here comes Joe Rabbitte hot on his tail. I've seen it all now – a Rabbitte chasing a Fox around Croke Park! ~ MICHAEL O'MUIRCHEARTAIGH

Lacrosse

I'm not a lacrosse guy. If they held it in my front yard, I'd move to my back yard. ~ TONY KORNHEISER

I thought lacrosse was what you find in la church. ~ ROBIN WILLIAMS

TARGETS

Darts

I hope for his sake he has a long and illustrious career. But when he finds out what women are all about, we'll see, won't we?
~ MARTIN ADAMS ON 17-YEAR-OLD WORLD MASTERS CHAMPION MICHAEL VAN GERWEN

Bobby George wears so much jewellery, he rattles to the oche.   ~ ANON

Jocky Wilson is the minimum of mass into which a human being can be contracted.   ~ NANCY BANKS-SMITH

[Phil] Taylor takes no part in sport. Instead, he plays darts. That is to say, he stands in a smoke-filled room and courts the acclaim of bawling swillers by tossing bunches of tiny arrows at a board. He walks seven feet, nine-and-a-quarter inches to retrieve his missiles and the same distance back to his mark. And that is the sum of his physical effort. By comparison, snooker is the decathlon and angling the Tour de France.   ~ PATRICK COLLINS

Look at his concentration – it's like someone has stuck a beard on a lump of granite.   ~ DAVID CROFT ON MARTIN ADAMS

Before a match I like to relax with 25 bottles of Holsten Pils and six steak and kidney pies.   ~ ANDY FORDHAM

I won't be able to stop the drinking just like that but I've hopefully cut it in half, and if you cut what I drink in half that is a hell of a lot.   ~ ANDY FORDHAM

I used to be called 'The Whippet'.   ~ 30-STONE ANDY FORDHAM

In order to play darts, you need a dartboard and some darts.   ~ BOBBY GEORGE

His darts used to stick out like tulips in the board.
~ BOBBY GEORGE ON VINCENT VAN DER VOORT

I wasn't nervous during the match but the streaker certainly affected my game. I just wish I'd got her name and address!

~ SHAUN GREATBACH AFTER A STREAKER INVADED THE OCHE AT THE 2001 WORLD CHAMPIONSHIPS

Only one word for that: magic darts.

~ TONY GREEN

He has a chance this afternoon to put history into the past.

~ TONY GREEN

I like that stage, although the carpet needs hoovering.

~ TRINA GULLIVER AFTER WINNING A FIFTH CONSECUTIVE WOMEN'S WORLD TITLE AT LAKESIDE

I was watching sumo wrestling on the television for two hours before I realised it was darts.

~ HATTIE HAYRIDGE

He is too patronising. He was going on about how he could not get a set of table and chairs in his Bentley, but I am driving around in a nine-year-old car and he's rubbing our noses in it.

~ CHRIS MASON ON PHIL 'THE POWER' TAYLOR

I had a bash at positive thinking, yoga, transcendental meditation, even hypnosis. They only screwed me up, so now I'm back to my normal game – a couple of lagers.

~ LEIGHTON REES

Well, as giraffes say, you don't get no leaves unless you stick your neck out.

~ SID WADDELL

The atmosphere is a cross between the Munich Beer Festival and the Coliseum when the Christians were on the menu.

~ SID WADDELL

There's no one quicker than these two tungsten tossers.

~ SID WADDELL

Three 140s on the trot – the last one was 100.　　　　　　~ SID WADDELL

Keith Deller is like Long John Silver – he's badly in need of another leg.

~ SID WADDELL

The way he's sweating, he looks like a hippo in a power shower.

~ SID WADDELL ON ANDY FORDHAM

His face is sagging with tension.　　　　　　　　　　~ SID WADDELL

His eyes are bulging like the belly of a hungry chaffinch.　　~ SID WADDELL

He's about as predictable as a wasp on speed.　　　　　~ SID WADDELL

He looks about as happy as a penguin in a microwave.　　　~ SID WADDELL

These guys look calm but inside they are as nervous as a vampire who knows there's a sale at the wooden stake shop in the morning.　　~ SID WADDELL

It's like trying to pin down a kangaroo on a trampoline.　　~ SID WADDELL

Even Hypotenuse would have trouble working out these angles.　~ SID WADDELL

He's been burning the midnight oil at both ends.　　　　~ SID WADDELL

You couldn't get more excitement here if Elvis Presley walked in eating a chip sandwich.　　　　　　　　　　　　　　~ SID WADDELL

That was like throwing three pickled onions into a thimble.　~ SID WADDELL

The fans now, with their eyes pierced on the dartboard.　　~ SID WADDELL

This lad has more checkouts than Tescos.　　　　　　~ SID WADDELL

When Alexander of Macedonia was 33, he cried salt tears because there were no more worlds to conquer. [Eric] Bristow's only 27.   ~ SID WADDELL

Bristow reasons; Bristow quickens; aaaah Bristow!   ~ SID WADDELL

Steve Beaton: the Adonis of darts, what poise, what elegance – a true Roman gladiator with plenty of hair wax.   ~ SID WADDELL

If we'd had Phil Taylor at Hastings against the Normans, they'd have gone home.
                    ~ SID WADDELL

William Tell could take an apple off your head, Taylor could take out a processed pea.   ~ SID WADDELL

Bobby George is like a Sherman tank on roller skates coming down a mountain.
                    ~ SID WADDELL

Cliff Lazarenko's idea of exercise is a firm press on a soda siphon.   ~ SID WADDELL

Jocky Wilson ... what an athlete.   ~ SID WADDELL

Shooting

When I take a gun in hand, the safest place for a pheasant is just opposite the muzzle.   ~ REVD SYDNEY SMITH

The fascination of shooting as a sport depends almost wholly on whether you are at the right or wrong end of the gun.   ~ P.G. WODEHOUSE

WHEELS

Cycling

I figure the faster I pedal, the faster I can retire. ~ LANCE ARMSTRONG

He's better about shaving his legs than I am. ~ SHERYL CROW ON LANCE ARMSTRONG

Cycling is cycling, but my boyfriend's a rugby player and that's a different ball game. ~ KIRSTY GALLACHER

We think the riders deserve to arrive at the Paris finish on a high note.
~ JEAN-MARIE LEBLANC, DIRECTOR OF THE TOUR DE FRANCE,
AFTER A SERIES OF DRUG SCANDALS DOGGED THE 1998 RACE

This is a pedigree group of men – they are holding on by the skin of their shorts.
~ PHIL LIGGETT

The weather is something of a damp squid. ~ PHIL LIGGETT

He's really having to dig deep into the suitcase of courage. ~ PHIL LIGGETT

And he's out there in front breaking wind for the rest of the peloton.
~ PHIL LIGGETT

Contour-hugging cycle shorts can cruelly expose anyone whose performance falls an inch or two short of an all-comer's record. You need a full kitbag to get away with this particular garb. ~ RICHARD LITTLEJOHN

Next week we'll be looking at the Tour de France – all those bicycles roaring through the countryside. ~ ANDY PEEBLES

The front wheel crosses the finish line, closely followed by the back wheel.
~ HUGH PORTER

In cycling, you can put all your money on one horse. ~ STEPHEN ROCHE

I don't care if you found out that he has a jet engine in his anus. He's the best that's ever been.

~ JON STEWART ON LANCE ARMSTRONG

The riders come out neck to thigh in slippery lycra with the sheen of deep space condoms.

~ JAMES WADDINGTON

They've kept his urine for a year. It's like a Chardonnay by then.

~ ROBIN WILLIAMS ON DRUG ALLEGATIONS AGAINST HIS FRIEND LANCE ARMSTRONG

Motor Cycling

It's kind of like tumbling around inside a giant clothes-drier.

~ DAVE ALDANA, ON FALLING OFF A MOTORCYCLE AT SPEED

Colin had a hard on in practice earlier and I bet he wished he had a hard on now.

~ JACK BURNICLE ON COLIN EDWARDS' CHOICE OF TYRES

Sorry I'm late, Brad, I was taking a dump.

~ COLIN EDWARDS TO BRAD PITT AT A PRESENTATION BEFORE
THE START OF THE 2005 UNITED STATES MOTO GP RACE

He doesn't like losing, like me. When I beat him a couple of times last season he had a face like a slapped arse.

~ CARL FOGARTY ON COLIN EDWARDS

You can always spot a motorcycle racer in a restaurant. He's the one gripping his fork with the first two fingers of his left hand.

~ KENNY ROBERTS

I crashed in the chicken and broke the fingers of my feet.

~ FRENCHMAN RAYMOND ROCHE, DESCRIBING HIS ACCIDENT
IN A CHICANE THAT RESULTED IN BROKEN TOES

It is definitely a peculiar motorcycle – sometimes it tells me it likes a track, other times it tells me it hates a track. We have a fight every now and again but then we make up.

~ VALENTINO ROSSI ON THE YAMAHA M1

The advantage of the rain is that if you have a quick bike, there's no advantage.

~ BARRY SHEENE

The conclusion is drawing to a conclusion.

~ RAY STUBBS

Motor Racing

If it were not for the fact I knew it would cost me a $10,000 fine, I would have put my fist in his face.

~ JEAN ALESI ON EDDIE IRVINE

What does it feel like being rammed up the backside by Rubens Barrichello?

~ JAMES ALLEN TO RALF SCHUMACHER

Michael Schumacher takes the lead, which he needs to if he's going to win this Grand Prix.

~ JAMES ALLEN

Zinedine Zidane retired with more glory than Schumacher.

~ FERNANDO ALONSO

I think NASCAR would be much more exciting if, like in a skating rink, every 15 minutes someone announced it was time to reverse direction.

~ JEFFREY ANBINDER

You always see gaps in racing. The trick is to make sure they are wider than your car.

~ MARIO ANDRETTI

I kind of like to have someone looking up my arse.

~ MARIO ANDRETTI, RELISHING TIGHT BATTLES ON THE TRACK

If everything seems under control, you're just not going fast enough.

~ MARIO ANDRETTI

Nigel Mansell should have 'Who Dares Whines' embroidered on his overalls.

~ SIMON BARNES

This might be the only race in the series where it takes longer to say the race name than it does to run the whole 250 miles.

~ NASCAR'S STANTON BARRETT ON THE 2005 ITT INDUSTRIES SYSTEMS DIVISION AND GOULDS PUMPS SALUTE TO THE TROOPS 250 PRESENTED BY DODGE

Auto racing is boring except when a car is going at least 172mph upside-down.

~ DAVE BARRY

Michael Schumacher, the finest driver ever to sit behind a Formula One car.

~ BBC NEWSREADER

He's got a ten foot ego and a four foot body.

~ NASCAR'S MIKE BLISS ON BOBBY HAMILTON JR

Racing is 99 per cent boredom and one per cent terror.   ~ GEOFF BRABHAM

And they spin off to destroy both their hopes of winning the British Grand Prix – Damon [Hill] for the second time in succession, [Michael] Schumacher for the first time in succession.   ~ DOUGLAS BROWN

And Eddie Irvine's tyre is only flat at the bottom.   ~ MARTIN BRUNDLE

This is a carbon copy of last year but reversed.   ~ MARTIN BRUNDLE

Jenson [Button] drives a car like he's pushing a spoon through treacle.

~ MARTIN BRUNDLE

Alonso's understeering like a supermarket trolley.   ~ MARTIN BRUNDLE

Looking at the way Karthikeyan's car was handling, I imagine his pit stop was for fresh underwear.   ~ MARTIN BRUNDLE

The mirrors are about as useful as a chocolate fireguard, on a Formula One car.

~ MARTIN BRUNDLE

I've crashed a Formula One car there – I've crashed a Formula One car in *most* places actually.

~ MARTIN BRUNDLE AT THE FRENCH GRAND PRIX

I thought the last two rolls were unnecessary – I'd got the message by then.

~ MARTIN BRUNDLE, AFTER HIS JORDAN CAR DID SEVERAL SOMERSAULTS AT THE 1996 AUSTRALIAN GRAND PRIX

The Germans once again have got their towels on the front of the grid, Schumacher and Frentzen.

~ MARTIN BRUNDLE AT THE 2000 MONACO GRAND PRIX

Being first out on the race track's a bit like being first up on the dance floor. You know everybody's looking at you.

~ MARTIN BRUNDLE AT A GRAND PRIX QUALIFYING SESSION

There's so many celebrities on this grid, I can hardly see the wood from the trees.

~ MARTIN BRUNDLE

There's two rules in Formula One. Rule One is 'Don't go against Bernie [Ecclestone] too often' and Rule Two is 'See Rule One'.

~ MARTIN BRUNDLE

—Murray Walker: First man out is Marques in the Arrows. Of course he's going out early to generate some media interest.
—Martin Brundle: I'm sure he would generate some interest if he went out in the Arrows because Marques drives for Minardi.

—Jenson Button: I was suffering a little bit with the balance of the car.
—Martin Brundle: Especially after the wheel fell off!

—Martin Brundle: First time for you on the grid of a Grand Prix?

—Frankie Dettori: First time in my life and I'm dying to get in that car. They got 900 horsepower in there, I only got one! You can smell the atmosphere growing and the smell of the tyres and the engines and I hope it's gonna be a fantastic race.

—Martin Brundle: Yeah, it must smell a whole lot better than the start of a horse race!

My wiener has never been so exhausted.

~ NASCAR'S KURT BUSCH AFTER WINNING THE OSCAR MAYER WIENERMOBILE RACE, 2005

If Ferrari are only sixth or seventh best next year, there is no reason to be with them – apart from having a nice company car. ~ JENSON BUTTON

She's pretty aggressive in our cars. Especially if you catch her at the right time of the month, she might be trading plenty of paint out there.

~ ED CARPENTER, INDY RACING LEAGUE DRIVER, ON DANICA PATRICK

Why are you always in red? Is it your lucky colour?

~ CHINESE JOURNALIST TO MICHAEL SCHUMACHER BEFORE THE INAUGURAL CHINESE GRAND PRIX

His is a car that goes like a Ferrari and is built like a tractor. It just never breaks down. ~ DAVID COULTHARD ON MICHAEL SCHUMACHER'S 2004 CAR

We may as well give ourselves names like Hulk Hogan and start battling each other in the paddock.

~ DAVID COULTHARD ON THE ONE-LAP QUALIFYING RULE INTRODUCED TO FORMULA ONE IN 2005

I am scared of nobody on the track. When I started racing my father told me: 'Cristiano, nobody has three balls but some people have two very good ones.'

~ CRISTIANO DA MATTA

Motor racing's less of a sport these days than a commercial break doing 150mph.

~ PETER DUNNE

You win some, lose some, and wreck some.

~ DALE EARNHARDT

Years ago, you used to get out and fight and run around and chase each other with a jackhammer and stuff like that. Those were the good old days.

~ NASCAR'S DALE EARNHARDT JR

I like visiting Silverstone – it's a reminder of what racing was like in the 1950s.

~ BERNIE ECCLESTONE

What have they done? Nothing. They've spent £14m on a car park.

~ BERNIE ECCLESTONE UNIMPRESSED BY THE IMPROVEMENTS AT SILVERSTONE

It does not matter to Formula One if there is no Grand Prix in the US. What do we get from America? Aggravation, that's about all. If you say good morning over there and it's five past twelve, you end up with a lawsuit. ~ BERNIE ECCLESTONE

Women should be dressed in white, like all other domestic appliances.

~ BERNIE ECCLESTONE ON LADY RACER DANICA PATRICK

It's the best thing to happen to a sport, that you have a superstar. In football there is always something to write about the Beckhams, same as people want to write about Rooney or Hooney or whatever his bloody name is.

~ BERNIE ECCLESTONE

Getting to know the Nürburgring was like getting to know a woman. You can't memorise 176 curves over more than 14 miles, just as you can't memorise 176 feminine wiles after a short acquaintance.

~ JUAN MANUEL FANGIO

One rumour: when Viagra mechanics popped the hood, they couldn't get it back down.

~ MARTIN FENNELLY ON WHY THE VIAGRA CAR FAILED TO MAKE THE LINE-UP FOR THE DAYTONA 500

Every car has a lot of speed in it. The trick is getting the speed out of it. ~ A.J. FOYT

—Larry Gogan: Name the BBC's Grand Prix commentator. I'll give you a hint: it's something you suck.
—Contestant: Oh, Dickie Davies.
(The answer was Murray Walker: Murray Mints)

Robby [Gordon]'s got a little problem going faster under caution than he does under green.

~ JEFF GORDON, NASCAR

Nigel Mansell is the only man who goes to Nick Faldo for charisma lessons.

~ NICK HANCOCK

I want to be a race-car passenger – just a guy who bugs the driver: 'Say, man, can I turn on the radio? You should slow down. Can I put my feet out the window?'

~ MITCH HEDBERG

The man is a millionaire but always looks like an unmade bed.

~ MELBOURNE'S *HERALD SUN* ON JACQUES VILLENEUVE

When you're at my end of the grid, nobody wants to know you. ~ JOHNNY HERBERT

I first had doubts at Melbourne this year. We all raced to the first corner and I thought, 'What's the hurry?' ~ DAMON HILL ON HIS RETIREMENT

Eddie Irvine is the Ian Paisley of Formula One. ~ DAMON HILL

Heinz-Harald Frentzen is one brick short of a full load. ~ DAMON HILL

I thought the world could only bear one Schumacher. Now we have two!

~ DAMON HILL ON LEARNING THAT MICHAEL'S BROTHER RALF WAS JOINING FORMULA ONE

What is this fixation – a kind of Schu fetish? ~ DAMON HILL

Winning is everything. The only ones who remember you when you come second are your wife and your dog. ~ DAMON HILL

Grand Prix racing is like balancing an egg on a spoon while shooting the rapids. ~ GRAHAM HILL

You meet a much nicer class of person when starting from the back of the grid. ~ GRAHAM HILL

Nigel Mansell is someone with about as much charisma as a damp spark plug. ~ ALAN HUBBARD

Jack [Brabham] could give the impression that he was a bit vague at times. He was quite good at that, particularly with anyone who wanted to talk about money. ~ DENNY HULME

The best thing about Italy is the border. ~ DENNY HULME

My first priority is to finish above rather than below the ground. ~ JAMES HUNT

It's a chess game played at 180mph, only each piece has a mind of its own. ~ JAMES HUNT

The only reason I ever walked up and down the pit road when I was a driver was to look at the crumpet. ~ JAMES HUNT

What people don't realise is that winning is easy. Losing is the thing that's bloody hard work! ~ JAMES HUNT

This car is absolutely hopeless – it's like driving a wet sponge. ~ JAMES HUNT

I wouldn't worry about your face, Niki – you were ugly in the first place!
~ JAMES HUNT TO NIKI LAUDA AFTER THE LATTER'S HORRIFIC CRASH AT THE NÜRBURGRING IN 1976

Damon [Hill]'s retiring like he overtakes. Will he? Won't he?　～ EDDIE IRVINE

I'd rather do 180mph around Monza than see an earwig.　～ EDDIE IRVINE

It's like when your girlfriend breaks up with you, she has to tell all her girlfriends about what's going to happen, but you don't know. That's the way it is here.　～ KENNY IRWIN ON HOW THE DRIVER IS OFTEN THE LAST TO KNOW HE IS BEING REPLACED

Even in moments of tranquillity, Murray Walker sounds like a man whose trousers are on fire.　～ CLIVE JAMES

The best way to make a small fortune in racing is to start with a big one.　～ JUNIOR JOHNSON

There is no point in having a complex about losing half an ear.　～ NIKI LAUDA

After the accident I am looking worse than some people are born – but at least I can say it was an accident.　～ NIKI LAUDA

The Chevrolet has had more nose jobs than Michael Jackson.　～ STERLING MARLIN

I don't know nothing about nothing, but what I know about, I know.　～ NASCAR'S MARK MARTIN

One zigged when he should have zagged.　～ MINARDI SPOKESMAN AFTER THE TEAM'S TWO CARS COLLIDED DURING TESTING

I was reading a book called *The Wisdom of Crowds*. I thought, 'If thousands of people are saying I'm a tosser, maybe they are right!'　～ MAX MOSLEY

There are two things no man will admit he can't do well – drive and make love.
～ STIRLING MOSS

I'm sure Sterling Marlin's hairpiece fell down in his face and he couldn't see me.

~ RYAN NEWMAN, APPORTIONING BLAME FOR A CRASH IN TEXAS

If you can't qualify in the top ten, 11th is the best you're going to do.

~ BARRY OLIVER

This guy has been in the grass so often the chipmunks know him by name.

~ PAUL PAGE ON PAUL TRACY

It's like trying to ride a bicycle around your living room.

~ NELSON PIQUET ON MONACO

Some of the ravines on the Monte Carlo Rally are so deep that if you topple over, your clothes will be out of date by the time you hit the bottom.   ~ TONY POND

Sure, I am one of the biggest stars in Finland. But we don't have that many.

~ KIMI RAIKKONEN

All I had to do was keep turning left. ~ GEORGE ROBSON, WINNING THE INDIANAPOLIS 500

The noise is constant and tremendous – like a woman's knitting club.

~ KEKE ROSBERG

Williams must be the only team in the business with more PR men than championship points.   ~ KEKE ROSBERG

Easter and Christmas would have to fall on the same day for our drivers to appear on the podium.   ~ PETER SAUBER

How has Formula One changed since my day? Less girls, more technology.

~ JODY SCHECKTER

I had enough problems passing a Minardi!   ~ MICHAEL SCHUMACHER

He overestimated his ability.

~ MICHAEL SCHUMACHER AFTER BEING SHUNTED OFF THE TRACK BY RICARDO ZONTA

I am the oldest driver in the field but it doesn't bother me because, fortunately, I'm not the slowest.

~ MICHAEL SCHUMACHER

Cornering is like bringing a woman to climax.

~ JACKIE STEWART

They name streets after guys like that – One Way and Dead End. He's just an idiot.

~ TONY STEWART ON NASCAR'S GREG BIFFLE

If horse racing is the sport of kings, then drag racing must be the sport of queens.

~ BERT SUGAR

Diniz In The Oven

~ *SUN* HEADLINE AFTER PEDRO DINIZ'S CAR CATCHES FIRE

Everything in Gilles Villeneuve's life moved at 200mph, whether it was driving, playing Monopoly, flying helicopters or spending.

~ PATRICK TAMBAY

Never punch a guy when he still has his helmet on. My hand's a bit sore right now.

~ CHAMP CAR'S PAUL TRACY AFTER A FIGHT WITH FELLOW DRIVER ALEX TAGLIANI

The drivers have one foot on the brake, one on the clutch, and one on the throttle.

~ BOB VARSHA

This is an interesting circuit because it has inclines – and not just up but down as well.

~ MURRAY WALKER

Knowing exactly where Nigel Mansell is because he can see him in his earphones.

~ MURRAY WALKER

With two laps to go then the action will begin, unless this is the action, which it is.

~ MURRAY WALKER

Mansell is gazing at him through his microphone.　　　~ MURRAY WALKER

He's in front of everyone in this race except for the two in front of him.

~ MURRAY WALKER

And now excuse me while I interrupt myself.

~ MURRAY WALKER

This would have been Senna's third win in a row had he won the other two.

~ MURRAY WALKER

Either that car is stationary or it's on the move.　　　~ MURRAY WALKER

The lead is now 6.9 seconds. In fact it's just under seven seconds.　~ MURRAY WALKER

The gap between the cars is 0.9 of a second, which is less than one second!

~ MURRAY WALKER

Alboreto has dropped back up to fifth place.　　　~ MURRAY WALKER

Warwick has overtaken Alan Jones and, in the process, moved up a place.

~ MURRAY WALKER

A mediocre season for Nelson Piquet as he is known, and always has been.

~ MURRAY WALKER

Mansell is almost metaphorically in sight of the chequered flag.　~ MURRAY WALKER

Into lap 53, the penultimate last lap but one.　　　~ MURRAY WALKER

The conditions at the Nürburgring are much better than last year's Grand Prix of Europe when the weather conditions were indescribably bad: driving rain, heavy mist and bitter cold.　　　~ MURRAY WALKER

I've just stopped my startwatch. ~ MURRAY WALKER

We're looking at the man who won in '83, '85 and '86, so this could be his hat-trick. ~ MURRAY WALKER

In case you're confused, Mansell has gone from seventh to sixth, from fourth to fifth, and is now third. ~ MURRAY WALKER

There's nothing wrong with the car except that it's on fire. ~ MURRAY WALKER

You can cut the tension with a cricket stump. ~ MURRAY WALKER

You can see now that the gap between Mansell and Piquet is rather more than just visual. ~ MURRAY WALKER

There is Michael Schumacher. He's actually in a very good position. He's in first place. ~ MURRAY WALKER

This will be Williams' first win since the last time a Williams won. ~ MURRAY WALKER

The European drivers have adapted to this circuit extremely quickly, especially Paul Radisich who's a New Zealander. ~ MURRAY WALKER

The beak of Ayrton Senna's chicken is pulling ahead. ~ MURRAY WALKER

Stewart have two cars in the top five – Magnusson fifth and Barrichello sixth. ~ MURRAY WALKER

Tambay's hopes, which were nil before, are absolutely zero now. ~ MURRAY WALKER

And Berger finishes his flying lap to begin a quick one. ~ MURRAY WALKER

This is lap 54, after that it's 55, 56, 57, 58.   ~ MURRAY WALKER

So this being Michael Schumacher's tenth race in his 151st year in F1.
~ MURRAY WALKER

Nigel Mansell is the last person in the race apart from the five in front of him.
~ MURRAY WALKER

He is shedding buckets of adrenalin in that car. ~ MURRAY WALKER

Do my eyes deceive me, or is Senna's Lotus sounding rough?   ~ MURRAY WALKER

I don't know what happened, but there was a major malmisorganisation
problem there.   ~ MURRAY WALKER

We now have exactly the same situation as we had at the start of the race, only
exactly the opposite.   ~ MURRAY WALKER

And now the boot is on the other Schumacher.   ~ MURRAY WALKER

And here comes Mika Hakkinen, double world champion twice over.
~ MURRAY WALKER

There's no damage to the car except of course to the car itself.   ~ MURRAY WALKER

If that isn't a lap record, I'll eat the hat I don't normally wear!   ~ MURRAY WALKER

With half of the race gone, there is half of the race still to go. ~ MURRAY WALKER

I imagine that the conditions in those cars today are totally unimaginable.
~ MURRAY WALKER

I make no apologies for their absence; I'm sorry they're not here.

~ MURRAY WALKER

A sad ending, albeit a happy one.

~ MURRAY WALKER

Mansell is slowing it down, taking it easy. Oh no he isn't! It's a lap record!

~ MURRAY WALKER

I don't make mistakes. I make prophecies which are immediately proved wrong.

~ MURRAY WALKER

Nigel Mansell will never win a Grand Prix as long as I have a hole in my arse.

~ PETER WARR, 1984

René Arnoux brakes like a bloody old woman in that thing.

~ JOHN WATSON

I really want to win a race this year. If I don't, then all the guys will start calling me Tim Henman.

~ MARK WEBBER

When the lights go green, he goes red!

~ FRANK WILLIAMS ON NIGEL MANSELL

The good news is that he is very, very quick. The bad news is that we can't afford him.

~ FRANK WILLIAMS AFTER NASCAR'S JEFF GORDON DID AN F1 TEST DRIVE

Michael Schumacher would remain a formidable challenge if he was driving a pram.

~ FRANK WILLIAMS

Driving a race car is like dancing with a chainsaw.

~ CALE YARBOROUGH

SELECTED BIBLIOGRAPHY

Douglas, Derek: *The Book of World Rugby Quotations* (Mainstream, 1991)

Exley, Helen: *Golf Quotations* (Exley, 1991)

Exley, Helen: *Tennis Quotations* (Exley, 1996)

Holt, Nick: *The Wit & Wisdom of Golf* (House of Raven, 2005)

Hopps, David: *A Century of Great Cricket Quotes* (Robson Books, 2000)

Liebman, Glenn: *2,000 Sports Quips and Quotes* (Gramercy Books, 1993)

Liebman, Glenn: *1,001 Golf Quips and Quotes* (Gramercy Books, 1995)

Lloyd, Guy: *The Wit & Wisdom of Football* (House of Raven, 2005)

Miller, Hartley: *You Don't Say!* (Andrews McMeel, 2005)

Milsted, David: *The Big Book of Sports Insults* (Weidenfeld & Nicolson, 2004)

Mullan, Harry: *The Book of Boxing Quotations* (Stanley Paul, 1991)

Parietti, Jeff: *The Book of Truly Stupid Sports Quotes* (HarperCollins, 1996)

Parietti, Jeff: *More Truly Stupid Sports Quotes* (HarperCollins, 1999)

Reynolds, Mark: *The Wrong Kind of Shirts* (Fourth Estate, 1996)

Sharpe, Graham: *Classic Horse-Racing Quotes* (Robson Books, 2005)

Shaw, Phil: *The Book of Football Quotations* (Ebury Press, 2003)

Tibballs, Geoff: *Do I Not Like That!* (Virgin, 1999)

Tibballs, Geoff: *50 Years of the Formula One World Championship* (Robson Books, 2000)

Tibballs, Geoff: *The Mammoth Book of Comic Quotes* (Constable & Robinson, 2004)

INDEX